Women of the Revolution

Kira Cochrane is a staff writer for the Guardian, writing regularly about feminist issues, and was women's editor of the paper from 2006–2010.

Women of the Revolution

Forty years of feminism

EDITED BY KIRA COCHRANE

guardianbooks

Published by Guardian Books 2012

4 6 8 10 9 7 5

Copyright © Guardian News and Media Ltd 2010

First published in Great Britain in 2010 by
Guardian Books
Kings Place, 90 York Way
London N1 9GU
www.guardianbooks.co.uk

A CIP catalogue record for this book
is available from the British Library

ISBN 978-0-85265-227-5

Typeset by Palimpsest Book Production Limited, Falkirk, Stirlingshire
Printed and bound by CPI Group (UK) Ltd, Croydon, CR0 4YY

In memory of Mary Stott and Jill Tweedie

Contents

Introduction   xvii

1970s

15 January 1971   3
The second sex
The Women's Lib movement is a search for meaningful identity
MARY STOTT

15 January 1971   6
How to be voluble, sexy and liberated
*An interview with Betty Friedan, the American feminists' leading
propagandist*
MICHAEL BEHR

18 January 1971   9
Why nice girls finish last
JILL TWEEDIE

29 March 1972   12
Shirley for President
*Shirley Chisholm challenges the assumption that a woman – and a black
woman at that – has no place in the White House*
WILLA PETSCHEK

19 July 1973   16
'I'm just a speaker. I've spoke to thousands. I'm glad I'm no cleaner
no more, it's bleedin' 'ard work'
May Hobbs, night cleaner, militant and author talks about her life in the East End
ANNA COOTE

12 July 1974   21
An unresolved strike
*'All Indian ladies respect older men. We thought that if we respected the foremen
they would respect us. We've learned a lot of things'*
ANNA COOTE

6 March 1974   26
Maggie May
MARY STOTT

5 July 1975   29
She has been through the gamut of radical chic New York experience,
from her days as a freelance journalist when she was an escort to
Henry Kissinger through a series of 'little marriages'
Interview with Gloria Steinem
CAROL DIX

12 December 1975   34
Brothers to blame
Susan Brownmiller talks about Against Our Will, her study of rape
TIMERI N. MURARI

15 March 1976   38
Too true confessions
Why the conference to turn attention on crimes against women failed
JILL TWEEDIE

    43
3 May 1976
Slave wages
JILL TWEEDIE

14 November 1977   49
Reclaim the night
The worst attack on a Guardian *woman writer happened in Mayfair. She went
out to buy a packet of cigarettes at 9pm and a man with razor blades in his
gloves punched her*
POLLY TOYNBEE

16 May 1978   55
Why the euphoria had to stop
The author of Patriarchal Attitudes, *first published in 1970, looks back on
eight important years*
EVA FIGES

16 May 1979   59
How different the history of world literature might look if mothers
were writers too
ERICA JONG

24 July 1979   63
Second thoughts
It appeared out of nowhere and it hit post-war France like a bomb. How does
Simone de Beauvoir see The Second Sex *now?*
JOHN CUNNINGHAM

20 August 1979   69
Even Liberal Jews had misgivings when the rabbi took a funeral service
in a bulging maternity dress
Interview with Julia Neuberger, Britain's second woman rabbi
LIZ FORGAN

1980s

5 December 1980   79
Now is the time to stand up and fight
A militant response to the menace of the Yorkshire Ripper
JEAN STEAD

                                                              82
5 May 1982
Letters from a fainthearted feminist
JILL TWEEDIE

23 July 1982   85
A day with Spare Rib
'Lesbianism is a central issue. It is an option all women need to know about and
think about'
POLLY TOYNBEE

10 December 1982   89
Ring of resolve to stop cruise
Greenham Common women plan to close the USAF base on Monday
JEAN STEAD

30 January 1984   96
Her life has had extraordinary ups and downs – from prostitute to
star, from street car conductorette to university professor
Interview with Maya Angelou
POLLY TOYNBEE

7 September 1984   100
A world away from women's liberation
Western feminism and women in the third world
SOON-YOUNG YOON

2 October 1984   105
Analysis of the political, social and economic progress of women
BARBARA CASTLE

18 December 1984   109
We have as much right as anyone to dine out
CAROLYNE SHAKESPEARE COOPER

2 April 1985   115
The double struggle
Black women and the fight against racism
CHINYELU ONWURAH

30 September 1987   119
Beloved people
Interview with Toni Morrison
REGINA NADELSON

19 May 1988   123
Behind the Lines: Ironing in the soul
*Twenty years on, what has really changed for women? Germaine Greer praises
motherhood. Her guests beg to differ*
POLLY TOYNBEE

29 December 1988   128
Handbag and rule
*Mrs Thatcher has never conceded one jot of her female identity. Yet in 1988 as in
all the years of her reign, she's not been slow in using it to swat an aberrant
male or two*
BRENDA POLAN

18 April 1989   133
An everyday guide to misogyny
*Women-haters are not freaks or outcasts, says the novelist Joan Smith,
but ordinary men*
ANGELA NEUSTATTER

25 October 1989   137
Awful wedded wives
What's the matter with married women? And why do we put up with them?
MONICA FURLONG

1990s

13 June 1990   143
A meeting of two worlds
Lifting the veil on Islamic feminists in the west
MADELEINE BUNTING

24 August 1991   149
My daughter begged me: Don't die
*In her first interview in Holloway, Sara Thornton talks about her life sentence for
killing her violent husband and why she stopped her hunger strike for her child's sake*
DUNCAN CAMPBELL

30 May 1992   153
The Gender Agenda
*She makes Martin Scorsese look laidback and Joan Rivers look polite. She's
aroused the fury of feminists, and the venom of the American academic
establishment. She's Professor Camille Paglia and she's also very funny*
SUZANNE MOORE

20 January 1993   163
Ordinary madness
*Thousands of abused women testify to systematic rape in Bosnia. But the Serbian
army is not made up of proven sex offenders, they are 'regular guys'. Are, then, all
men potential rapists?*
CATHERINE BENNETT

14 December 1994   171
Feminist under a fatwa
*The Bangladeshi writer Taslima Nasrin has been forced into exile with a price on
her head. Her crime, she says, is trying to free her countrywomen from slavery*
LINDA GRANT

23 November 1995   175
The princess and the pain
*Forget the future of the monarchy, divorce, the constitution. The most important
thing Diana did was to give countless silent women a voice*
BEATRIX CAMPBELL

21 December 1995   178
Yea, though I walk through the valley of discrimination
Three years ago, the church took a bold, brave step towards reversing Christianity's
2,000 years of patriarchy. Being at the forefront of such change was always going
to be hard
MADELEINE BUNTING

9 October 1997   183
Chamber of horrors
This week, the government announced it will take action against opposition
MPs who make sexist comments in the Commons. A PC fuss about nothing?
ANNE PERKINS

24 October 1997   185
Pro-lifers have lost but won't give up
DECCA AITKENHEAD

29 January 1998   189
Dear Bill and Hillary
The whole world is talking about it, but what do American women really think
of the presidential affair?
ANDREA DWORKIN

2 February 1998   192
All white now
Take a closer look at the picture painted in the press of Britain's New Feminism.
See any black women?
HEIDI SAFIA MIRZA

10 August 1998   195
Get a life, girls
What's missing from women's lives is interests other than men
ELIZABETH WURTZEL

13 February 1999   200
The power of one
Talk shows made Oprah Winfrey rich and famous. But now she's having second
thoughts. Maybe talking is not enough
MAYA JAGGI

8 November 1999   213
The promises feminism made, and broke
BELL HOOKS

2000s

22 July 2000   219
Trailblazer of feminism
Interview: Sheila Rowbotham, a pioneer who got lost in the 80s but is being
rediscovered by a new generation
MELISSA BENN

27 July 2000   231
Sisters of mercy
For 21 years, Southall Black Sisters have campaigned in defence of women jailed for
killing violent men
MELISSA BENN

5 February 2001   235
'When the woman in the witness box began to cry, I cried too'
Police believe David Mulcahy may be Britain's worst serial rapist – we hear from
one of his victims
DIANE TAYLOR

1 September 2001   240
Stitched up
What happens when a power feminist becomes a parent? For Naomi Wolf , it
meant the birth of two children, rage at the way women are treated – and an
explosive new book
KATHARINE VINER

25 May 2002   251
Abortion: still a dirty word?
JULIE BURCHILL

1 July 2003   254
What women want
Equal pay for equal work is a noble demand, so why does feminism seem so
embarrassing these days?
ZOE WILLIAMS

6 November 2003   257
Brutal legacy of war in Congo
Harrowing evidence of systematic sexual violence against girls and women
surfaces as fighting recedes
EMILY WAX

24 November 2003   262
Buy your son a Barbie for Christmas
The desire to make little boys more masculine is becoming worse and worse. This can only spell bad news for women
NATASHA WALTER

22 May 2004   267
The sexual sadism of our culture, in peace and in war
The Abu Ghraib images have all the hallmarks of contemporary porn
KATHARINE VINER

13 December 2004   271
Two to the power of 2 million
We black women face a double whammy when it comes to political representation
HANNAH POOL

2 March 2005   274
Life after birth
Breeding women may play havoc with the rota. But isn't it worth a bit of bother to keep a few of them in the workplace?
EMILY WILSON

10 December 2005   277
A year of killing
All the people featured on the following pages met their death in one year at the hands of partners or ex-partners. The overwhelming majority are women
KATHARINE VINER

17 February 2006   294
This bawdy world of boobs and gams shows how far we've left to go
In the new raunch culture, the freedom for women to be sexually provocative has usurped genuine liberation
ARIEL LEVY

18 February 2006   298
Embarrassment of riches
When female health workers won a colossal £300m equal pay claim last year, few cared to share in their celebrations. Why?
BEATRIX CAMPBELL

6 April 2007   307
How the web became a sexists' paradise
Everyone receives abuse online but the sheer hatred thrown at women bloggers has left some in fear for their lives
JESSICA VALENTI

8 June 2007   312
What would Beth Ditto do?
Today's dilemma: How should I respond to catcalls in the street?
BETH DITTO

28 July 2007   314
The really bad girls
*Those who collude in the public degradation of gifted young women are beneath
contempt*
BIDISHA

11 December 2007   316
'You're consenting to being raped for money'
*Appalled at the sanitised picture The Secret Diary of a Call Girl paints,
a woman who charges for sex describes her life*
EMINE SANER

22 December 2007   322
Porn is screwing up young men's expectations of sex
*The revelations about Manchester United's party reflect the parlous state of our
supposed sexual liberation*
MARINA HYDE

15 February 2008   325
Banda sisters
*In one of India's poorest regions, hundreds of pink-clad female vigilantes are
challenging male violence and corruption*
RAEKHA PRASAD

22 February 2008   329
Mothers need not apply
Maternal profiling is illegal in the UK – but it is flourishing
VIV GROSKOP

21 March 2008   334
I was only telling the truth
*When Rachel Cusk wrote A Life's Work, she was shocked by the vicious reaction it
provoked from other women. The experience forced her to question herself as a writer
and a parent*
RACHEL CUSK

17 December 2008   342
'We are the future'
So many men were killed during the Rwandan genocide that women have increasingly found themselves in positions of power. How is that changing the country?
CHRIS MCGREAL

30 January 2009   346
My sexual revolution
Thirty years ago, a group of radical women began arguing that all feminists should be lesbians
JULIE BINDEL

11 May 2009   351
'When I was growing up, one or two girls were beautiful but it wasn't an aspiration. That was what movie stars were for. It wasn't essential for all of us'
Interview with Susie Orbach
DECCA AITKENHEAD

24 July 2009   358
Time for a good scrap about what our feminism really is
Bring on 'infighting' if it means rigorous, honest debate about what we believe
LIBBY BROOKS

16 April 2010   361
'I have a rebel gene'
Nawal El Saadawi has braved prison, exile and death threats in her campaign against female oppression. She isn't about to give up now
HOMA KHALEELI

2 August 2011   366
What is the link between the media and eating disorders?
We all know that the way the media judge women's bodies is sick – but how directly this leads to eating disorders is less clear
HADLEY FREEMAN

12 August 2011   370
Layla's story: jailed after reporting a sexual assault
In 2009, Layla Ibrahim told police she had been the victim of a savage sexual assault. So why did she end up in jail?
SIMON HATTENSTONE AND AFUA HIRSCH

23 December 2011   381
Bruised but defiant: Mona Eltahawy on her assault by
Egyptian security forces
Mona Eltahawy's tweets about her assault in Cairo made global headlines. Here she tells her full, extraordinary story for the first time
MONA ELTAHAWY

Introduction

I began editing this anthology with the thought that, through the Guardian archives, it might be possible to produce a strong, straightforward guide to feminism – a collection that would work as an introduction to all the thinkers, ideas, debates, sisterhood, in-fighting and triumph that have marked the forty years since the first ever women's liberation conference was held in the UK. I thought that it might look something like a textbook: here an interview with Gloria Steinem, there an instructive piece about abortion law.

In some ways it does. These pages do, indeed, include an interview with Steinem and one with Germaine Greer, another with Betty Friedan, another with Maya Angelou. But I quickly remembered that the Guardian isn't actually written like a textbook. And so, for instance, I found a very interesting piece about abortion, but it wasn't a measured discussion of the law – it was Julie Burchill's wild, witty column about having had five terminations herself. I found Jill Tweedie, in 1971, upbraiding the nascent women's liberation movement for being too nice; Polly Toynbee writing about the horrendous physical attacks that had been suffered by female Guardian staffers; Carolyne Shakespeare Cooper skewering the tendency for black women to be stereotyped as prostitutes; Suzanne Moore having an uproarious time interviewing Camille Paglia; and Andrea Dworkin, writing of the Bill Clinton sex scandal, that she had 'a modest proposal. It will probably bring the FBI to my door. But I think that Hillary should shoot Bill and then President Gore should pardon her'.

As I leafed through the material, I realised our archive was actually even richer, more interesting and exciting than I'd imagined. I also realised that, while it might not paint a straightforward picture, it could provide a patchwork of the shifts in women's lives, of the path from the issues facing women in the 1970s to the issues facing us today – many of them, of course, very similar. There are articles here, over the course of four decades, about equal pay, rape, domestic violence, abortion, maternity rights, pornography, political representation and prostitution, all territory that continues to be debated and fought over with impressive commitment.

The anthology traces the route from the feverish feminist campaigning of the early women's liberation movement of the 1970s, to Margaret Thatcher's rule, when solidarity and socialism were pushed to the margins. It takes in the alleged post-feminism of the 1990s (how can you live in a post-feminist world if you've never lived in a truly feminist world?) and the exciting, energetic activism of the present day. And it does this through interviews, reporting, personal stories, and opinion pieces. In that sense, nothing like a textbook at all.

But I hope it will act as an introduction to, or a reminder of, the importance of feminism, and its continued relevance today. The reason I wanted to edit this anthology was because, during four years as women's editor of the Guardian, I have seen the feminist movement in Britain – and far, far beyond – go from strength to strength, with campaigns popping up locally, nationally, internationally, changing laws and minds and lives. I've seen women take to the streets for the annual Reclaim the Night and Million Women Rise marches in the UK, a trove of new British feminist books being published, and such interesting, pioneering changes abroad as Rwanda electing a majority-female parliament. Change just keeps coming, and usually only as a result of those dedicated individuals and groups who are willing both to raise their heads above the parapet and devote dogged hours to the cause. All in the service of one radical belief: that women are human beings, and deserve to be treated as such. Long may they continue – and may many more of us join them.

Kira Cochrane, August 2010

1970s

One of the more crippling aspects of being a woman –
and an Englishwoman to boot – is the continual and largely
unconscious compulsion to be nice.

Jill Tweedie

The second sex

The Women's Lib movement is a search for meaningful identity

Mary Stott

When I was a girl I wished dreadfully that I had been born earlier so that I could have been a suffragette. Now I wish I had been born later, to involve myself in the essentially youthful ferment of Women's Liberation. This seems less odd to many of my contemporaries than to many women young enough to be my daughters, who are apt to mutter that they have all the freedom they need, thank you, and what is there worth fussing about? Well, what is the Women's Liberation fuss about?

It is a search for an identity as a human being, a deeply felt, often inarticulate, protest at being typecast by sex from birth to death. It is nothing new . . . Mary Wollstonecraft wrote about it in 1792; Florence Nightingale acutely felt it, though she never called herself a feminist; it was what brought women out in their thousands in the suffrage campaigns of the early years of this century.

And then, in the years since the second world war, with so many obvious restrictions on women's freedom of action, so many limitations of their status removed, the current of feeling seemed to dissipate. Why is it flowing again? Here are some of the explanations:

1. A swing of the pendulum: A 'back to the home' swing after the war was natural and was greatly reinforced by the dominant

psychological opinion that the total devotion and constant presence of the mother was necessary for the mental health and well-being of the child. From the time Betty Friedan wrote her Feminine Mystique (1963) analysing the effect on women of this 'back to the true feminine role' doctrine, the pendulum began another swing.

2. The Pill: For the first time women are not only freed from the inevitability of conception, but in charge of their own sex lives. The fundamental nature of this psychological revolution is only just beginning to be realised.

3. The population explosion: The effect of this on intelligent young women is to make them realise that, as Brigid Brophy bluntly put it, they are no longer needed basically as 'breeders'. Therefore they have to find a new role, a new place in society.

4. Protests: The younger generation is in a turmoil of protest against the values of our society but many young women have found that in protest movements – particularly civil rights – men have expected them to play the traditional, supportive role. This almost certainly was the spark that fired the dramatic Women's Liberation groups in America.

The 'leadership', if one can call it that, seems now to be coming down on the side of 'respectable' campaigning. A mass demonstration is planned for March 6, gathering in Hyde Park and marching, with banners, slogans, and floats for the marchers' children, to Trafalgar Square via Harley Street, Curzon Street, and Downing Street, to hand in petitions. This demonstration will concentrate on four demands:

1. Equal job and educational opportunities.
2. Equal pay.

3. Free contraception and abortion on demand.

4. 24-hour nursery facilities.

Most of these points are acceptable to the old-established women's organisations, and their support is to be sought. 'We want to be regarded as a serious movement' and 'we want to recruit every woman's support' are the things that are now being said.

Two problems arise. Has the loosely-knit Women's Liberation movement the resources, financial, organisational, practical, to mount a really effective mass demonstration? Will it have to evolve into a tightly-knit organisation, training people to lead and fulfil a variety of roles?

If Women's Liberation concentrates on 'reformist' demands, can it really achieve its aim of changing fundamental attitudes? It will need very clever publicity to get home to the woman in the shopping street that '24-hour nursery care' is not just something that would be a convenience to her, but would give her the chance to be a different kind of person – if she wants to.

But 'consciousness' – the realisation of being 'the second sex' – comes in many different ways. And once the sting has penetrated, nothing looks quite the same. The suffragettes went to prison, hunger struck, and suffered the barbarous cruelty of forcible feeding in their hundreds because they felt so deeply about that essential symbol, the vote. Is there anything that Women's Liberation would hunger strike for, die for? Not yet, but perhaps in time . . .

15 January 1971

How to be voluble, sexy and liberated

An interview with Betty Friedan, the American feminists' leading propagandist

Michael Behr

The tall, elegant young woman in the black Stetson hat who stopped me outside the Rockefeller Centre in New York, had something important to hand to me. That is to say, it was important to her and to hundreds of thousands of women like her in the United States who are still waiting for the Civil Rights Act of 1964, which promises equal employment rights for women, to be enforced. The paper she pressed into my hand argued her case in passionate, if slightly smudged, prose; it also demanded 24-hour a day child care centres and the freeing of abortions from restriction.

And the fact that these women of New York are enthusiastically stomping their case on the sidewalks and the streets of the city, is the achievement of one woman more than any other – Mrs Betty Friedan, author of The Feminine Mystique; founder of NOW (National Organisation of Women); and today the woman most likely to succeed in bringing a useful notoriety to the activities of Women's Liberation. Taxi drivers recognise her, journalists crowd into her press conferences, and the lectures which she delivers at university campuses all over the US are a sell-out.

And yet the restless mind and over-driven body of the 49-year-old woman who might be called the founding mother of the Women's Liberation Movement, (a loose grouping of over 100 women's associations) carries the burden of a strange set of paradoxes – she has been all but disowned by her own organisation, NOW, who nevertheless cannot do without the publicity she brings them; her crusade for deeper and fuller lives for women has resulted in the ending of her own 20 years of marriage; and her real calling, that of a writer, has been pressed into the background by her increasing, almost unceasing, political activities.

The Betty Friedan of today is a voluble, sexy, Jewish woman who can dress herself up with splendid effect and attract intelligent and distinguished men as her admirers – she is also a woman whose face is a magnificent map of the emotions, generated by nearly half a century's ardent living. Born in a small town in Illinois, even as a schoolgirl she found difficulty in reconciling a brilliant scholastic mind with the functions expected of women in the twenties. Her student days in the 30s brought her even less contentment: there were unhappy love affairs, one of which terminated a promising research fellowship at Berkeley.

It was in New York, in Greenwich Village, where she worked as a journalist, that she met her future husband: Carl Friedan, volatile and bohemian director of experimental theatre projects, and perhaps, the catalyst who was to open out her hidden drives and frustrations – possibly even helping her to dramatise them. Later, after a second child was born, and Carl had joined the Establishment as an Adman, psychoanalysis relieved her of other hidden aggressions. 'I was appalled – I admitted to myself for the first time that I actually hated my mother. She was a promising journalist who sacrificed her career to keep house for my father, a small-town jeweller. Next I had to admit that I was following in her footsteps. Work saved me – I freelanced dozens of magazine articles – but always with the knowledge that I was silently battling with Carl to do it. He couldn't help resenting the money I earned.'

The outcome of 10 years' upheaval, both emotional and intellectual, was her bestselling book The Feminine Mystique (1963).

It was her touchstone, and she put everything into it: the frustrations of marriage, child-raising, housekeeping, that she had experienced herself, and observed her contemporaries from college experiencing: the disappointments of a brilliantly promising intellectual career; the bitterness of a warm and vital woman whose talents had made her seem 'different' and therefore unacceptable to the boys and men she grew up with.

'I really believed in that book. It started as a magazine article on the unhappiness of all us housewives, and grew over five years in the writing to a whole statement of my beliefs. My publishers took it grudgingly – they'd long ago regretted their original advance to me – and I had to hire a public relations firm to sell it. My God, how I pushed it! I went on every television talk show in the country – once I really got mad, and just yelled out "orgasm!" as loud as I could in the middle of a programme. It was the only way to stop some man from needling me. Anyway, the hard-sell worked – the book sold by the millions and made me over $100,000. I was called a militant radical. That would make some of the women's liberation laugh now – they think I'm a real reactionary square.'

Betty Friedan is a woman. She has no hatred or resentment of men, as some later recruits to Women's Liberation have. She states publicly and repeatedly that a world of aggressive maleness is as unattractive to men as it is to women. Privately, she says the same about aggressive femaleness. A compulsive talker, garrulous, and often off the point, she nevertheless convinces by her unashamed acceptance of what it is to be a human being. She's emotional, even contradictory, but if she's wrong, it could be about the 'wrong' things – because on the 'right' ones, she's doing fine.

18 January 1971

Why nice girls finish last

JILL TWEEDIE

One of the more crippling aspects of being a woman – and an Englishwoman to boot – is the continual and largely unconscious compulsion to be nice. Nice and kind, nice and fair, nice and tidy. Nice. Always ready to understand the other point of view. Always careful not to give a wrong impression.

It would be a tragedy if the still embryonic Women's Liberation Movement in this country sank without trace into the amniotic fluid of niceness, but already I detect some signs. The women directly concerned with organising the March 6 demo, though they point with pride to the massive WL movement in the US seem not to have learned very much from the performance of their American sisters. They bend over backwards to be fair. ('We must be very careful not to assume that if a woman is refused a job it is sexual discrimination' – why? It's not our job to worry about fairness.) They talk too much about wanting to be taken seriously; they say too often how much they deprecate extremes and shudder with refined horror at bra-burnings and at SCUM and WITCH. Not at all the image we want, they say, metaphorically crooking their little fingers and adjusting their petal hats. We don't want to go to jail, or worse, be laughed at.

The tendency among these ladies is to sneer at the Germaine Greers of the movement and, indeed, it is easy enough to carp at sweeping generalisations and lack of careful factual research. But anger, neurosis, insights, obsession and extremism is where it is at and women will have lost the battle before it has begun if they reject all this and concentrate their energies only on concrete injustice. Reforms like equal pay, equal job opportunities, free contraception, better nursery schools, have needed implementation as long as I can remember, and armies of hard-working, dedicated women have been pushing them forward as long as I can remember, too, and a great deal longer. The only new ingredient Women's Lib ever had to offer was the intellectual recognition of an imprisoned psyche and the realisation that when that inner battle is fought and won, concrete injustices crumble at the roots.

And that is not done by being nice. American liberationists did not surge into life thinking of the other chap's point of view or making constant efforts to be fair, moderate, cool and ladylike. They succeeded by being prejudiced, unfair, immoderate, uncool, and devastatingly unladylike and they came up with the only symbolic image of the movement so far – bra-burning. A small and risible thing, perhaps, but their own. Yet even this causes a throwing up of hands in England – one girl commented last week, among general agreement, that she hoped no one would freak out that way on such a serious demo.

In fact the whole point of bra-burning seems to have vanished from some English liberationists' minds. Have they forgotten that, hilarious though it may be, the bra is a presentation pack, two breasts, gift-wrapped, to please the customer, with as many human variations as possible camouflaged under the implacable stitching? And by rejecting bra-burning (or any other symbolic act in favour of the concrete) they reject anger almost before it begins. Ah yes, there was a faint smell of burning there a while ago, but we're glad to report that it's now well under control.

American Women's Liberationists go to extremes, but I cannot personally think of any widespread injustice that has been remedied by plodding worthily down the middle of the road, smiling and smiling. The argument against extremism, however non-violent, is that you risk alienating people who might otherwise support your cause, but does this hold water? Where have all those potential supporters been over the last 2,000 years? Nodding sleepily in their corner, rousing only to growl about extremism when disturbed by a particular extreme. But by actively alienating some people (or not caring if you do) the debate is immediately polarised: furious reactions prod previously uncommitted women into action and if you are sure of the justice of your cause it must be better to have people thinking of it with initial anger than not thinking at all. As to the fear of derision, that is anger in another guise.

Another hurdle for nice, reasonable English ladies is to realise that nice, reasonable English gentlemen are, to some extent, the Enemy. There are, for instance, very few women 'free' enough to pursue a cogent emancipation argument in the presence of a man (granted he isn't the Hunchback of Notre Dame), without feeling a terrible urge to soften the hard edge, to persuade him in subtle ways that, after all, you're lovely when you're angry. This weakness – a resignation to the sexual object role – must be recognised and accepted quite coldly by women, and they must protect themselves carefully from it until such time as they are more secure.

Ladies, unite. Let us cherish our freaks and fanatics, cultivate our obsessions, hone our anger to a fine point and never, never, listen to anyone who says, 'be reasonable'. Our own voices will tell us that too often, as it is.

29 MARCH 1972

Shirley for President

Shirley Chisholm challenges the assumption that a woman – and a black woman at that – has no place in the White House

WILLA PETSCHEK

She strides down the shabby streets of Manhattan's Lower East Side, opens the door of a shop selling magic potions and voodoo charms, and marches inside. 'Hello mom, hello sister, I'm Fighting Shirley Chisholm, the only black woman in Congress. I'm running for the presidency of the United States and I need your help. Please vote for me.'

A dark-skinned woman cries 'We're with you sister' and Mrs Chisholm moves on. Outside a Chinese grocery offering bean curds and eggs in brines, she repeats her spiel. A young white house-wife pledges her support and a bearded student promises Mrs Chisholm his vote in the New York primary in June.

Straight-backed, regal, and with an almost messianic belief in her own abilities, the fiery representative from the Bedford Stuyvesant slum in Brooklyn is challenging the notion that the American people will not vote for a qualified candidate simply because he is not white or because she is not male.

For days that start at dawn and end past midnight, she is on the road, campaigning in 15 states and speaking on campuses, but the route is uphill all the way. Black male politicians have refused to endorse her – 'They're no different from white politicians and it's difficult tor them to accept the fact that women are human beings,' she says scornfully. In addition, her campaign lacks what she terms Madison Avenue packaging and money: other Democratic contenders are spending a million dollars apiece on the primaries while so far she has raised only $50,000.

Standing on a street corner, her bifocals planted firmly on her nose, Mrs Chisholm rails against liberal candidates such as Lindsay, McGovern, and McCarthy who complain she is splitting the votes of blacks, women, and the young. '"Why don't you get out?" they say. And I say "George, John, and Gene, you all look alike to me – you're all white, you're all male. I'm the only unique one who's running. Why don't you flip a coin and one of you get out instead?" And the crowd roars "Sock it to them Shirley."'

Whatever the outcome of her campaign, Mrs Chisholm's bid for the presidency is a natural progression in her extraordinary career. Blessed with a shatterproof ego ('Thirty-six men have been President of the United States and I am better than all but six or seven of them') and wholly independent ('unbought and unbossed' is the slogan she used when elected to Congress) she has fought the political machine for 20 years and come out on top.

'My rise has been constantly fighting. I've had to fight doubly hard and of the two handicaps being black is much less a drawback than being a woman,' she says passionately into the microphone, her clipped Caribbean accent a legacy of her parentage and early childhood.

Born 47 years ago in the Brooklyn district she now represents, Shirley was the daughter of a West Indian immigrant couple, her father a labourer in a hessian sack factory, her mother a domestic worker.

When she was three, Shirley was sent to live with her grandmother in Barbados while her parents struggled against the Depression back home. Her earliest heroine was the suffragette Susan B Anthony. Jeered at by male hecklers during her street corner campaign she quotes Miss Anthony: 'The hour is come when women will no longer be the passive recipients.' 'That always stops them cold,' she says happily. 'Women have to learn to flex their political muscles. You've got to flex your muscles to get what you want.'

Graduating from Columbia University, she became a teacher – 'what else could a black woman do' – and later the distinguished director of a daycare centre and educational consultant to the city's Bureau of Child Welfare. She also became active in Brooklyn Democratic politics.

Elected to the Senate in 1964, she was the second black woman to sit in the Assembly, the first being the wife of a Harlem businessman whose chief accomplishment in four years was getting the legislature to decide on an official New York State anthem. Mrs Chisholm (and it is definitely Mrs not Ms: 'I don't get hung up on these things – sure I'm part of the woman's movement but there are other issues that are far more important') quickly acquired the reputation of being a maverick, a designation which delights her. She sponsored the first bill offering unemployment insurance benefits to domestic workers and initiated the SEEK programme, a higher education plan to give state scholarships to poor, bright, black, and Puerto Rican children.

The real breakthrough came in 1968 when she was elected to Congress, beating James Farmer (the nationally known director of the Congress of Racial Equality) by two and a half to one – the ratio of women to men voters in the district. Her battle was fought from a sound truck. As she recalls it: 'The truck would pull up to a housing project or a group of stores and I'd get up there and say "Ladies and Gentlemen, this is Fighting Shirley Chisholm coming through." Meanwhile my female workers would hand out literature – a couple of thousand pieces at each stop. I have a theory about campaigning. You got to let people feel you.'

As the first black Congresswoman ever elected to the House, she was furious at being assigned to the agriculture and forestry committee. 'I guess all the gentlemen in Washington know about

Brooklyn is that a tree once grew there,' she snorted to her husband, Conrad, a New York City welfare investigator to whom she has been happily married for 22 years and who is active in his wife's campaign.

Outraged, she took her case to the next meeting of the House Democratic Caucus and after an unprecedented battle was switched to Veterans' Affairs, hardly her first choice but nevertheless a victory. 'At least,' Mrs Chisholm told reporters, 'there is a veterans' hospital in Brooklyn and I intend to use my position on the committee to make people more aware of their eligibility for the hospital and other veterans' benefits.' She also established a reform in abortion law and quickly became known for her outspoken comments on racial and social inequalities.

'One thing the people in New York and Washington are afraid of is Shirley Chisholm's mouth,' she says forcefully, her head in its elegant wig nodding, and her listeners cry 'Right on Shirley'. She describes herself as a standard bearer for all those minorities and women who have been powerless in a political system dominated by white males. Clenching her fist she talks about black and Spanish-speaking farm workers who cannot afford enough food for their own children, and of the American Indian 'whom we exorcised from the human race'.

Her campaign programme demands immediate withdrawal from Vietnam and a qualified amnesty for draft evaders, more money spent on welfare, and legalisation of pot. But her number one concern is foreign aid. 'Women all over the country have come up to me to ask if I'd give all the taxpayer's money to other countries the way male presidents have.' She says only that she is opposed to foreign aid for dictatorships and countries which don't clamp down on drug traffic.

Mrs Chisholm insists she is gunning for the presidency but says privately that her 'more realistic goal' is to win enough delegates to force leading candidates to adopt her programme at the Democratic National Convention in July. An alternative possibility would be the vice-presidency. She says that anyone who wants the votes of her delegates will have to nominate a black for vice-president, a woman to run the Department of Health, Education, and Welfare, and an Indian as Secretary of the Interior – 'the American dream come true'.

'Join me on the Chisholm trail,' she begs, her voice rising with evangelical fervour. 'We can make the real America heard at last. The black alone can't do it. The young people alone can't do it. The women alone can't do it. But together all these groups are rising up together in yearning and frustration to get their share of the American dream and participate in the decision making processes that govern all our lives.'

19 JULY 1973

'I'm just a speaker. I've spoke to thousands. I'm glad I'm no cleaner no more, it's bleedin' 'ard work'

May Hobbs, night cleaner, militant and author talks about her life in the East End

ANNA COOTE

Three years ago May Hobbs was a cleaning lady and trade union militant. Today she is an author and co-opted star of the media-conscious elements of Women's Liberation.

May Hobbs put night cleaners on the map. Until she started shouting, people barely knew they existed. She founded the Cleaners Action Group and gathered considerable support from the women's movement and leftwing political groups. Many of the night cleaners were unionised and the campaign reached its high-spot last summer with a successful and well-publicised strike at the Ministry of Defence.

Meanwhile the night cleaners put May on the map. She is now a regular speaker at women's rights meetings, where she comes across like Jack Dash at a Rotary Club lunch and is loved for it. She appears frequently on television. Foreign journalists fly in to interview her. A shrewd publisher asked her to write a book about her life in the East End. It comes out next week. The book will be made into a film. Another book is planned . . .

She lives in a ramshackle old council house in Hornsey with Chris, the man she's been with for the past 14 years, and four good-looking, scruffy kids. They all wander in and out making mugs of tea and she sits in a corner of the settee and talks.

'I'm getting like you lot now,' she says. 'I'm just a speaker. I've spoke to thousands. I can't be people's spokesman no more – they've got to be their own.' She's stepping down from the cleaners' campaign. 'We've got people like Maria Scally and Myrtle. They're potential leaders. If they think you're going to do their thinking and running about for them, they're quite contented to let you get on with it. But as soon as you say "Right you are, you're on your own," they zoom. And this is how it should be. I'm no cleaner no more. I'm glad I'm not a bloody cleaner no more, it's bleedin' 'ard work.'

She wishes that more ordinary women could be offered the plat-form that she has been given. For instance, she last spoke at a meeting organised by Women in Media to herald the report stage of Lady Seear's sex discrimination bill: 'You know what gave me the needle at this last meeting? We had a beautiful black woman there. She was a nurse, she had a sick child and she had to do night cleaning and she had problems with her husband who wouldn't pay ... she would have told a marvellous story. From two o'clock until five o'clock I tried to get this woman up on the stage and they wouldn't let her up. They kept saying there's all these poetry readings. Why the hell did they have the Joan Bakewells there? And why can't they say to Shirley Williams: "I'm very sorry but you can speak for 24 hours a bleedin' day and there's a woman here who wants to tell her story . . . ?" Why do they have all these nice blah-de-blah people? What is it? Does it make good press publicity?'

Whatever Joan Bakewell and Shirley Williams have got, May Hobbs evidently has it, too. 'I always get roped in some way or other. They don't ask me to speak on the cleaners so much now, it's more on women's things, which I rather like. Also by going to these meetings it learns me a bit more, you know.'

She first confronted the issue of women's liberation three or four years ago when members of the women's movement started to help her with the night cleaners' campaign. When she speaks on the subject, she doesn't bother with polemics or profundities. It's all straightforward, emotional stuff. It's the way she says it that counts. She can seize any meeting by the scruff of its neck and shake it into a frenzy of foot-stamping and applause.

More than anything, it's her amazing cockney oratory that has brought her to prominence. And prominence has its perks. 'There's thousands of women who've had the same life as me; maybe worse. But would I have ever been able to get this book published if I'd have been Maria Scally or just another little housewife, or May Hobbs six years ago?'

She has written her book in a matter-of-fact conversational manner: she describes Hoxton, the East End community where she was born; her childhood in foster homes; the dead-end factory jobs she was forced into when she left school; her brush with the law which took her to Holloway for a month; the arrival of her kids amid constant evictions from one dismal, high-priced flat after another; and finally her involvement with the night cleaners' campaign. She deals with the campaign briefly, since it occupied only four of her 35 years. The second half of the book consists of a series of yarns about petty crime in the East End, which don't appear to involve her at all.

'If I do write another book, I'll write it about the cleaners. I can incorporate the whole campaign into it, but I'll write it in a story form, as if it's 'A Week of the Office Cleaner,' so it'll be more interesting to read. But I ain't going to write another one if this is a flop.'

This one took her about seven weeks to complete. Some bits she wrote herself. Others she told to Chris and he wrote it down as she spoke. 'Me and Chris have worked together all the way through. People have said "Why is she always with Chris?" But the thing is we do everything t'bleedingether. If I wasn't on the picket line, he was on it and the girls came to rely on him as much as they did on me.'

They both belong to the Communist party, although May admits she seldom goes to the meetings. 'I got in for the simple reason that I thought well you've got to work on these things, not keep on moaning about them and when I got in I thought thank god I'm in because it does need some bloody altering!'

May's real politics seem to lie in her activities as a self-appointed guerrilla social worker and troubleshooter. 'People come round to us with problems. We had a young mum round the other day, an unsupported mum with two kids and she told me about her electric. She'd taken nine quid out of the meter. She'd only seen her social worker that day and I said "Why didn't you tell the bleedin' social worker?" and she said "Well, I was frightened." Why? Because they talk that much more different. They've not had the experience of them women, having no bread on the table and not having no shilling for the meter, and then they wonder why in some cases the women have to break the meter open. To them it's wrong. But if your kid's bloody hungry, well fuck the meter. Wallop, it's open. This is what it's all about. When it comes to it; you cross the bridge. So I told the social worker who just said "Make sure it don't happen again," and now the Welfare's going to pay.

'If people are homeless they come round to us first. There was a young couple, they'd been sleeping in a van. They came round to us, for us to tell the Welfare that they've been sleeping in a van. Now they've got a council house. When my mate Sheila was evicted she had seven kids. Round she come, she brought all her kids in. "How can you tell them ponces?" she said. That's what Sheila used to call the Welfare. "They're not interested in our problems, it keeps them employed, don't it?"'

With all this to cope with, May says she's 'too bleedin' busy to go out to work'. What's more, Georgia Brown and Midge Mackenzie are making a film of her book and she's helping them write the script. 'Georgia Brown is being me. Why not – she come from the East End, don't she?'

So May Hobbs, night cleaner, militant, and author becomes May Hobbs immortalised on celluloid. May Hobbs working-class hero. But the radical elements of Women's Liberation do not want heroes and stars, and she is beginning to come in for a bit of criticism. 'I got this letter saying would I like to go to the Women of the Year function and I'd be sitting at the top table with all the celebrities. These women said, "Surely you're not going are you May?" I said, "Fuckin' right I am, it's a free nosh!" It's only in the last six months to a year that I've been invited to all these posh restaurants and posh dinners. The point is they've had it all. And just because, god, you know what I mean, just because I want a little bit of it now, they all get the needle and say I shouldn't go.

'When I saw that people like Mary Wilson and Lady Harewood was going to be there, I felt quite honoured to be invited among all that lot. I won't get all titivated up for it. I'll have me hair done because I like having me hair done. I've got one long dress that I've worn to every bloody thing that I've been to, and I shall wear that. So why should people have a go at me because I've been invited? I'm going because it's a free eat. Wherever I'm invited, if it's a free nosh-up May's there. Anyway, I just think it's nice. You come home and you've got something to talk about.'

12 JULY 1974

An unresolved strike

'All Indian ladies respect older men. We thought that if we respected the foremen they would respect us. We've learned a lot of things'

ANNA COOTE

'My sister-in-law, this is her first job. When she came to the factory they put her on training at £18 a week. After four weeks the foreman said: "Now you're on your own." He told her she had to complete 200 machine parts a day to earn about £22 a week. There were six ladies doing the same job, but they only had to complete 150 a day for the same money. She could never manage 200, so she was still earning £18 a week. Every day the foreman came to her and said: "If you don't do 200 you'll get your cards." Once she came home crying. She is afraid she won't get another job if she is sacked.'

Sobhna Doshe speaks very little English. She is a slight, timid woman of 22, who looks no more than 16. Jayshree, who is a year younger but almost fluent in English, speaks for her. The two women are Ugandan Asians and employed at the Imperial Type-writer Company at its Leicester factory. They have been on strike for the past 12 weeks.

They are among 600 Asian workers who have walked out and stayed out – since the dispute began on May 1. The majority are women and they have proved themselves stalwart supporters. It has been no ordinary strike. The white workers at the factory have refused to support it. The Transport and General Workers' Union (to which most of the factory employees belong) has refused to make it official. It held an inquiry two months ago, but has not yet produced a report. Six pickets have been arrested, refused legal aid and fined. The magazine Race Today has launched a national support campaign. Next Monday, the strike is expected to make news again, as the factory reopens after its annual holiday and the pickets return to the gates.

The company is owned by Litton Industries, a multinational corporation based in Los Angeles which also controls Olympic, Triumph and Adler typewriters, and manufactures navigation and data processing systems for the US armed forces. Between 1968 and 1972, it doubled its workforce at the Leicester factory in order to introduce assembly-line production. This coincided with the exodus of Asians from Kenya and Uganda – who now make up a substantial proportion of Imperial's 1700 employees. 'This is not a racial dispute, it is a workers' dispute,' Jayshree Doshe insisted. She and a group of other women described the issues behind the strike. The workers are paid according to a system of piecework and bonuses based on 10-week averages which is so complicated that none of them understands it. 'You get different money each week and you never know how much to expect. When you think you are going to get more, you get less.' They are regularly timed at their jobs and as they get more proficient their quota is increased, but not their pay. They are frequently switched from one job to another or given three or four jobs to do at once. They claim that white workers get the better jobs, faster promotion and are seldom expected to do more than one job at a time.

On average, the women are paid about £19 a week and the men £25. The company has recently redesignated a number of 'men's jobs' as 'women's jobs' at considerably lower rates, which suggests it is preparing to soften the impact of the Equal Pay Act.

One of the women's main grievances is the way they are treated by the foremen. Jayshree explained: 'There is no tea break, but there is a tea machine and we can help ourselves. Whenever we go to get tea, the foreman is always after us, saying "Come on girls, stop wasting time; get back to work." Some of the ladies are afraid of the foreman and they don't dare to argue. Some are afraid even to go to the toilet because the foreman is rude to them. If he thinks they stay too long, he says: "What are you doing in there? Hurry up." But a white woman can stay in the toilet for 10, 15 minutes and he doesn't say anything.'

'He treats us like children,' said Shardaben, a widow of 32 with three children to support. 'We used to treat him like God. All Indian ladies respect older men. At first we thought that if we respected the foremen, they would respect us. We've learnt a lot of things.'

Their middle-class Hindu upbringing was a poor preparation for industrial strife. They had been taught to defer to their elders, particularly to men, and to accept their husband's word as law. In addition, they had to tackle a foreign language in order to query a wage system so complex that it would defy a British-born economist. Few of them had jobs in Uganda: waged labour and trade unionism were beyond their experience.

When Jayshree came to the factory two years ago, she filled in a form saying she wanted to join the union. 'Only three months ago they sent me my card. I thought they must have forgotten, but then I discovered that my dues had been deducted from my wages all along.' Until the dispute began, she had no idea what a shop steward was.

There are only 18 in the factory – one for every 200 workers. The Asian workers never knew when elections and meetings were taking place and they assumed the stewards were appointed by the factory convenor, Reg Weaver. One woman had been working at the factory for five years and didn't know the convenor's name. They had difficulty distinguishing the union officials from the management. 'There is one lady in our department, a shop steward. If you take a complaint to her she talks to the foreman and then she comes back and says: "Sorry. I can't help you." If you say you want more money, she says: "Wait until next week." They always promise "next week".'

As a fighting mood developed among the Asian workers, they nominated two of their own people for election as shop stewards Both were vetoed by Weaver on the grounds that they had not been in the union two years (a rule dating back to 1941 which is considered obsolete by most branches of the union). When they walked out on May 1, the union virtually ignored them.

The strikers are demanding democratic election of shop stewards; a new wages system which does not result in low wages, overwork and bonus-cheating; equality of opportunity with white workers and an end to petty discrimination. They also want to return to work without victimisation. The union is in an embarrassing position, as it also represents the white workers who oppose the strike. Weaver has warned that if the strike leaders return to the factory after a settlement, there will be a massive walk-out of white workers. From the strikers' point of view, this looks as if the union is taking a racist position and accepting management plans for victimisation (the company has said it will not re-employ 24 unnamed 'ringleaders'.)

George Bromley, the district secretary of the TGWU, has consistently opposed the strike and attacked the leaders. He told me that Leicester had absorbed successive waves of immigrants and there had never been any trouble until 'this lot' arrived with ideas above their station. 'They've had an easy time out there with swimming pools and servants. They're not used to British industrial life.' As for the two-year rule, he agreed that 'a blind eye could be taken' but he was not prepared to do so. 'I don't want to bother you with esoteric doctrine, sweetheart, you know what these rules are like, they can be complex.' How was he planning to work out a solution? 'What can I do? I don't know what they want. I don't think they want to go back to work.'

Twelve weeks is a long time to stay out without union backing. Most of the strikers have been unable to get any social security, although they should be entitled to benefit for their dependents. Shardaben has been refused money for her three children. It is only because they live in 'extended' families that some of them can keep going. But where several members of the same family are on strike the extended family system is a positive disadvantage. Many have continued to work out of financial necessity although they support the cause.

The women I met seemed determined to stay out until their demands were met. They had learnt a lot, certainly. They were no longer afraid of the foremen, nor of the management, and they were learning how to assert their rights. But there were only two women on the strike committee of nine and they still deferred to the men. Equal pay was not one of the strike demands. They were under the impression that the Equal Pay Act would solve that problem for them and were unaware that the management had ways of avoiding it. However, they plan to set up a women's committee when they return to work, in order to deal with their own particular problems.

Meanwhile, racial tension in Leicester is growing. White people who live near the factory have begun to display open hostility. The strikers are waiting for the union to produce its report and they hope it will back their demands and start negotiations on their behalf. They insist that they want to remain within the TGWU and that the differences between black and white workers are merely the fruits of divide-and-rule tactics employed by the management. But they are feeling isolated. 'The trade unions keep saying it is wrong to build separate black unions. But where the hell is their support?'

6 MARCH 1974

Maggie May

MARY STOTT

I once startled the sixth form boys of a grammar school by saying that it was on the cards that the pretty girl whose legs they eyed as she got on a bus might one day be their boss. That was three years ago. I don't think I imagined the emanation of hostility, and as I have never heard a word from their headmaster from that day to this I have always supposed he rather regretted inviting me.

I wasn't surprised that clever, ambitious boys winced away from the idea that they might have to take orders from a woman. I was staggered, astounded, that in such a short space of time the climate of opinion could have changed so much that the boys' equally clever and ambitious older brothers, uncles, and fathers had willingly, eagerly, bent their necks to the yoke of Margaret Thatcher. Not one of them, surely, was so purblind as to suppose that they were electing an attractive new image-maker who could be manipulated by men? They knew, they must have known, that they were giving a tough and astute politician power to hire and fire, to promote and emote, to elevate and humiliate, and indeed, within days she had sent Peter Walker and Robert Carr packing.

That's politics. Willie Whitelaw or James Prior would have done similar. But the new leader of the opposition is a woman. Suppose it had not been politics but business. (And, indeed, if Ms Thatcher ever becomes prime minister it will be a matter of earning power.) How would you like to get the boot from a female, sir?

The revolutionary implications of Margaret Thatcher's election have been largely glossed over by men. Within a few days the Word in Edgeways radio panellists took their cue from Brian Redhead and discussed the topical theme 'leadership' for 50 minutes, without referring to the choice of a woman as leader. It struck me as exceedingly odd, but I suspect now that it will take more than a few weeks for men to accept and discuss openly that things can't be quite the same again, because a basic brick has been removed from the edifice of beliefs and prejudices about the roles of women. The committee of the Carlton Club, for example, must be protecting itself by a sort of deliberate amnesia after having had to admit Ms Thatcher to membership. On what ground can they stand when any other distinguished woman comes knocking at the door?

'The custom of the trade,' so to speak, will no longer stand up as a justification for keeping women out of top jobs – or any other kind of job. A few years ago, Barbara Castle said at a dinner given in her honour by the Fawcett Society when she was minister of employment: 'We have conquered the credibility gap.' Perhaps she was a bit premature ... but only a bit, because now the bounds of belief have been limitlessly stretched. Why not a woman director-general of the BBC or the CBI? Why not a woman chairman of the BMA or the Coal Board? Why not a woman as editor of the Guardian or Times or as conductor of the LSO?

As to Ms Thatcher herself – she is certainly a rare phenomenon but equally not unique, except in so far as every human being is unique, in brains or beauty. I do suspect that part of her success lies in the fact that she looks entirely feminine in the nicest possible and most English way ... blonde hair, blue eyes, pretty complexion, pretty, very photogenic, and practically indelible smile. Her choice of clothes is tasteful rather than exciting. She is the very picture of an ideal wife for a Conservative MP. Moreover, her voice is sweet and low; it is impossible to imagine her sounding shrill, indulging in a temper tantrum, or bursting into tears. Or, indeed, the age-old arts of Eve. She is said to hate being called unfeminine. Well, it all depends on what you mean by feminine. Her kind is no threat either to wives or to conventional-minded men. Professor Higgins might have created someone exactly like her as his ideal Galatea.

It isn't surprising that Ms Thatcher's election has not been greeted with triumphant fanfares throughout the whole length and breadth of the women's movement. She has never declared herself as a campaigning feminist, much less a liberationist. Unlike other women members of her party, she did not speak in favour of Willie Hamilton's anti-discrimination bill at either of the debates in the Commons. When she was minister of education she told a deputation from Women in Media that she did not believe there was any discrimination against girls in schools or colleges which could be remedied by act of parliament. She surely would not agree with Roy Jenkins's view that there should be positive discrimination in favour of women to help them to catch up. It will be interesting to see Ms Thatcher's reaction to the equal opportunities bill which Mr Jenkins has promised to lay before the House very shortly. My guess is that it will be distinctly cool, perhaps even critical. Almost certainly less sympathetic than Robert Carr's reaction if he had still been shadow home secretary.

For Margaret Thatcher is the very epitome of the self-made woman who believes that any woman worth her salt can also get unaided to the top.

If Margaret Thatcher had been a kind of Francoise Giroud

(minister for women's affairs in the French government) she would not have had the remotest chance of sitting in the front seat of the front bench, and I believe it is much more important to the future of the little girls now at school that she should be there than that she should turn aside from the battles with the Treasury and the Foreign Office or talks with foreign heads of state to give equal pay or equal opportunities a helpful push along.

That's the job of us unmeritorious females who, unlike Ms Thatcher, have too often taken no for an answer and are prepared to fight to see that our daughters won't do the same.

5 JULY 1975

She has been through the gamut of radical chic New York experience, from her days as a freelance journalist when she was an escort to Henry Kissinger through a series of 'little marriages'

Interview with Gloria Steinem

CAROL DIX

Gloria Steinem was a guest on a New York late-night TV talk show chaired by Jimmy Breslin. Author of The Gang That Couldn't Shoot Straight, and one-time co-mayoral candidate with Norman Mailer, even this most confident man was made to wriggle nervously in his seat by Ms Steinem's presence. Would she show him up for the obvious male chauvinist that he is?

Breslin conducted his defence well, showing he was on her side. He said the Women's Movement had already had an untold effect because he knew a Congressman whose wife taught in the evenings and he refused to go for drinks with the boys because he's got to get the kids' dinner and put them to bed. And that, even in International Women's Year, is presumably a lot.

Gloria Steinem was mild and sweet-tempered on television, gentle with Breslin's sensitive ego. That morning I had been along to the offices of Ms magazine, which she co-founded and largely edits, for an interview. Her life is still a constant round of magazine work, lecturing and public appearances, and she is getting quite tired of doing too much. 'I don't mind going on TV when I can express myself, but I get tired of bad write-ups. People magazine said we had gone underground because I refused them an interview. They just are not used to being refused.'

She is still news because, in spite of certain suspicions, women have not been indifferent to the notion of their liberation, and because Ms has now achieved the status of a full three-year run.

Ms (pronounced Miz) is solid and serious, which makes its achievement more of a surprise. And it is run on strictly professional lines. They run a regular feature on lost women, cover politics, sport and ideas; review (very well) fiction, cinema and art and have recently exposed discrimination in the UN.

Ms has the 13th floor of an anonymous Lexington Avenue block. The only sign of nonconformity is the replacement of No 13 with Ms when the elevator lights flash up. The working environment is the usual: open-plan layout with some cubicle offices to house the staff of 50. Some men do walk about, quite happily, and one toddler crawls about. The telephones are painted yellow but apart from that the atmosphere is quite stark and anonymous.

Gloria Steinem became a household name as the 'glamour girl' of the Women's Movement because she has a deep and gritty voice, and is very attractive. She never felt the need 'to walk round in army boots and cut off her hair' to avoid being a sex object. Contrary to the image that has been coming over here about New York-style feminists – that they are frighteningly butch and terrifyingly liberated – Steinem is remarkably unusual. She still wears her hair long, sits behind large blue-tinted glasses and surprised me by the fact she wears panstick and pale pink lipstick. Whoever would have thought of the spokeswoman for feminism wearing pale pink lipstick?

She is 39 now, and comes from Ohio, the daughter of an itinerant antique salesman and newspaper reporter mother, and granddaughter of an early feminist. She has been through the gamut of radical chic New York experience, from her days as a freelance journalist when she was escort to Henry Kissinger, and appeared in magazines at openings and events. Her non-married state is well-known, as is the fact she had an abortion, and has been through a series of 'little marriages'. Unlike some of the movement's stars, she has not suffered from the exposure. 'I was an experienced journalist already,' she explains, 'so I knew it was all shit. I mean, I know journalists are cynical of notoriety and that's healthy really.'

She led the way to revolt by writing articles in the late 1960s about Playboy Bunnies, the new marriage, and the moral rearmament of Betty Co-Ed. The beginnings of Ms magazine, though, were fraught with doubt and fed by desperation. Precisely because Steinem was a well-known journalist, it had not escaped her notice that she was still expected to cover fashion or pop stars, and that politics and even profiles of authors were usually left to men. If she wanted to write an article about the emerging feminist movement, then magazine editors would say: 'Oh, my dear, we did our feminist article last year.'

'Most of my energy at that time went into not writing about fashion, food and children. So I began to go out and speak to community groups and on campuses out of frustration,' she says. It was from those meetings that the idea of a new magazine for women grew. The women who co-founded it all took a leap into the unknown, for no one knew whether it was needed or realistic.

Pat Carbine left McCalls and took a huge cut in salary – 'it meant giving up her stock option too'; Nina Finkelstein came from book publishing; Letty Cottin Pogrebin had been a publicist; Harriet Lyons was on Fan magazine; and Mary Peacock had edited an underground 'anti-fashion' magazine.

'Few of us,' says Steinem, 'had been working up to our capacity. Nina had been fired for being uppity.' Nina Finkelstein adds: 'I'd been working for 25 years and I'd never found the sense of personal dignity and freedom that came with this job. Still, it wasn't an easy decision. Letty came to me and said: "Where's your head at?" and I didn't know. I'd never named myself a feminist at that time and we weren't going to be paid at first.'

Gloria Steinem gave up a position in journalism which had previously seemed unattainable. New York Magazine, edited by Clay Felker, had taken her on as a political reporter. She wrote a column called City Politic in which she was able to give her personal analysis of the New York scene. She covered Eugene McCarthy and George McGovern's presidential candidacies, adding her liberal voice to their other backers; and supported, as might be expected, the California grape pickers, Angela Davis, the Black Panthers, Eskimos and Indians.

Then, in November 1968, there was a meeting of a New York women's group called the Redstockings which she covered for her column.

'I was exceedingly dumb for a long time. I'd always understood what made me angry about the Playboy Club, or the double standard of not being able to do political writing or being sent out for coffee. Before that Redstocking meeting I had thought that my problems and experience were my own and not part of a larger political problem.

'Thanks to other women, I began to understand. It was as if a light bulb had connected.'

I asked what she felt about dropping political reporting in favour of writing for women. She said: 'I was reporting the traditional political situation, and feeling proud of myself, when I began to realise that it was only about white males over the age of 35, with the occasional black or token woman. As soon as you see that politics is in our daily lives then it changes your viewpoint. I once worked for ABC-TV and they said: "We don't want you to limit yourself to women and blacks." That's an awful lot of the world.'

The politics of daily lives is brought into their office. At Ms there is no receptionist, nor do secretaries sit filing their nails or reading romances. They type their own notes and letters, and answer their own telephones. One national paper said that Ms was going broke because Steinem had answered her own telephone.

They earn reasonable living salaries, they say; and pay their contributors less than the New York Times but a lot more than underground papers – and the same rate goes for professional as for unknown writers. They receive 300 or 400 unsolicited manuscripts a year and read them all. They have published, for example, a new marriage contract which just came to them in the mail and a short story from an unknown woman who won a prize and a book contract after its publication. 'It's nice to see it all blossom,' reflects Steinem.

Some of the profits are siphoned off into the Ms Foundation, a charity for sponsoring other women's groups and projects. Money also goes into the foundation from the publication of a Ms Reader and a record/book/TV show promotion called Free To Be You and Me. Is that for children? 'Well, yes,' says Steinem, 'but I like it.'

Financially, they have succeeded beyond belief. They began with backing from Clay Felker who carried the pilot edition in the centre pages of New York Magazine (those issues now sell for $25). The owner of the Washington Post, Katherine Graham, invested $8,000 and they were backed by Warner Communications (film, TV, records, car rental and parking lots) to the tune of $1m. 'Most small magazines,' she explains, 'begin on $3m and hope to break even in their first two or three years. We broke even after one year, on $1m.'

Circulation is now about 400,000 after a starting point of 250,000, and the staff know that they reach beyond the card-carrying feminists because only 15% of their readers belong to women's groups. 'A magazine is easy. It's passive and friendly. It drops through your door every month, so it's no hard commitment,' she says.

'We want to reach women all over the country and of all types. We're no different to them. We started from one room, with orange crates for desks, and a gesture of faith from the people coming to work for us. Mostly, though, we were consumed with not failing, otherwise people would say: "See, the Women's Movement is meaningless." That was typically female, to be consumed with not failing rather than with success. Or should I say, "culturally typically female",' and she laughs at her mistake. You don't have to be an ogre to be a feminist and a success.

12 DECEMBER 1975

Brothers to blame

Susan Brownmiller talks about Against Our Will, her study of rape

TIMERI N. MURARI

The dust-jacket portrait of Susan Brownmiller, author of Against Our Will: Men, Women and Rape, showed her as an attractive, gently smiling woman. The contents, however, are a different matter entirely.

Three days of reading a thoroughly well-documented book on the history of rape was a disturbing experience: somewhat like walking through a minefield scattered with a few squibs but also some psychically – for the male anyway – damaging explosions. The main theme of her book is that rape is not a sex act, nor does it have anything to do with the male-female relationship. Rape is a male-male power relationship, whether it takes place in war, in gang rapes, or by a single individual down a dark, grim alley.

Ms Brownmiller is energetic and articulate and, as she describes herself, 'combative, wary and verbally aggressive'. She is also uncompromising and put me immediately at unease by stating she preferred the company of women to men. She is a slim, tousle-haired woman of 40, unmarried by choice, who laughs a lot, sometimes nervously and sometimes with genuine humour. She is going to need a lot of that humour to keep her going for already the book is rocketing up the bestseller list, publishers are reverently murmuring that paperback rights will range around half a million dollars, and she is now embarked on a marathon coast-to-coast publicising trip.

'I was brought up an old-fashioned New York liberal,' she says. It is only occasionally, as if it's a lapse in manners, that she falls into using feminist dialectic jargon. 'My conception of rape had been conditioned by my background. Rape was a sex act, rape was the act of a deranged mind. I didn't believe that rape had anything to do with the feminist movement.

'In 1968 when I covered a black on white rape trial, I took a very political view and believed that the black men were the victims of society. I didn't even interview the female victim. Then, in 1971, when I helped to organise a Rape Speakout, I thought there would be no contribution from the women in the audience. But the women did want to talk about what happened to them or their friends, and it was in this discussion with my feminist sisters that I discovered that rape was a male-male power relationship. I'm a woman who changed her mind about rape.'

Brownmiller, who'd been approached often by publishers because of her writings in Esquire, Village Voice, and other magazines to 'do a book', changed her mind so emphatically that she decided she was going to write the definitive history of rape. On the advice of her publishers and agent, she signed a contract to deliver the manuscript within a year, but at the end of eight months she found she'd only begun to research a shadowy and obscure subject. The reason for the shadow, she says, was because all history had been written by men, and they'd lightly skipped over the subject. She ran out of money but fortunately a foundation came to her rescue with a grant.

'My publishers said: "Don't bother about source notes",' Brownmiller says with a laugh. 'But the serious writers I met in the New York library, where I did all my work, said if I was wanting to be taken seriously I had to include every source. It was in some ways a depressing experience, but also quite exhilarating.

'You'll be interested to know how I researched my information on English rape. I'd seen a television programme on Culloden made by the BBC and the name just stuck in my mind. So when I began on the English section, I checked Culloden and found this book by John Prebble. For British law, I found nearly everyone referring to Brackton, and I couldn't find out who he was. I kept going farther and farther back, until I found two books in Latin by Brackton. I nearly gave up.' Thankfully, for her, she found that Yale had only recently done a translation on the 13th-century jurist.

The book bludgeons the reader with the gruesome details and footnotes of man's inhumanity to woman, and, in a chapter on homosexual rape, on man himself. Brownmiller herself has never been raped and decided not to have children.

'It's an interesting question,' she says. 'If I did have to have a child I would prefer to have a girl. I would bring her up to be a marvellous woman. I would teach her . . . ' She becomes irritated when I remind her that the question I had put to her concerned how she'd bring up a son. 'I wouldn't have a son,' she says fiercely and briefly. I feel that someone with such fierce determination might well be able to control the choice of sexes within her. I still want to know how she'd bring up the boy.

'I don't know,' she says shortly. 'I have friends who have sons, and they try to bring them up to be, well, men. To compete in the world, to use their fists, to be boys. They don't know how else to bring them up. If they try to teach them to be something else, they're frightened the boy would become a homosexual.'

Brownmiller seldom mentions her father. She is enormously proud of her mother who worked all her life as a secretary. However, she does have a theory that most strong women have father fixations. In this she refers to Patty Hearst who she believes was influenced greatly by her grandfather and her father.

'Upper middle class women like Patty Hearst nearly always have strong fathers,' Brownmiller says. 'The mothers are nearly all decorative and spend most of their lives socialising and doing very little. Can you imagine how much Patty must despise her mother who rushed over to the jail saying "My baby, all is forgiven."' She shudders.

She is justly proud of Against Our Will. After she'd finished it, she and seven of her 'sisters' wrote a comedy screenplay on the feminist movement. What amuses her most is the deference being shown to her by her publishers and everyone else. Everyone wines and dines her now, and every magazine wanted to read her book. She refused to show it to Playboy and Penthouse. Her principles were very strong, much to the surprise of her publishers.

In the final chapter Ms Brownmiller describes how she took karate lessons and how she intends to defend herself if a man does try to rape her. She believes all women should take karate lessons.

'All two and a half billion?'

'Yes,' Brownmiller says quickly. 'It's the only way women can deny rape in future. We must learn to defend ourselves.'

It may be a man's quibble, but I feel it's too American a solution. The woman strapping on her gunbelt and walking down the street at high noon to face her ancient enemy. The only result of the confrontation surely would be an escalation in violence. Maybe it would be best to change the thinking of men, as she would her hypothetical son?

'No,' she says, 'men won't change. I'm more concerned with women.'

15 MARCH 1976

Too true confessions

Why the conference to turn attention on crimes against women failed

JILL TWEEDIE

Simone de Beauvoir called the International Tribunal of Crimes Against Women a 'great historic event' where 'women across the world would show, together, their awareness of the scandal of their condition.' It was a fine idea. A lot of women slaved to get it together, a lot slaved at the tribunal. Many women met many other women, talked, exchanged experiences, addresses, know-how. Emotion and subjectivity were not shunned. No one nodded off through boredom, only through complete mental and physical exhaustion. But by its own yardstick, the tribunal came somewhere near failure. There were very few non-Europeans. Very little precise information. Very little wish to spread what information there was. A solidarity among some women served only to mark its lack among others.

The Women's Movement suffers from a surfeit of democracy. It is controlled so much by the women that it is no longer for the women, only for those with the loudest voices and the most obsessive grievances. Priorities of suffering are lost in the melee as the strong trample the weak, as the wounded victim whispers while the merely bruised screams. Those appointed to defend priorities stand down, more terrified of being accused by the powerful of dictatorship than reproached by the weak of betrayal.

True victims need the spotlight of the world focused on their plight. But one whole day was laid waste by the action of one French woman journalist who rushed the platform and informed the audience that a man from her paper had been appointed to write about the tribunal. She demanded the instant banishment of all male journalists. The spotlight of the world flickered and died. Third world women, battered wives, all those who desperately wanted their cases heard beyond the walls of the Palais de Congress were out-voted to protect some of the most articulate women of the west. Is there such a word in English, said a Danish woman to me, as sister-fuckers? There is now, I said.

A well-organised and uninhibited group of lesbians came complete with large placards. 'I love only women.' 'I am a lesbian – what are you?' Some women, infuriated, come out with their own placards. 'I am a woman – what are you?' Imagine a tribunal of black people protesting their oppression and allowing black homosexuals an entire morning and many long interruptions to state their case. If being a lesbian is a problem, sisters, how does it line up with torture, prison, endless pregnancies, starvation, dying children, rape, a lifetime of brutality from a violent husband? An Australian, white, tells an American, black, that she is a lesbian. So am I, honey, says the black woman. But are you going to relinquish the power you have to help us, by saying so?

Americans usurped too much space, too: vociferous out of all proportion to their numbers, their actual suffering or their understanding of the causes of other women's suffering. American women work extremely hard and they have an enviable flair for organisation. But when, time after time, an American voice announces that she represents Britain, France, Belgium, or wherever, irritation sets in. To hear an American lecturing an Englishwoman upon the use of the speculum is enlightening:

'With it, you can see if your cervix is infected.' 'And if it is, I go to a doctor?' 'No way. You can treat it yourself. If you go to a doctor he'll burn your cervix (whip out your womb, cut off your breasts).' The Englishwoman looks bewildered and no wonder. American doctors have an overwhelming financial incentive, and it well behoves American women to know it. An Englishwoman's problem is more likely to be medical inaction. Moral: advice combined with ignorance produces paranoia in the advisee.

Most of the evidence given at the tribunal was in the traditional women's movement format of true confessions. It is a format completely unsuited (if not increasingly outdated) for a very large hall and very large audiences who cannot take up points and are therefore reduced to clamour. The listener must either accept the testimony in blind faith or have unanswered questions flicker in her mind, causing unease, frustration, and suspicion. I want to believe women but I cannot believe all women, just because they are women.

Spontaneous testimony has other drawbacks. Contradictions flourish and remain unresolved. One woman pleads for abortion on demand, another against forced sterilisation. One says lesbianism is normal for all women; another that women in her country are lesbians because they have so little contact with men. One says women are censored, their voices unheard. Another implores us to support censorship and stop pornographic films showing rape that will certainly incite further rape. A third, from Portugal, where no such films exist, says rape in her country is a normal female experience. The abyss between white and black women looms large.

'You white women are fighting to get out of your homes, away from your television sets and your children, to work. We black women are working our asses off so we can get back in our homes, watch television, and look after our children.' Obviously, here, freedom of choice is the issue, but the aims of each group of women can easily be held against the other, obstruct the other.

Much of the testimony is heart-rending. Some so glib, so suspiciously vague that it detracts from the whole. An American Indian girl receives an ovation after her story about a conviction for second degree murder. Her speech is tin-pan-alley sobstuff. She was found guilty on Mother's Day by an all-white, all-male jury. She is an Indian, a minority, a woman, a mother. Indians, she says, are being killed every day in the States. Perverts roam the playgrounds of America freely, every day. The actual facts of her case – who she shot, how many she shot, and why she shot – remain unexplained. Women are implored to write in her defence and I dare say hundreds will. Even, I dare say, hundreds should – but not on the evidence she gave at the tribunal.

Women who were frightened, untravelled, unused to speaking, older, had a tough time putting their cases. A 51-year-old battered mother of nine children from the Irish countryside is trembling, totally confused and in no condition to storm a platform and push aside young, well-muscled militants stoned on ego-boosting adrenalin. She, the English battered wives, and the women of the Women's Aid Federation, were near desperation at times, unable to make themselves heard in the bedlam of Sarah Bernhardts.

Eventually they got a quiet and sympathetic hearing, but it was touch and go.

No reasonable man who had been allowed to listen to such testimony could have failed to feel bitterly about his fellow men, could have failed to want change. The Catholic church, a male institution if ever there was one, emerged as one of the prime instigators of crimes against women, indicted time and again by women from Catholic countries as the dictator of their bodies and minds, the instantly traceable source of every horror from rape to femicide, whether in Ireland or Puerto Rico, Belgium or Spain. In Rome, the men sit and debate the saving of souls. At their feet, the ruined women lie, souls in the Czarist sense. The Pope's serfs.

What, in the face of even one such total power (not mentioned, for fear of trouble, in the original manifestos) could the tribunal achieve? It is a fine car body with no engine, no power. An Israeli MP gets together with a Syrian woman. They talk of the condition of women in their countries, they talk of the horrors of war, of menfolk loved and killed. Women listening have tears in their eyes. Can feminism combine where men divide? You are my sister, you are dear to me, we kiss, we cry. And the war will go on.

Reluctantly, now, it seems to me that any international meeting of women is more likely to produce division than cohesion. Our problems are too disparate, too tied to our particular societies, to be solved outside. International action is only effective on relatively trivial issues – demonstrations against the film Story of O, for instance. As one Belgian feminist, active in her government, put it: 'just take a simple thing like social security. Yours is based on need, ours on work. Both require different tactics, how can we get together on that?'

Better, then, to stay at home and work out our own problems there. Each internal victory provides ammunition for victory in another place. If women drive buses, work in the docks, practice medicine in one country, the men of another have a harder task of arguing that their women cannot do the same. If the girls of England have equal education, that provides a touchstone for other women to use as they can or wish. Feminism is encouragement by women for women, it is an accumulative process, an internationalism by example, not by bull-in-a-china-shop action, intervention by tourists who do not know the battlefield or the female army's needs.

If you win your fights I, strengthened by your success, will the sooner win mine.

3 MAY 1976

Slave wages

JILL TWEEDIE

To many women in the Women's Movement, the Wages for Housework campaigners come over like Jehovah's Witnesses. Open any door marked Liberation and behind it is a woman with a Wages for Housework badge on her bosom, ten thousand leaflets in her hand, a fanatical gleam in her eye and her foot wedged firmly in the jamb. At any meeting concerned with women's rights there will inevitably be a Wages for Housework stall piled higher than any other with literature, buttons, posters, and statistics.

Selma James and her sister enthusiasts in Italy and France, America and Canada harangue conferences, shout from soapboxes, gesticulate on television, burn with a strange fever. In Brussels, the evening before the tribunal, what was the first sight that met my eyes? A short square silhouette bent under a rucksack struck full of plac-ards, trudging up the hill from the station. Who's that? Who else. Rosie from Wages for Housework.

On the street corner they go down well. Within the movement and, often, among career women without, they set up a high level of irritation. Eyes roll heavenwards, figures slump in seats as yet another campaigner leaps for the platform. Myself, I have felt the same irritation, even at times hostility. A non-starter, I said. Who needs it, I said. I mean, I thought that was exactly what we didn't want, housework confirmed as women's work. Give us wages for it and we're really trapped, we'll never get out of the home.

What did I want to get out of the home for? Well, to do some-thing rather more fulfilling than housework, of course, Also to find out who I was – you don't discover who you are by staring at your reflection in polished lino. Also to win some economic independence so that choices can be made and, if driven, others told what they can do.

When I first married I stayed at home, did housework, and looked after my children. My husband was as generous with money as his salary allowed. He gave me labour-saving devices to make my house-work easier. Thank you, I said. Thank you. You are good to me, I said. Did he say that to his employer every time he picked up his wages? His money was his by right. Mine by virtue of his generosity.

I worked for seven years cleaning the house and caring for the children so that he was free to earn the money to support us all. But when divorce came, he took away all the things he had bought: the house, the labour-saving devices, the savings. Because after all, when the chips were down, they were his. He left his job too but the boss didn't take back the house and the labour-saving devices and the savings. Well, of course not. He'd worked for them, hadn't he?

The law is different now but why, then, was my own work as invisible to me as it was to everyone else? I didn't work, I explained to others. I was just a housewife. The only lesson I learned was that next time round I should do real work, outside work, paid in real money that couldn't be taken away. Besides, housework is what all women do and if all women do it, where am I among them? Me, the individual, a person apart from the biological trappings that are all the qualifications needed for being a housewife and mother. Now I am a free woman. I am not a slave.

What is a slave? A slave is a person who is not paid for working. In ancient Greece, a slave did housework, cared for children, served the men, worked their fields and was sexually available. In the old South, in America, ditto. If they had a good master they lived comfortably, wore nice clothes, were kindly treated, ate good food and thanked their lucky stars. If they had a bad one they got the bare minimum necessary to keep them working and were sometimes killed. Many women all over the world today do housework, care for children, serve their families, work the fields, are sexually available to their masters and are not paid for this work. If they have a good master they live comfortably, wear nice clothes, are kindly treated, eat good food. If not, they get the bare minimum, are frequently beaten, often raped and sometimes killed. But they do not call it slavery, they call it marriage. They do not call themselves slaves, they call themselves housewives.

I was a housewife. My mother is a housewife. My grandmother was a housewife. I come, in other words, from generations of slaves. But I do not care for that definition of myself, I have turned my face away from it. Slaves are stupid and inferior people because they do stupid and inferior work, work that no one pays them for. I fought to work at a proper job and I know it is a proper job because I am paid to do it. So now I am a free woman and you, if you are a housewife, are the slave. And when the Wages for Housework women come along my skin prickles. Housework? What's housework to do with me? That is my slave past, the state I struggled to discard, that state I do not wish to be reminded of, the thing about myself that I despise. The thing about you I despise.

House slaves in the old South who had good masters and were comfortably kept despised field slaves. When you are all slaves, you have to find someone worse off than you to despise or how do you keep your self-respect? There are blacks in the States today, who are doing well enough in the white man's world, who do not thank you if you remind them of their slave past. It makes them extremely irritable, even downright hostile. It is better to forget all that, forget the masses of poor blacks, put a distance between yourself and them. I think their skin must prickle as mine does at the mention of wages for housework. For my own self respect I must turn away from the thought of the masses of women who are doing unpaid housework.

Of course, I still do housework. I shop, I cook, I clean, I sew, I minister to my children. I wash all our clothes. But if I do it all really efficiently and quietly, if I pretend well enough that I am not doing it, if I wave in front of you my other persona, my paid job persona, then maybe I shall deceive you into not noticing that though one hand turns the pages of a book, the other is washing dishes in the sink. Maybe, if you are a career woman too, we can get together and joke about the housewives because only by rejecting them can we be sure we are no longer slaves.

Women who have read this far and who are housewives, cleaning, cooking and caring for a husband and children may well be very angry. You may say you enjoy your work, that the world would be a better place if all women stayed at home and did what you are doing, that there is nothing more valuable to society than making a good home for a man and children. I say unto you: if this work is so valuable to society, why doesn't society pay for it? It pays for every other type of work it considers valuable. You say, because the best things in life are free, because love is free and given freely. And I say unto you, right on. Money cannot buy love, no one can pay you to cherish your husband and children. But the laundry, the scrubbing, the sewing, the ironing, and cooking, and shopping? Do fathers not love their wives and children? And yet they are paid for the work they do to keep those wives and children. If you employed a housekeeper and you grew to love each other and she to love your children, would you call her in one day and say I tell you what, I think you love us now so I won't pay you any more?

We all know that the majority of women who work outside the home do it because they must. The poorer the woman, the more likely it is that she works. But housework continues. They have two jobs. I have two jobs, we expect reasonable pay for one and nothing for the other. But these days more men are taking on two jobs because more men are fighting for custody of their children in divorce and more men and children are being deserted by their wives, mothers of those children. These men, unlike women, have never been slaves. However hard their work, however soul-destroying, they have always been paid for it. They know that they love their children but they are not confused by that into thinking that the drudgery involved is an absolute part of that love. Talk to any one of them and you will discover they think they should be paid, compensated, helped, something. At the very least they expect to be able to boast or to demand sympathy. Most of them get it. Most women don't.

Well, I said to Selma James, shifting irritably about. Even if you accept the idea of wages for housework it is quite utopian to imagine that any government, of whatever shade of pink, is going to provide those wages when women are already doing housework free. Yes, she said, that is utopian. Governments rarely or never give anyone anything for the asking. They give only when there is no alternative but giving. The women of Iceland withdrew their labour for 24 hours last year and they threw their country into chaos. Mmm, I said.

And then again, I said, if women got wages for housework,

wouldn't their husbands say, right, you're getting paid for it, do it. Wouldn't we lose what little freedom we have to do our housework when we see fit and as much as we see fit? I wouldn't want my husband wiping his finger along the mantelpiece and finding me lacking. Selma James said why did I think that would happen more if I were paid than if I wasn't. If a man knows he's paying for a woman's work, isn't he much more likely to criticise than if he knows someone else is paying? But suppose he thinks, well, she's getting paid, I'm not going to share my wage with her? That depends on the relationship, said Ms James. Besides, we can do that now, when you're earning nothing.

But, but. If I am paid, as a woman, wages for housework, then I must do it and I don't want to. But you are, anyway, said Ms James. If housework is paid, then everyone knows it is a job. When it is not paid, everyone thinks it is as inseparable a part of being a woman as a womb or a vagina. There is no placard on a vagina that says 'I have sex with a man and I also wash his socks.' There is no notice on a womb that says. 'I bear children and also cook their meals.' Society puts the placards there because it is extremely convenient for society to do so. Payment for housework puts housework on the open market, just another job that anyone can do. And isn't that where most women would want it? Isn't that where most women who can afford to, put it?

If you find that you feel as deeply uneasy and dismayed as I did when I first heard the arguments for wages for housework, ask yourself why. What is it about the idea of wages that is so unsettling, even obnoxious? I cannot presume to answer for you. My own answer? I do not want to think about the anger I actually feel about 'women's work'. I do not trust myself not to direct it at my husband and children in lieu of taking action. My only way of accepting that work is either to ignore it, shut off my brain and try to do it like a robot, or pretend to myself that I do it for love and therefore am good.

What do I feel? The horrid resentment of the mind bred to slavery and faced with freedom. Wages for Housework? Let them eat cake.

The family allowance is, as yet, the only money paid to women for their work. It is very little and even that little is threatened. Wages for Housework are campaigning for more.

14 NOVEMBER 1977

Reclaim the night

The worst attack on a Guardian woman writer happened in Mayfair. She went out to buy a packet of cigarettes at 9pm and a man with razor blades in his gloves punched her

POLLY TOYNBEE

On Saturday night groups of women in cities all over the country took to the streets. They called their campaign Reclaiming the Night, and they walked through Leeds, Manchester, Bradford, York, Nottingham, Brighton, Salisbury, Guildford, Bristol, and London. They were campaigning against the increasing dangers for women in the streets at night. They want to reclaim their right to go where they please when they please, without fear. Many of them were women who had themselves been raped or otherwise attacked in the streets.

Every year the street crime statistics get worse, and more and more people, men as well as women, are beginning to develop a siege mentality about urban living. Women, of course, are at much greater risk. Last year there were 1,094 reported cases of rape, and

10,901 cases of indecent assault on females, 89 people were murdered by complete strangers. (The rest of the 493 homicides were committed by family, friends, or lovers.). There were in all 77,748 crimes of violence.

Sir Robert Mark in his last report on London crime breaks down his statistics more precisely. Last year there were 180 rapes and 149 violent assaults on females in London. Violent personal robbery, ie mugging, rose by 37% in a year, and there were in all 12,613 such robberies.

Saturday's campaigners were organised by the women's liberation movement. They were not asking for a change in the law, or even for greater police protection. They were campaigning for a change in society's attitudes towards women, no less. They argue that women are subject to attacks because men are encouraged, at all levels, to regard women in a predatory way, and women are encouraged to be passive and helpless.

In London they chose Soho for their demonstration, as they regard pornography, and displays of women as objects and not as human beings, as partly responsible for the increasing number of attacks on women. For a long time they have plastered stickers reading 'This degrades women' over posters of naked women in underground stations. They are anxious not to be associated with Mary Whitehouse-type censorship. They aren't asking for any change in the law, but they are trying to influence the way people think. They believe that if people had a proper respect for women, pornography would wither away.

As a campaign it seemed to be ideologically sound enough but tactically and politically a hopeless gesture. The political naivete would be almost pathetic, if it weren't for their sincerity and earnestness. What's the good of taking to the streets to change the whole way society thinks, without making a single demand for specific changes in law, its policing, or in the allocation of money? They say they have no faith in the law.

It is also hard for them to muster publicity, since they have no faith in the male chauvinist press. They will only speak to the press as a collective, and as a result have difficulty in speaking on the telephone. And it is not so easy for collectives of women to get into the Guardian offices any more. Ever since a Women Against Rape demonstrator bit one of our security guards during an alter-cation over whether or not her group should be allowed in, the officers have been doubly wary of large groups of women. The Reclaiming the Night group are anxious to stress that they have no connections at all with Women Against Rape. Indeed, although the whole aim of Saturday night's demonstration was to bring publicity to the cause, the women involved were loath to say exactly what they were going to be doing, when and where.

The fact remains that they are right. Women are becoming more and more restricted in their movements, especially at night. Of course everyone is threatened, but women far more so. Public transport, underground trains in particular, dark, insanely designed underpasses, and empty streets present threats that keep women at home. The women's liberation movement was enraged when a Bradford police officer advised all women not to go out alone at all, even in the day.

I never used to be much afraid. Although I live round the corner from the tube station once described as the worst muggers' black-spot, I hardly ever worried about it. I sometimes feel uneasy walking at night, but I am not afraid enough to stop walking alone at night. But since an incident a year ago I am much more alert and aware of the danger than I ever used to be.

It wasn't even night time. It was a quiet Saturday afternoon and I was changing trains on my way home at Stockwell tube station. As I stepped on to a train, alone on the platform I thought, two boys ran up and jumped on behind me. The train was about a third full. The boys began jostling and shoving me, and I thought they were just playing around, until I saw one of them snatch my purse out of my bag. As I turned to grab it back he handed it to his friend who started to run off with it. I caught him by his coat and held on.

They both pushed and shoved me but it didn't really occur to me to let go of his coat. I shouted at the other passengers that he'd got my purse and would they please help. No one moved. No one said anything. The doors of the train were trying to shut, but they were standing in the way and keeping them open, and I still had hold of the coat. I think they saw a guard coming as they suddenly dropped the purse, threw me across the carriage, leapt out of the train and ran away.

As the train moved out of the station I was so angry and upset that I screamed and ranted at the passengers in that carriage. 'Why didn't you help? Why didn't you do something? Why didn't you at least shout?' No one said a word. They looked away, tucked their heads into their newspapers, behaved as if I was a mad woman harassing them.

I approached one man, who had been sitting within inches of where it had happened, and I challenged him. 'I didn't see,' he said, and blushed as the other passengers stared at him. I challenged another man. 'I was asleep. Never saw a thing,' he muttered.

It was then that I became really afraid. That's what people say about New York, but I always thought in England that any number of law and order minded decent citizens would come to your assistance but it's not so.

I started wandering round this office to find out how many other women have had some kind of unpleasant experience. I was astonished to find, among the small number I asked, how many of them had frightening stories to tell.

Janet Watts, feature writer, was attacked in daylight one morning walking through Regents Park on her way to work. As she came to a secluded place she heard a pounding of feet behind her, and an enormous, 'gorilla-sized' man pounced on her from behind, grabbing her breasts. She screamed, and he ran off, leaving her much shaken.

Felicity Roskrow, Guardian Diary secretary, was pursued down a dark road outside her home, and a man jumped on her and grabbed her round the neck. She struggled and screamed, and he ran off.

Lindsay Mackie, reporter, alone in her ground floor flat awoke one night to find a man by her bed. He pulled back her bedclothes and warned her not to make any noise. When she raised her fist to him he took fright and ran away.

Caroline Tisdall, art critic, has been attacked three times. The last time was in the underpass at Shepherd's Bush, on her way to a television broadcast at the BBC. Four youths approached her from behind, and one of them grabbed her. She swung round with such force and indignation that they were surprised, and ran away.

The worst attack, though, on a Guardian woman writer happened in Mayfair. She'd rather not have her name printed, as she feels she's managed to put the whole thing behind her. She went out to buy a packet of cigarettes at 9pm and a man with razor blades in his gloves punched her face and made criss-cross cuts all the way up her legs and hands. Eventually she got away, covered in blood.

I haven't counted the large number of indecent exposings, bum pinchings, and touching-ups which may be infuriating, but aren't frightening. After finding so many attacks by just asking a handful of people, I am beginning to become more alarmed myself.

I've always tried to avoid getting involved in the great noise that the women's movement has been making about rape. It seems to me perverse, and somehow irrelevant to pick one fairly infrequent crime to campaign about, just because for them it represents symbolically the way they feel all men treat all women. It reminds me of the great American fundraising campaigns for sickle cell anaemia. This is a form of leukaemia that only attacks black people. It is not, of course, the disease that most black people die of, by a long shot, but because it only affects blacks, it has become a strong political cause.

The group of women who came to talk about Saturday's demonstration said that rape was only the extreme edge of a spectrum. One woman said. 'It starts with the "Hello darling" and wolf whistles and it goes right through to rape. It's exactly the same kind of sexism.' Perhaps that's true.

I've never had any doubt that wolf whistles and provocative taunts in the street are intensely aggressive. I never know how to deal with it. Usually I just try to maintain an absurd sort of dignity and pretend I haven't heard. If I smile back, I feel angry with myself inside and even more vulnerable. Perhaps it's silly to mind about it, but now I come to think about it I find I do feel indignant that women walking along the street minding their own business should be teased and forced to respond.

These women also believe that rape is at the root of all sexuality as we now know it. It is not that they regard every man as a potential rapist. It is not as simple as that. They believe that all our views about sex are centred around the idea that men should dominate and rape is the natural extreme conclusion of that kind of sex.

One girl said rather touchingly, 'We don't exactly know what sex would be like if you took away the idea of male power and domination, because our own heads have been so conditioned with this notion, but we believe it must be possible to make sex about something other than power.'

The Hite Report appears to be having great influence. They say that if the female view of sex were generally accepted instead of the male aggressive and predatory view, there would be no more attacks on women, no rapes, no fear.

Still, that's rather a complicated message to take out on to the streets. Until the feminist millennium, women are in danger of having their lives increasingly restricted by real danger and their own fear of it.

16 MAY 1978

Why the euphoria had to stop

The author of Patriarchal Attitudes, first published in 1970, looks back on eight important years

EVA FIGES

My book Patriarchal Attitudes first appeared in June 1970, and it is just a decade since I started work on it, motivated as much by a wish to stir women out of their apparent passivity, their acceptance of an intolerable status quo, as by anger at a society dominated by men who discriminated against women in so many ways. I worked in isolation, against the stream (or so I thought), with no literary models to guide me.

Simone de Beauvoir's The Second Sex had been published a generation earlier, but when I re-read the book it seemed inadequate and oddly uncommitted: female sexuality remained shrouded in an ambiguous fog of uncertainty and the nature/nurture argument was not really tackled head-on. With hindsight I realised that my entry into womanhood had been influenced for the worse by reading it. Only Betty Friedan's The Feminine Mystique provided a few rough guidelines.

By the time my book was published in the early summer of

1970, a few months before Germaine Greer's popular bestseller The Female Eunuch, the first echoes of the American women's movement were beginning to reach Britain from across the Atlantic, and my intellectual isolation was suddenly over.

While working on the book, I found myself under constant attack, and even people who might have been expected to approve had reservations. If I was not downright wrong-headed, then at least I was being unladylike in not pulling my punches. One paperback publisher, who had bought and expressed warm admiration for my novels, rejected the book before publication of the hardback because he thought that I had 'a chip on my shoulder', since I had problems as a divorced woman with two children. But in the months after publication a massive postbag from all over the country told me that thousands, perhaps millions of women appeared to have the same chip: that for years women had been nursing a secret rage which society required them to repress for fear of ostracism and ridicule.

All sorts of women began to speak out in the early 70s. Women's workshops sprang up all over the country; almost every college had its feminist group; and women's associations of long-standing and of all kinds suddenly joined the growing chorus demanding women's rights on a whole range of issues: an end to discrimination in education and employment, equal pay, abortion on demand, nurseries and creches.

The jokes and mockery took some time to die down, but there was no doubt that the tide of opinion was turning. The publisher who had accused me of having a chip on my shoulder bought the paperback rights and declared himself 'proud to be associated with a great cause' to his assembled salesmen, not least because feminist books sold like hot cakes as women sought to reassess their roles and men tried hard to keep up with them, anxious not to be labelled male chauvinists.

That was the first stage. The second stage came when the two major political parties, who had contemptuously thrown out several private members' bills on sex discrimination as unworthy of serious attention, discovered that women could no longer be relied upon to vote with their husbands. Fifty years after the woman's vote had been won as a result of a long and bitter struggle, it had at last begun to matter. The Labour government introduced and passed its own Sex Discrimination Act in 1975.

The early 70s were undoubtedly exciting, almost euphoric days for those actively involved in the women's movement. First and foremost, women had found each other; not since the suffrage movement had women worked together with such a sense of communion and unity of purpose.

Our sense of excitement and joy had another reason: we knew that our message was radically different in style and content from anything that had gone before – that women's liberation would mean men's liberation and a whole new set of social and cultural values. We had another reason to feel euphoric; it is not often that you push a rock as big as a mountain and feel it shift. Within a miraculously short space of time the ridicule had turned to respect, and the legislation we had been demanding appeared like a white rabbit out of a magician's hat.

The mood has changed now, for a number of reasons. Firstly, the novelty has gone, and women actively engaged in the struggle are no longer parading the streets. They are engaged in the tedious struggle of trying to make the new legislation work, in bringing test cases to courts and tribunals. Inevitably, there is disillusion and disappointment. To make matters worse, the whole mood of the country has changed. At a time of public spending cuts when many teachers are unemployed it makes no sense to demand free nursery schools for all children. The rising unemployment figures have had an intimidating effect on women's demands for equal job opportunities.

Individual women, particularly those in the professional classes, do and will use the new legislation to improve their status, but an invisible (because they do not register as unemployed) army of working class women has been driven back to the kitchen sink by the job shortage.

So how much has actually been achieved since 1970? I think the real victory, perhaps the only one, has been a fundamental change in awareness and social attitudes. Young girls are beginning to have wider expectations: many no longer see marriage as the be-all and end-all of their existence. And a movement which was often accused of being middle class, and which certainly began amongst middle-class women has nevertheless succeeded in reaching the factory floor. Women workers have staged small courageous strikes for sexual equality, doomed to failure though most of them were for lack of male support.

But the march to sexual equality is proceeding at a snail's pace. In 1970 women's earnings as a proportion of men's earnings were 54.8%, and by 1976 the gap had narrowed by less than 10% to only 64.3%. Meanwhile the absolute cash differential between men's and women's earnings had actually widened from £13.50 in 1970 to £25.60 in 1976.

Progress in other areas has been equally slow. The position of divorced and separated women bringing up children on their own has improved in terms of welfare and cash benefits, but creches, nursery schools and job opportunities have become more remote with economic depression and high unemployment.

The change of awareness in itself presents a danger to progress. Just because we have learned to observe the verbal niceties, address women as Ms and make knowing little jokes about 'chairpersons', we may be taken in by appearances and forget the reality. We are in danger of being lulled into a sense of premature complacency: we may have won the first battle, but we are still a long way from winning the war.

16 May 1979

How different the history of world literature might look if mothers were writers too

ERICA JONG

Only a man (or a woman who had never been pregnant) would compare creativity to maternity, pregnancy to the creation of a poem or novel. The Muse is a stern taskmistress and will withdraw her favours from the lazy, slovenly or self-pitying artist. Nature, on the other-hand, is all-forgiving. Any womb, any woman, may be the vessel for her continuance.

Creativity demands conscious, active will; pregnancy only demands the absence of ill-will. Perhaps the desire to equate them arises from the artist's ancient wish that creativity be as effortless, easy and unconscious as the creation of a foetus. Or perhaps the male artist's desire to equate the two arises out of his envy of the female ability to generate life. Like most forms of envy, it is absurd. One might as well envy the hummingbird for being able to stand still in mid-air, or the flounder for having two eyes on one side of its head.

Whatever joys there are in pregnancy (and there are many) they are not the joys of consciousness, not the joys of intellect, not the joys of art, not the joys of civilisation. Pregnancy is perhaps most enjoyable to the over-civilised, over-intellectualised woman precisely for that reason.

Certainly this was true for me. All my life I had mistrusted my body and over-valued my mind. I had sought a very high degree of control over my environment and my body – a degree of control perhaps best represented by the fact that I never became pregnant, not even 'accidentally', until well after my 35th birthday, and well after having spent a year or more consciously wishing and trying to become pregnant.

I had dreaded pregnancy as a loss of control over my destiny, my body and my life. I had fantasies of death in childbirth, the death of my creativity during pregnancy, the alteration of my body, the loss of my intelligence through mysterious hormonal sabotage, the loss of my looks, my energy, my robustness.

But I ought to have known that the ruler of the cosmos is nothing if not a joker – and all the opposite things happened. My face grew thinner, my skin clearer, my eyes brighter. I never felt sick or lacked energy. I worked as hard at my writing as I ever had in my life – and, in fact, worked with greater consistency.

Pregnancy felt particularly good to me, I think, because it was an affirmation of life for one who had once been prone to a romantic infatuation with death. It was a turn from romantic to classic, from martyr to survivor, from self-destroyer to self-affirmer, from worshipper of sickness to worshipper of health.

I think that to a large extent the artists and intellectuals in our society worship illness, as if it were illness that conferred art rather than art that conferred a temporary reprieve from illness. In part, this is one legacy of 19th-century Romanticism, but in part it also stems from the misconception that the mind can only be nourished at the expense of the body – as if health were a finite commodity (like oil or electricity) and one could only fill one area by depleting others. In fact, the contrary is true. Both creativity and health are self-replenishing; the more they are used, the more they flourish and regenerate.

I belong to one of the first generations of women artists for whom pregnancy is not compulsory (despite the psychological pressures for motherhood that still do exist) and therefore one of the first generations of women artists to be able to examine the paradox of artistic creativity v biological generativity. Neither George Eliot nor Jane Austen had that option. Even Edith Wharton and Virginia Woolf were not really able to regard child-bearing as a choice. In their time the only way for a woman artist to combat the Victorian stereotype of 'the angel in the house' was to turn around and become the devil (or else to assert that they were mothers of books, and thus had fulfilled the ideal of womanhood, albeit in another way).

For years I was determined not to have a child precisely because many of the women writers I admired most had not had children. Yet the worm of desire for a child gnawed at me constantly and gnawed at my poems as well. Having a child seemed to me a rite of passage (without which one could still certainly be a perfectly fulfilled woman, prolific artist and spiritually developed person), but also without which one would have failed to have one of the crucial experiences of the human race.

But still, I hesitated. Child-bearing had always taken too much of a toll on women. It had meant jeopardising the things writers needed most – peace, quiet, a lack of interruptions. It had meant diluting passions which one wanted undiluted for one's work. It was not only the drudgery of child-bearing which seemed threatening to art, but the pleasures. Babies are most distracting when they are most pleasurable. Besides, it had taken me years to free myself of the guilt I felt towards my parents and the men in my life when I shut myself away to write. How would I ever deal with the guilt created by a creature who needed me for its physical survival?

I will never be able to claim that I sacrificed all to have a child, but then I am not quite sure that rearing a child in such a spirit of sacrifice is a favour either to the child or to the mother. All I know is that I did the only thing I could do at the time. For the first 35 years of my life, writing was so much more important to me than anything else, that I could not risk any turn of fate that might jeopardise my own still shaky self-confidence as a writer or my need to establish a sense of vocation, regular work habits and a pattern of self-discipline. Women who bear children before they establish these habits of work may never establish them at all. Having been defined first as mothers (rather than as writers) they may never be able to see themselves in another light and the demands of their children may always drown out the demands of their books.

The very fact that no generation before ours has really been in a position to challenge the lie that creativity and generativity are one and the same makes us privileged beyond any earlier generations. And that privilege rests almost entirely upon motherhood remaining optional for us. It is the key to all our freedoms – even the freedom to dwell seriously on the meaning of pregnancy and childbirth.

I think we have never quite considered the implications of the fact that most of the literature about pregnancy and birth has been written either by men or by women who forswore child-bearing in order to do their creative work. Pregnancy and birth were considered minor, foolish, 'female' subjects, and women writers who aspired to the heights of Parnassus often disdained them as their male mentors had taught them to do. So the lie that creativity and generativity were somehow interchangeable continued unchallenged for generations.

So, now we stand at a literary crossroads made entirely possible by childbirth having become a choice. All efforts to withdraw that choice must be seen as efforts to put women back into the mute rage from which they have so recently begun to emerge.

The history of world literature is the history of the literature of the male, the white man, the aristocrat, the affluent bourgeois, and the childless woman. How different it might look if mothers were writers too.

It would certainly put an end, once and for all, to the notion that books are like babies, and babies even remotely are like books.

24 JULY 1979

Second thoughts

It appeared out of nowhere and hit post-war France like a bomb. How does Simone de Beauvoir see The Second Sex now?

JOHN CUNNINGHAM

In the afternoons, she used to go over to Sartre's place to write, but in the mornings she worked away in her own room in the rue de la Bûcherie. She'd put up new red curtains and bought some green bronze lamps. Outside, life teemed: along the street, dogs barking in the vets' clinics – one of these establishments boasted the patronage of the Duke of Windsor; North Africans brawling in the Café des Amis opposite her window.

There were, for a time, the weekly letters from Chicago, though the affair with her American lover was in its declining throes. There was, and had been since student days, her enduring relationship with Sartre. There was the matter of growing old: 'Forty. Forty-one. Old age was growing inside me. It kept catching my eye from the depths of the mirror. I was paralysed when I saw it making its way towards me so steadily when nothing inside me was ready for it.' And the matter of being a woman, the exploration of which was involving two years' work on The Second Sex.

It is exactly 30 years since Simone de Beauvoir's monumental study of women appeared out of nowhere in the sense that it was spawned by no feminist movement; there was no spate of women writers at work on aspects of the same theme. Its origins were personal to her because she decided that, before embarking on her autobiography, which has since appeared in four volumes, she needed to unwrap the myths which surround women and to place womanhood in its proper social and philosophical context.

The Second Sex hit a country slowly recovering from war like a bomb: the first volume sold 22,000 copies in one week; the second, a few months later, did well also, and led to accusations of all kinds, particularly indecency. Being roughed up by some of the critics was one thing – and as a member of the Left intelligentsia, De Beauvoir was used to that – but there was a separate assessment by readers. She was pelted with barbs accusing her of being a lesbian, a nymphomaniac, an unmarried mother, a frigid old maid by men, some of whom signed their missives 'Very active members of The First Sex'.

Part of the furore was because women's emancipation had come more slowly to France than to other West Europe countries, or to the United States. In the late 1940s when she was writing, there were, De Beauvoir estimated, as many abortions as births: 300,000 low income women a year needed abortions; it was a society where country girls 'half consenting, half revolted' lost their virginity in wayside ditches; where, for the middle class, there were still more arranged marriages than in other West Europe countries. France was in the grip of the Church and of a 19th-century Gallic machoism.

A law which demanded a wife's obedience to her husband was repealed only seven years before The Second Sex appeared; up to the time she was writing, De Beauvoir noted that adultery committed by a wife was held to be a legal offence – leading to the paradoxical situation in which sexual adventures were 'easier' for married rather than single women. Even at the present time, many young middle-class women of strict behaviour marry 'so as to be free!'

Her view of marriage is horrifying. In the 1940s, it was still traditionally an institution which was 'forced much more tyrannically upon the young girl than the young man'. Some middle-class daughters were left incapable of earning a living; the choice was either to 'remain as a parasite in her father's home or to take some menial position in the home of a stranger'. Even for girls with education, the odds were weighted against an independent career because of the economic advantages held by men. To her husband, a woman is presented as a sexually submissive dependent. 'It is still agreed that the act of love is a service rendered to the man; he takes his pleasure and owes her some payment.'

De Beauvoir's method, in over 700 pages, is that of a lucid and learned prosecuting counsel, laying indictment on top of indictment to prove her case that women, in every manifestation of their being and their sexuality – girlhood fantasies, young wives, women living vicariously through their sons, older women with young lovers, lesbians, mystics, even – are man's passive, disadvantaged victims with little idea of their own identity and almost no chance to explore it.

But as well as this, women have come to be accomplices in their collective repression. 'The real reason why she does not believe in liberation is that she has never put the powers of liberty to a test: the world seems to her to be ruled by an obscure destiny against which it is presumptuous to rise in protest'. All very well for De Beauvoir to take that line, critics have said over the last 30 years, for she has been one of the lucky elite. Her family wealth brought her education; education brought her freedom, both intellectual and sexual, so that she has been able to survive, without marriage and motherhood, and to sustain, on mutually favourable terms, a central relationship with Sartre for over 50 years.

Her comments on pregnancy and child-rearing are suspiciously sour: 'Even if the woman deeply desires to have the child, her body vigorously revolts when obliged to undergo the reproductive process.' And when a child is born: 'For while maternal devotion may be perfectly genuine, this, in fact, is rarely the case. Maternity is usually a strange mixture of narcissism, altruism, idle day-dreaming, sincerity, bad faith, devotion and cynicism.'

A generation later, De Beauvoir is not retreating from this harsh view. Three years ago, in an interview with the German feminist Alice Schwarzer, she said the sight of grandmothers having to look after children at a time when, without other responsibilities they could have a moment to themselves, made her glad to be childless. She added: 'Motherhood today is a real slavery . . . And when, in spite of everything women want a child, they should have it without marrying. For marriage is the greatest trap of all.' The mother-baby bond is something which De Beauvoir thinks is still a 'dreadful mystification' in which a woman vainly uses her children to get the love and tenderness denied by her husband.

In the book, the relentless indictment allows no scenario of sexual fulfillment for women, from the first encounter onwards. Sexual initiation is portrayed as an ordeal: 'Woman is penetrated and fecundated by way of the vagina, which becomes an erotic centre only through the intervention of the male, and this always constitutes a kind of violation.' Even in married life, love and erotic fulfillment are divorced for many wives. 'If her husband has succeeded in awakening her sexuality, she will want to enjoy the same pleasures with others because she has no special feeling of attachment for him.'

Presumably in many societies these sentiments are growing less true by the year. Yet, perhaps perversely, De Beauvoir now points to a danger in the climate where mutually satisfying sex is the norm. She told Alice Schwarzer that responsiveness could be a greater danger than frigidity. 'The worst is when women have the misfortune to find sex with men so pleasurable that they become more or less dependent on men. This bondage can be an additional link in the chain which binds women to men.' The ideal, as she has come to see it, is a bisexual ability to love a man or a woman without anxiety, compulsion, or obligation.

De Beauvoir is now in her 72nd year and she is continuing in the same vein. In a Le Monde interview in January she stated that the women's movement was making good progress; it had been almost non-existent 10 years ago yet there was some deterioration in the overall position of women. Rape was now more common: true, there was more publicity about it, but there had been a rise in absolute numbers. There was, too, a 'hostility in men which is led precisely by the emancipation of women. It makes them much more aggressive and much more dangerous than they have ever been.'

There is now more pessimism from her, for she confessed that she had 'always thought the victory of woman would be linked to the advance of socialism. Now I see that socialism is a dream. It exists nowhere. The countries we call socialist nowadays are nothing of the kind.' Only in Russia were there hopeful signs – 'but even when she (the Soviet woman) is a big boss or a great surgeon, a woman has still to do the housework, the cooking and the shopping.' And the entry of women into teaching and medicine had devalued these professions so far as Russian men were concerned.

The lack of change in France is the reason why in recent years she has become involved in the women's movement. And, as the author of what has been described as the Bible of Modern Feminism, the sisterhood has received her well. For The Second Sex has been widely read, but not always closely studied. In the interview-film of her life, which opened in Paris in January, she says that the book came about not because she was a feminist but because she wanted to make a theoretical study of women. She became a feminist comparatively recently, after the book was taken up by the movement.

The theoretical framework is existentialist; she wanted to analyse her own life in existential terms, so she had to discover how being a woman affected her choices. One of the possible titles she discussed with Sartre was The Other Sex (she relates this in Force of Circumstance). It would have been a key title. In the existentialist ethic, individuals see themselves as the 'subject', others are 'objects'. In the male view, the masculine self is the 'subject': women are relegated to being 'other' or 'object'.

Man is essential; woman is inessential. This acceptance by women turns them into passive beings, and all is lost. 'Allowing herself to be an object, she is transformed into an idol proudly recognising herself as such; but she spurns the implacable logic which makes her still the unessential,' De Beauvoir writes. The theory is that man can break the reproductive cycle and re-order the world in line with his own choice; women are shown to have less control over their own bodies. This is how De Beauvoir lambasts her own sex. Sexually, a woman is 'absorption, suction, humus, pitch and glue, a passive influx, insinuating and viscous: thus at least, she vaguely feels herself to be'.

This leads De Beauvoir to denigrate women and to deify men: she comes to see man as the 'norm' and women as an aberration: she postulates that women live vicariously through men, seeing them as saviour-heroes. This doesn't invalidate the book, but the existentialist promise is a distortion of the argument. De Beauvoir is given to saying that femininity to her personally has never been a burden or a handicap. But then she has succeeded in her enterprise on male terms which she has been waiting to accept. La Grande Sartreuse is ahead of her sex.

20 AUGUST 1979

Even Liberal Jews had misgivings when the rabbi took a funeral service in a bulging maternity dress

Interview with Julia Neuberger, Britain's second woman rabbi

LIZ FORGAN

Every morning of his life an orthodox Jewish man repeats the following prayer: 'Blessed art Thou, Oh Lord our God, King of the Universe, who hast not made me a woman.' Happily for Rabbi Neuberger, minister of the South London synagogue, Progressive Judaism does not use that prayer. Happily for Rabbi Neuberger because God did make her a woman, one of two in England to have been ordained as rabbis.

In the eyes of the Chief Rabbinate and the Jewish establishment, they are an unacceptable absurdity, in spite of the fact that rabbis have no priestly functions and therefore the principal obstacle to female Christian clergy is not present. 'Do you put a horse in the pulpit?' asked Rabbi Gold of Leeds when asked for his views on the ordination of women. In orthodox synagogues, women are not allowed to read from the Law, they are seated apart from men, they do not count as people for the purposes of constituting a minyan or quorum of 10 necessary for a full service. They may not sing, wear the prayer shawl, be witnesses at weddings or initiate divorce proceedings. Women are revered and honoured in the home but the synagogue is something else. The idea of appointing a female rabbi is – in orthodox eyes – simply unthinkable, at odds with deeply held beliefs and traditions so long established they have passed into instinct, though it should be said that it is only one of the many features of Progressive Judaism which provokes such feelings.

Julia Neuberger has long since come to terms with that disapproval. It was not her idea to be a rabbi, she explained. She was reading Assyriology and Hebrew at Cambridge at the time, with a view to becoming an archaeologist. But since Jews in Iraq and Turkey, the two places she most wanted to dig, were being actively ill-treated she decided it was not a promising career.

It was a tutor (male) who suggested she consider the rabbinate instead of becoming a Hebrew academic. Four years after Cambridge she graduated from the Leo Baeck College, two years after Britain's first woman rabbi, Jacqueline Tabick. She had a choice of three jobs on graduation and chose South London where she had served as a student rabbi. 'I liked them and they liked me. They are pretty radical and so am I.'

She comes from an observing Reform household in Hampstead, and was 'fairly religious' until the age of 15 when she went through what she calls an anti-semitic phase. She could easily have opted for an academic life but enjoys the pastoral duties of a rabbi, even though it means driving 15,000 miles a year round the 580 members of her congregation who live scattered between Clapham and Kingston. She teaches, leads services, looks after proselytes, preaches sermons about anything from the Boat People to the energy crisis, and performs all the usual rabbinical duties including officiating at circumcisions ('but not actually doing them . . . ugh').

Her congregation, she says, are entirely used to the fact that she is female though, since traditionally even Liberal Jewish women tend not to go to funerals, there were a few misgivings about Rabbi Neuberger actually taking funeral services in a bulging maternity dress a fortnight before her baby was born. 'There was no real reason why not. I think they just thought it looked funny; it sort of asserted one's femininity rather. Anyway it was too bad. I had five funerals in the last two weeks I was working and had to take them so I did.'

The birth of her daughter, Harriet, in June was the fulfilment of half an ambition. 'I always meant to have my first baby and get my PhD by the time I was 30' (she is 29, but the PhD is progressing slowly). It was also a bit of a relief for certain members of the congregation. 'You know – "she's normal after all". They tend to think I'm a bit fierce and I seem to be less frightening since I had the baby.' Harriet's nursery is now papered with the hundreds of letters and cards that poured in from a joyful congregation. Emancipation is all very well but motherhood is still an extra-blessed state.

The only serious problem about breaking with the tradition of male rabbis was that she had to invent her own uniform to wear in synagogue. She hit on a black suit, white shirt and a black Kangol beret with the bobble cut off. A Cambridge MA gown comes in useful for funerals.

It was the headgear which proved most difficult. Since she wears a prayer shawl she thought she ought to cover her head but a skull cap looked ridiculous on her springy blonde hair and her usual taste in hats tends to be large and floral. The Kangol beret, she says, is perfect.

To understand how Julia Neuberger and her congregation take all this so calmly while orthodox Jews would call it an abomination, it is necessary to grasp how fundamental are the differences between Progressive Judaism (Liberals and Reformed) and the Establishment (United Synagogue).

For Mrs Neuberger and other Liberal Jews, the 613 commandments, which the observing Orthodox perform to the letter, are part of an evolving, dynamic religion whose rules in the last analysis are a matter for the individual conscience. 'I don't think it would be right to say you don't need to perform any of the laws – that would be nonsensical – but I feel very strongly that it's up to every person to define what of Jewish custom and Jewish law he or she is going to practise. You must decide each one on its merits and things of merely traditional practice affecting only oneself, like the dietary laws, should be a matter for the individual. (She does not observe them.)

She is strict about observing Jewish festivals and the Sabbath – not in terms of refusing to switch on lights or put a match to a fire, but she does not, for instance, do any writing on a Saturday. The family always has a meal together on Friday night and they do not celebrate Christmas or Easter, even to the extent of a Christmas tree or jollities for the children. Her Sabbath observation is based on a belief that the good life includes one day a week set aside for rest and refreshment. 'I don't write on a Saturday because for me writing is part of my normal work. If I were a professional gardener, I wouldn't garden.'

All very sane, but is it Judaism? Might she not just as well be a social worker or a scholar? 'No, no. Part of it lies in a tremendous loyalty to the Jewish people (mind you, it's difficult to explain what I mean by that because it's not a matter of God's chosen people. I don't think that's a very inspiring thing to be told and anyway, chosen for what? In a sense that's meaningless). The idea is you live a particular life but that lies within Judaism and within Jewish teaching. I feel very strongly that my people have suffered and if I can help . . . I suppose to keep them together, certainly to create a form of Judaism that is consistent with 20th-century life, then I think that is an important thing to do. I just don't think it is going to go on being possible to be orthodox. I may be wrong, but I don't.'

Her husband, Anthony, a civil servant like her father, fortunately shares most of her attitudes although he is not, she says, a particularly enthusiastic synagogue-goer. She thinks the congregation takes a more indulgent view of this than they might with a rabbi's wife – 'they expect the man to be doing something else.'

But how does a woman like Mrs Neuberger, who has assumed a professional status in Jewish life, confront other women in more orthodox denominations who accept that women cannot read from the Law because menstruation renders them unclean and who live by a set of laws that define her sex in ways she herself would not countenance – and what of the ultra-Orthodox who shave their heads on marriage, take ritual baths to purge their tainted bodies and consider birth control and even a career to be forbidden to them?

'The ultra-Orthodox absolutely hate us of course.' But although the divisions between Orthodox and Progressive are deep and there is a lot of hostility between them, the strange thing is that on the whole women from most wings of Judaism get on very well together. People on the whole are friendly – but on unofficial terms.

Progressive Jewish women are anxious to demonstrate that their stance is defensible on historical and theological grounds, not just wishful pragmatism. 'The role of women in Judaism has changed at various times' says Mrs Neuberger. 'We know that in the Middle Ages, for instance, men and women did sit together in the synagogue: the division came later. I think it's fair to say that the idea always was that women had their children and their place was in the home but I don't think they were restricted from public worship in the way they seem to be now.

'We know from the Talmudic Law that a woman is not obliged to perform a religious duty that has a fixed time attached to it – but it doesn't actually say that she isn't supposed to do it. There is no authority for preventing women from reading from the Law – or not one that one couldn't argue with anyway.'

Rabbi Neuberger's powers of argument are patently formidable but it should be said that even within Liberal Judaism there are differing views. Rabbi David Goldberg, associate minister at the Liberal Jewish Synagogue, for instance, wrote recently in an article not unsympathetic to Jewish feminism: 'There are no two ways about it. However generous first- and second-century rabbis were in their appreciation of the woman of virtue . . . nevertheless they accorded to women the same legal status as slaves, minors and imbeciles.'

Julia Neuberger is more optimistic. 'There is a lot of literature about the attitude of rabbinic law towards women and the apologetics are extraordinary. They will, for instance say that a man blesses God for not making him a woman because he is grateful to God for insisting that he performs all the commandments whereas a woman doesn't have to.

'Frankly I think that is so much eyewash. Those blessings make it pretty clear that men consider themselves superior, as does the business of only counting men for the minyan, but many other things which are supposed to be ancient rules dictating male superiority I don't think really are. Anyway, we believe in progressive revelation, that in each generation God reveals his will in a different way. It didn't all happen on Mount Sinai.'

There are still women who allege that even Progressive synagogues discriminate against women, but only in the United States has Jewish feminism really become a serious movement. There, a group of Orthodox women have formed their own minyan and run their own services. Women have produced prayer books written in non-sexist language where God is addressed throughout as You to avoid having to use He or Him. 'Some of the stuff is just unreadable, which is a shame,' said Mrs Neuberger. 'But I think there is a value in redoing the Haggadah, the Passover order of service book, because it is very male orientated.'

Julia Neuberger, despite her professional success, still has about her an air of the Cambridge undergraduate. She has a bouncy way of talking that accelerates constantly into gales of laughter that would be girlish if she wasn't so intelligent; she has a way of leaping upon a well-known argument before it has even taken shape like a bright pupil coming to the point of an essay.

It was so when I started on the ancient question of whether survival was better safeguarded by infinite adaptability or by rigid adherence to tradition. It was familiar territory to every Jew, this argument, and she saw it coming a mile off. 'What do you mean by tradition?' she pounced. I had barely begun on the Polish ghettoes when there was a sharp 'Oh' and she was off.

'It's not true. If you look at what the ultra-Orthodox Jews are wearing now, they are wearing 18th-century Polish and Russian dress. What then were they wearing in the 18th century? Was it 16th-century Polish dress? What has happened is that it's frozen in the 18th century. I think the fact is that orthodoxy was so frightened by the Enlightenment that they withdrew into themselves.

'Until roughly then Judaism was a dynamic religion. Really it would be possible to say that the natural form of Judaism is some form of progressive Judaism. If you look at the ultra-Orthodox in say Stamford Hill, yes, they haven't changed but the question is how long haven't they changed for?'

She finds the current return to tradition in Judaism, in Islam – even in British politics – terrifying. 'I don't think it's healthy and personally I don't think it's any kind of answer to anything. If I'm serious about it I suppose that's why I say I'm a radical. I didn't feel part of that at all and as many Jews, Progressive as well as Orthodox, become more and more out on a limb.

'I think we're frightened of looking forwards, so let's go back to these nice comfortable traditions of the past. I agree many of those traditions are absolutely lovely and there's no reason why one shouldn't observe them but one must examine one's motives for observing things – and if the motive is so that you can occupy your mind with those and not think about other things then I reckon you ought to examine your motives again.'

1980s

It is just not good enough for some women to make their way to the top and then for us to say that the doors are open to all of us. They are not.

Barbara Castle

Now is the time to stand up and fight

A militant response to the menace of the Yorkshire Ripper

JEAN STEAD

Not much point in being sugar and spice and all things nice, is there, if it ends up with a one-pound hammer smashing into the back of your head?

I suggest that the time has come for primary schools to get some supervised mixed infant fighting courses going in the playgrounds. Small girls learning that a mixture of brain and muscle can defeat small boys will go a long way towards avoiding in future the degrading fear and dependence now being felt by the women in West Yorkshire because of the Ripper attacks.

It might also engender in the male population generally a healthy physical fear of women instead of an irrational fear of their tongues. We need more Amazons around, or simply some characters like those in The Romans in Britain who never went anywhere without a large stone which they used to attack any strange man who came near them.

If this seems unduly pragmatic, or to be encouraging lawless behaviour, then I can only point to the guidance of our judges. The law, on the whole, believes in the value of deterrence. Wherever there is an outbreak of a particular crime, judges recommend 'deterrent sentences' of unusual severity and claim that this usually stops the epidemic in that area.

A spokesman for Women's Aid in Leeds said that even if the

Ripper is caught, that will not stop the fear that women have of going out at night on their own.

'There are still rapes and attacks on women all the time, and we have to get all the women's groups together and decide on a long-term course of action,' she said. 'The men here say that this killer is a maniac, he is one in a million, and not at all typical of men in general. That may be so, but the male view here is that if a woman is attacked, she must have been asking for it. The same is not true of attacks on men.'

'You get a lot of awful jibes from men,' said another woman. 'If a woman is battered, they say she must want it or have done something to deserve it.'

The days when Mrs Whitehouse and friends were the only ones against pornography are gone. The Leeds women, in their recent demonstrations through the street, threw red paint at the screen during a showing of Dressed to Kill, a film in which women are the object of the violent attentions of a male transvestite psychiatrist.

When violence against women is the standard entertainment of local cinemas, is it truly sensible to deny that it has not become part of the established cultural pattern of our day?

Feminists in America protested about Dressed to Kill because, though it was a clever film technically, it had, as is usual in films of violence, women as the victims.

Women are easy to frighten. Most of them go through life terrified of the dark, of sleeping alone, of being in a railway carriage alone with a man. They form relationships with men, sometimes for life, simply to have a handy bodyguard. It really isn't any way to go on.

After the Leeds demonstration following the latest Ripper killing, which called for a curfew for men – 'because why should we be the ones who always have to stay in at night?' – a male reader from Surrey wrote to the Guardian: 'Those so-called feminists who appear to think that brawling can be excused because it serves a progressive cause are just fascists in everything but name, and it's about time that radical thinkers exposed them as such.'

This provoked many angry replies from women, including one who had been on the demonstration and pointed out that one man had walked into their midst and hit her when she said there should be a curfew on men.

The violence she had experienced on the march, she said, had been provoked by men.

All this is not at all meant to under-rate the courageous protectiveness being shown by many men in West Yorkshire, and indeed, throughout the country. It is meant to suggest that women might start to emulate their virtues. Karate classes have been the norm for women in many areas of London for a decade and they are starting to think about it in Leeds.

It is only recently that policewomen have been allowed out of the confines of traffic work and child crime, and they are quickly showing ready skill and courage as markswomen and in tackling dangerous criminals.

The search for the Ripper has become a focus for feminist thinking that will be far reaching. The first lesson is that women have to stop clinging to men as their only support and to learn to band together. Even if a male curfew might serve no purpose in catching the Ripper, as a temporary measure it might at least display a gesture of goodwill by men towards the miserable women of Leeds. A few nights away from the pub wouldn't do them any harm and it might help them to imagine how it feels to be a woman.

An excerpt from Poem for Jacqueline Hill, written by a woman poet in Leeds and currently being distributed by women all over the north of England.

'No woman is safe:' (It is the police this time)
'No woman should go out after dark' – then in a whisper:
'but we men can.'

The voices ride in on the wind
that butts against the walls –
(Walls vulnerable as our skulls) –
'No woman is safe' –
The voices climb in as draughts through the cracks –
'Women' (it is all men speaking now)
'fear the dark, stay at home,
we cannot answer for the consequences
if you get on buses;
leave us the hunting paths in the city jungle –
be good: be stupid: never, never be free.'
and we remember
the woman, who was, or could have been,
our sister, student, colleague, friend, neighbour

5 MAY 1982

Letters from a fainthearted feminist

JILL TWEEDIE

Dear Mary,

Daffy Murdoch's just been regaling me down the phone about when she and her husband weren't speaking and he started coming home later and later from the office. On her own again for the umpteenth evening, something snapped. She broke six plates, pulled out every drawer, spread out all her worldly goods across the floor, turned their tiny hall into the St Valentine's Day Massacre with red paint, up to and including bloody handprints smeared down the walls, left a note cut out of newsprint saying: We Got Your Wife, and departed. Give him a fright, she thought. So straight away she rang her mother, her mother betrayed her and when she came back he wouldn't say a word to her for weeks. Just like old times it was, she said.

And then there was my American friend Dorrie Carrie Bogvak, when she first had the twins and things were tough all over. She got so desperate slaving over a hot two-ring stove that, one afternoon, she emptied meatballs in tomato sauce and all the mashed potatoes on the floor, unplugged the Baby Belling, stuck it on top of the mess, picked up the babies and did a flit, leaving a note for her old man saying Your Oven's In the Dinner. But, as she said, what man's going to take you on with three-month-old twins when even their rightful and legal father is none too keen, so she had to patch it up, poor dear. Or, rather, mop it up.

Would that I could afford such drama but I can't, because of the children. They are my hostages to fortune but also to any chance of plain marital speaking. The luxury of an all-out bang-up shouting match can't be had when they're around. I tried launching into a mini-scene with Josh, the evening of the morning he broke my heart with his remarks about Irene being more feminine than me, but Ben came in just as my voice was hitting a thoroughly therapeutic High C and I had to pretend I was midway through The Hills Are Alive With the Sound of Music.

That night, I tried a bit of hissing under the sheets but my hisses were drowned by Josh's snores. How can I make him realise the extent of my wounds? I lie beside him, sniffing, and all he does is occasionally brush my side of his face like I was an early mosquito. Obviously he thinks if he just keeps saying cheerful, everyday things like what a nice day and Martha, this shredded wheat is delicious, I'll come round.

But I won't, this time. Now he's changed his tactics. Ignoring the fact that he's cut me to the quick with his gushings about Irene and is probably having an affair with her, he says why are you looking so glum, Martha? and I say because and he says oh God, you're not still on about that, are you? You wouldn't believe, Mary, how hard it is to make your loved one realise that your life's blood is sploshing at their feet. In view of this I have no alternative but to take up your kind offer and absent myself until such time as Josh understands the near-fatal blow he has delivered. Telling him over the top of the Telegraph only makes me feel a nag as well as everything else. Josh. What? You've broken my heart, Josh. You what, Martha? I'll tell you one thing, Martha, that Tony Benn ought to be shot at dawn, Martha.

You said in your letter I should come to you if the going got rough and it couldn't get rougher. I won't stay long, I promise, how can I, with Ben still a child in all but feet? The baby will have to come along, of course, but he's in a quiet phase at the moment and even his shrieks are quite thoughtful and don't last that long. I've told Helen I've got to leave Annie's Attic. She said oh dear and sighed a lot and talked about how they always told her she shouldn't rely on married women. No man could have said better.

Big Noreen is going to take over while I'm gone. Just remember, take the baby out of the chest of drawers before you sell it, I said, and she shook all over. She told me when her Born Killer gets on her wick, she hits him over the head with a bottle and that rearranges his brains nicely, know what I mean. As for old Charlie After-Shave, when I shouted in his ear that I was off, he gripped my hand and said 'give them Argies hell'. Well, at least he's got his wars straightened out now.

Jane and Ben took the news calmly. Just popping up to see Mary, I said, only for a few days. Jane said who's going to cook the meals for me and Ben said I need a new pair of Levi's, Mum, and could Flanagan stay while you're gone. Martha, sadly missed by one and all, tra la.

I haven't let Mother know my plans, she'd only be confirmed in her lifelong view that I was born a runaway wife. Why can she always be relied upon to take my husband's side against me? If anyone ever dared to take Father's side against her, she'd swat them into a fly paste. I did ring her yesterday, in a weak moment, but I only got Father shouting who is this when I said hullo Father, so I gave up. Lorna wasn't exactly supportive, either. When I dropped round to her Funeral Home to say cheers, be seeing you, she put on a cadaverous voice said today happened to be her 15th wedding anniversary and what a good thing some women took their vows seriously and stuck by their husbands, in spite of marital infidelities on a scale that I, Martha, wotted not of.

But Lorna, I said, you're the one having an affair. I beg your pardon? she said, rigor mortis setting in. Lorna, you told me about it yourself. Ah, she said, that one. You don't want to take any notice of that one, Martha. My old man doesn't and he never had it so good.

Whatever that means. Anyway, Mary, I'm leaving my Dear Josh letter on the mantelpiece, which I expect the cat will eat, and I'll be with you all in Sebastopol Terrace this time Thursday as ever was.

Yours, darkening the door, Martha

23 JULY 1982

A day with Spare Rib

'Lesbianism is a central issue. It is an option all women need to know about and think about'

POLLY TOYNBEE

In the beginning, back in 1972, few people thought Spare Rib had much of a long term future. It came out of the era of OZ, IT,

FRENDZ, and INK, the 60s underground press. The original founders had worked for these publications, but were angry to find that women were no better treated by the alternative than by the straight press. At the time its appeal to feminist women seemed too limited to stand much chance of survival.

Now, 10 years later, its circulation is 35,000 and is still growing and Penguin has just published a mammoth anthology, Spare Rib Reader. As the women's movement has expanded, so has Spare Rib. There is a full-time staff of 10 women. They are paid so badly that they wouldn't reveal the actual sum, but they all get the same amount. There is some discussion about whether they should pay themselves more since, they say, such low pay self-selects those who are financially dependent on those with whom they live.

I went to see them with some trepidation. People like Frank Johnson of the Murdoch Times, who took a mocking swipe at the Guardian women's page only last week, may regard us as wild women, but Spare Rib, from the other side, consider us beneath notice. Spare Rib Reader, chronicling the women's movement of the last 10 years, gives the Guardian just one mention – for a sexist ad the paper carried by Hertz in 1973. Jill Tweedie also gets one mention, for having mocked a women's group in Tufnell Park in 1969.

So it was a pleasant surprise to meet two of the longest serving members of the collective, Sue O'Sullivan and Ruth Wallsgrove, and find them neither ferocious nor contemptuous but open and welcoming. The office is a cluttered, cheerful, open plan room in a grim old warehouse converted into workshops in London's Clerkenwell, inhabited mainly by alternative organisations of one kind or another.

Feminist posters line the walls – For a Taste of Sweet and Sour read Spare Rib every month. They explain that theirs is a 'non-patriarchal, non-hierarchical' structure. There are no stars, and no drudges. The collective members hardly write themselves these days, preferring to regard the magazine as an outlet for other women, most of whom are not writers.

The women's movement has no structure, no umbrella organisation, no headquarters. It consists of a myriad groups scarcely connected. But Spare Rib is its main notice board and journal. It chronicles events, provides news of women's groups around the world, carries small ads for coming events, contacts and jobs. Larger ads that pay half the cost of the magazine promote handbags, vibrators, books, feminist jewellery, dungarees. Trade unions ply for members, with NUPE showing a picture of dinner ladies, and TASS a harassed woman at a desk. Spare Rib is scrupulously uncritical of any feminist manifestation – so long as it is leftist and alternative, but those who are outside that boundary get short shrift.

Sue O'Sullivan, a 40-year-old American, explained her view of the Guardian women's page kind of feminism: 'The Guardian is liberal and reformist. It's the same as all liberals, and moves with the fashion. It was more feminist when it was safer to be so, but now we have hit hard times, with the Thatcherite backlash, you are of course, retreating, as we knew you would.'

The foreword to the Penguin Reader talks of the magazine's wish to reach out to all women, of all classes, and especially those outside the movement. But Spare Rib reads like an insiders' manual. The nature of the staff may have something to do with it. Although their average age is 31, only five of them have to care for children, and some of those care for friends' children. The majority of the women are lesbian by coincidence, not design, they say. There is one black woman, and they are currently advertising for two more – never mind the Race Relations Act.

'We are writing more and more about lesbians and black women,' says Ruth Wallsgrove. How does that make it accessible to most women, when by their own acknowledgement only 5% of women are lesbian, and 3% black?

'It helps all women to identify with the struggles of these

minorities,' Ruth Wallsgrove replied. 'Because women are oppressed themselves it is easy for them to identify with black women who are even more oppressed. And lesbianism is a central issue for all women. It is an option all women need to know about, and think about.'

The cover of the June issue of Spare Rib is enticing – 'What the women's army is really like from the inside.' The article, however, is disappointing. It is the inside story of three women thrown out of the army for being lesbian, and tells little of army life apart from its anti-lesbianism. The June editorial begins, 'Unlike General Galtieri Margaret Thatcher does not – yet – head a fascist military dictatorship. But they do share certain characteristics . . . '

The news section carries articles on abortion in Spain, hysterectomy, morning-after pills, German anti-war feminists, homeworkers, women and unions, plastic bullets in Northern Ireland, the feminist League for Animals' Irreducible Rights, and more.

The magazine is written heavily in Left-Speak, that curious jargon of Marxism that sounds only half translated from the German. Everyone is 'fighting' or 'struggling' in this 'arena', or that 'forum', 'confronting' the 'contradiction' and the 'violence' of the 'system'. There is not much jargon that springs from feminism itself, beyond 'male chauvinism', 'sexism', 'macho' and 'patriarchal'.

I asked if all the women in the collective called themselves socialists. No, I was told, some were radical feminists, some socialist feminists, some revolutionary feminists and some Marxist feminists. Were any of them not of the far Left? The question puzzled them. 'You can't be a feminist and a capitalist,' Ruth Wallsgrove said. 'Why not!' I asked. 'Because,' she answered, 'feminism is about freeing women from oppression, and capitalism oppresses all women. Capitalism feeds on patriarchy and you can't get rid of one without the other.'

Spare Rib Reader contains all that is best in the magazine. Here are collected lively, serious, well written articles, recording the various phases and moods of feminist thought over the last 10 years. There are some excellent historical pieces, articles on women's images, and women at work. A powerful section on women and sex has brave articles reaching the same conclusions as the Hite report on women's sexuality, long before the Hite report was published.

Oddly enough, the book doesn't really give the flavour of the magazine. I assumed that some moderate Penguin editor had got a hand on it and cleaned up the image – but no, the collective made the selection themselves. Lesbianism, separatism and even Marxism feature far less in the book than the magazine. When it came to choosing the highest quality writing, the wilder exotica fell away. The two women I spoke to were surprised at this. 'Perhaps,' one of them said, 'it's just a lot of that is old stuff, and we've got a lot tougher now.'

10 DECEMBER 1982

Ring of resolve to stop cruise

Greenham Common women plan to close the USAF base on Monday

JEAN STEAD

A few women sleeping under plastic sheeting in subzero temperatures at the Greenham Common RAF base near Newbury have become the unexpected focus for the Western disarmament movement. At conferences and meetings in Western Europe, the United States, and from part of the Eastern bloc, messages of support to 'The Greenham Common' women are sent.

They arrive by every post outside the main gates. This is a strange phenomenon, for the women belong to no identifiable group. They are not attached to the Labour party, to CND, or to any other organisation. They have no communication system – apart from a bike ride to the nearest pay telephone kiosk. Yet they have become an embarrassment not only to the 501 Tactical Missile Wing of the US Third Air Force, which actually occupies the base behind the RAF camouflage, but to the British government and to Nato. Next December the base is scheduled to receive the first consignment of cruise missiles in Europe.

The women have twice been evicted and can no longer have tents or caravans because of the common by-laws. Twenty-three of them have just served prison sentences for nonviolent action at the base.

The Americans, usually ready enough to put their case, are holding back this time. 'We regard this as an internal British matter,' they say when questioned about the base. 'As such it is a matter for the appropriate British authorities to deal with. We have no jurisdiction. It is an internal political debate.'

This is the policy line that has been laid down.

Every subordinate US commander on every US base in Britain has been told to take the same line. The appropriate British authority is the Ministry of Defence, which has leased the land to the US Third Air Force. They don't trouble to give reasons for the blackout. Each American base in Britain has a public affairs department for liaison with the public, but requests for interviews are passed to the Ministry of Defence. The 'appropriate officer' at the MoD says at present that 'the answer is no' – and that is that. Freedom of information there may be but not where the delivery of cruise missiles – which will be under American control – are concerned.

In the 15 months since 40 of them and their children walked 140 miles to the base, to protest at the heart of the nuclear theatre weapons modernisation programme in Europe, the Greenham women have inspired other peace camps at other bases. No one took them very seriously at first. They seemed an isolated and slightly unrealistic crew. But they had gone there for one reason – and that united them and made them stay. CND meetings were not enough. They did not trust the Labour party to carry out an anti-nuclear programme and, in any case, by the time they were in government, they thought, it would be too late. They wanted to get away from the lonely depression of thinking about the Bomb by themselves. They went where the action was going to be – and they are going to stay.

The first harassments and evictions brought support from all over the country, and other women left jobs and homes to join them. The protest, intended to last a few days, carried on. The women came out of prison and went back to the camp. This time it is harder, for officially they cannot camp on the common land and have only roughly rigged-up plastic sheeting and a few vans to sleep in. The vans have been lent by supporters.

To begin with, the camp was mixed, but the women found that the men were starting to run it, expected them to cook and clean, taking over the demonstration they wanted to be their own. So the men were asked to leave. Then their image was tarnished by a visit last summer from a noisy group called the Cosmic Carnival. Newbury council still has outraged memories of this. The carnival mercifully went on its way, but then CND wanted to take them over as a 'project'. That might have meant forms and committees and being taken over again, so the women politely said no.

They have been evicted both by Newbury council and the Department of Transport, who share the land outside the base. At present, they are on the common land – part of the tiny fraction still left to the council at present led by the Conservatives. The rest of the common has long since been lost to the Ministry of Defence and the Transport Department.

The worst may be yet to come. The council is taking them to court for trespassing on council-owned land under the Law of Property Act of 1925 and the Order of Limitation under the Act – criminal laws which will bring criminal sentences if they are found guilty. The council will also seek a high court injunction to stop them ever returning to the common.

Commoners do have some rights on the land, but they are restricted. A deed of declaration made in 1939 gave them the rights of taking air and exercise and there are other rights the council is a little vague about, like grazing animals and cutting turf. This will have to be decided in court.

There are no rights to camp, and the women's pathetic attempts to manage without proper shelter will be a key issue in the case. The council will have the approval, not only of the base, but also of the Department of Transport, which took over part of the common to give better visibility when it built the A339 trunk road past the camp in the 60s.

But all this will not happen until after the weekend, a period which marks the third anniversary of December 12, 1979, when a number of Nato countries in Europe decided to install American cruise missiles – including West Germany, Italy, Holland, and Belgium. For the last four, they will be the first nuclear weapons on their soil, able to reach the Soviet Union, as opposed to battlefield weapons, hence the importance of the anniversary.

The decision was taken with a 'zero option' – that they would not be delivered if the Soviets removed the SS20 missiles deployed in Eastern Europe.

On Sunday the women plan to encircle the whole nine-mile perimeter of the Greenham Common base with a chain of women holding hands. They estimate they will need 8,000 for this, but the message by word of mouth seems to have spread like a brushfire, and their worry now is how they will cope if 20,000 arrive. Each woman is being asked to bring what means most to her as a symbol of life – flowers, photographs of their familes, bits of baby clothing and to hang them on the wire and concrete fence. It is a daunting prospect for those who will have to take them down.

All the women who have just come out of prison for their beliefs give coherent accounts of why the peace camp means so much to them. Christine King, one of four daughters of a Rhondda security guard, who went to prison with her sisters, said that at the June anti-bomb rally in London it suddenly seemed like a pointless re-run of a familiar scene.

'Someone started talking about non-violent direct action, and I knew that was what I had to do. We started in the Rhondda, asking for support for Greenham in the shopping centre, and got an amazing response. Every time the women there were in trouble, they'd phone and we'd be down. We spent weeks at a time sleeping at the camp.'

Simone Wilkinson left her comfortable Isle of Wight home, husband, and son and daughter, aged 12 and 11, to support the Greenham women. 'There seemed no point in doing anything at all if the children were not going to have any future.'

This feeling started when she was eight months pregnant and met a Japanese girl from Hiroshima at a party in London. The girl told her that in Hiroshima women were never congratulated when they became pregnant. People just waited silently for nine months to see whether the baby would be normal – because of radiation effects which still persist.

'I couldn't get it out of my mind. The local CND group didn't seem enough – it was not actually doing anything to stop the missiles coming. For the first time, at Greenham, I felt I could physically do something.'

The women there are quite confident of this. Sarah, an ex-social worker from Sheffield who has been there for practically the whole period of the camp, is quite confident of this. Her face is quite calm when she talks about it. 'This is where I feel at peace because I can see what is going on. I know we shall see them coming and I know we can stop them.'

Despite the desperately hard conditions, the women seem blooming with health. 'You get used to the cold,' they say. Visitors start to shiver after a few hours.

They used to have painted banners and emblems, but the rain washes them away. People have brought plastic sacks of clothing, but these have become soaked with rain as well. Drying their clothing is the biggest problem. But they have supporters in Newbury who lend dryers and offer them showers and baths.

They explain how they have changed since they came to the camp. 'It is difficult for many women to learn that they can change things on their own, without men, and that is why they feel helpless in the nuclear crisis,' said Sarah, the former social worker. 'We have all changed since we came here. We know we can survive on our own, run our own camp, and we know that we have the strength to stand up for what we believe in. We know that cruise missiles won't arrive here, because we can stop them.'

Americans on the base are forbidden to talk to them or look at them. They drive past with their children, eyes averted. The women have met one or two, however. 'They told us they are getting themselves posted home before cruise arrive because they can't stand it,' said one. They have also talked to workmen building the huge concrete structures in the middle of the base. 'We have tried to persuade them that building housing for missiles is wrong. One or two have left.'

Prison reinforced their determination to carry on. Holloway, they said, they found a completely inhuman place. Most of the inmates, they said, were either Irish, black, or very young, and inside for what seemed minor offences. Some women were moved from one prison to another because of their unsettling influence in trying to convert other women prisoners to the cause of nuclear disarmament.

At the open prison near Maidstone, Katherine Barker, an ex-student from the London College of Printing, told how they persuaded the governor to let them show a video of a film on the effects of nuclear war by the scientist Helen Caldicott. The governor said the inmates wouldn't understand it, that it was too technical – but they did. They were converted, though the prison officers did not appear to be.

Now they are out of prison, they are much in demand by radio and television and to speak at public meetings. But they are also busy with the organisation of Sunday's demonstration. That is not surprising, for on Monday they plan to close down the base completely. Non-violent action needs training and planning, and they do not want anyone to get arrested who has not decided beforehand that they are prepared to go to prison.

The plan is to lay down at all the entrances to the base so that transport cannot get through. If lifted away by police, they hope simply to return and lie down again. They are likely to get hundreds of volunteers. They are asking that men should not take part, but should help instead in giving the support the arrested women will need – looking after children or transport or providing medical treatment.

The reason they do not want men to join in is simple. They think that if they do, the demonstration will become violent. That may happen in any case, but not if the women of Greenham Common have their way.

30 January 1984

Her life has had extraordinary ups and downs – from prostitute to star, from street car conductorette to university professor

Interview with Maya Angelou

POLLY TOYNBEE

Since 1969, the book has now gone into its 16th hardback and its 25th paperback edition. It is required reading in every college and university in the United States. But by some bizarre oversight, no one thought to publish it over here – until Virago, with their usual perspicacity, did so today. I Know Why The Caged Bird Sings, by Maya Angelou, is a remarkable autobiography, the story of a pitifully poor childhood in a backward cotton-growing part of Arkansas.

Maya Angelou has had a life of extraordinary ups and downs. She has been a prostitute, a madam, the first black conductorette on the San Francisco street cars, night club singer and dancer, star in Porgy and Bess, poet, civil rights worker with Martin Luther King, bestselling author, and now Reynolds Professor of American Studies at Wake Forest University in North Carolina, with strings of honorary degrees and awards to her name.

The title of the book suggests she knows the secret to surviving catastrophe. The reader is left stunned and puzzled. Could anyone else but her have overcome such a catalogue of disaster and disadvantage to emerge a tower of strength, a dynamo of inner energy?

Six foot tall, majestic, she still moves like a dancer. Her voice has a rich mellifluous boom: a singer's voice. She carries with her an awe-inspiring air of authority, a flash in the eye of experience and command, and she laughs with warmth and exuberance.

The art of autobiography is a rare talent. How easy to chronicle such a powerful story of injustice and horror and expect the tale to tell itself. But Maya Angelou's book is lyrical and contemplative, a knowing exploration of herself as well as an account of a hard life in the Deep South. Indeed, her publisher, pressing her to write the book, finally succeeded when he said 'Anyway, it's almost impossible to write autobiography as literature.' That challenge made her sit down and write. Literature it is.

Maya was three, her adored and adoring brother Bailey four, when they arrived in the small poor town of Stamps, Arkansas, with tags on their wrists addressed 'To Whom It May Concern'. Their parents in California had divorced, and they were being bundled off to their father's mother. 'The United States had been crossed thousands of times by frightened black children travelling to their newly affluent parents in the Northern cities, or back to grandmothers in Southern towns.' Marguerite Johnson, her name tag said ('Maya' came from when Bailey taught her to walk and said, 'This is my sister. Mya sister,' and it stuck.) The children clung together through all their vicissitudes, fiercely loving and protective towards each other.

Their grandmother, Sister Henderson, devout elder of the Christian Methodist Episcopal Church, owned the only black store in Stamps, and land too, lived on by the 'powhitetrash'. Sister Henderson's power, pride, severity, religion and sheer survivalism dominate the book. They were poor, scrimping, just managing, but the cotton-pickers were half-starved. On the other side of the tracks, the whites of Stamps were so far away and remote she rarely saw one and didn't think of them as real human beings. Bussing began long before civil rights. The black children were bussed a long way to the poor black school.

At eight she and her brother were summoned back to their mother, who was then working the clubs and casinos of St Louis. Here Maya was raped by her mother's lover. With a clarity and honesty, she describes how the seduction pleased her, her own half-complicity, until the brutal horror and agony of the rape itself. When she came out of hospital the man was put on trial. She said in court that he had never made advances to her before, which he had. He never served his sentence, as he was lynched and beaten to death the next day. Overwhelmed by guilt, sure she had caused his death, she became mute. She spoke not a word to anyone but her brother for five years.

All her life since then she has suffered occasional mutism. She becomes tongue-tied, unable to speak a word. 'It beckons me,' she says. 'I feel it coming. It is a temptation, to listen to sounds and stop speaking.' To her listeners that sounds extraordinary, with all her fluency, her rich vocabulary, a love of words. She has learned now, she says, to sense its onset, and refuse to give in to it.

The children were packed off back to Stamps, where Maya was beaten for insolence for refusing to speak, but stayed silent. In spite of that she was top of her class, star pupil, graduating at 12, when the only future for black girls was a college to learn domestic skills in preparation for service to whites. She spoke again at 13, taught by a friend to read poetry aloud.

The children were finally called back again to their mother, now in San Francisco. They arrived, country hayseeds, in a world where some blacks were affluent, schools integrated, life fast and hectic. At 15 she left school and decided to work on the street cars as a conductorette. Her mother pointed out that no blacks did that job. She fought with the street car company, persisted, struggled, refused to give in, and eventually got the job on her own at 15.

Her family, she writes, were so beautiful, and she felt plain gawky. Looking at her now, that's hard to imagine. Her wide apart eyes and expressive face defy plainness. They said she was so clumsy she'd trip over the pattern on the carpet. At 16 she read The Well Of Loneliness and confused lesbians with hermaphrodites. Looking at her own body, six foot tall, big boned, underdeveloped breasts, deep voice, big feet, genitals she thought deformed because she had seen no other, she thought she was turning into a lesbian. To prove it one way or another, she accosted the best looking boy in the class in the street and propositioned him baldly: 'Would you like to have sexual intercourse with me?' He obliged, briefly, and they didn't speak again. But she got pregnant – and managed to hide it from her mother until three weeks before the birth, so that she could still get her graduation diploma from school.

At this point the book ends. The rest of her life follows in three further volumes, not yet published in Britain. They describe how, after the birth of her son, she had to forgo a scholarship, refusing to give up her son to her mother. Together they sank into low life in San Francisco, using prostitution for survival.

She learned to dance in night school, and then to sing, and her career took off, taking her to New York, and round the world with Porgy and Bess. She met Martin Luther King: 'I was bowled over by him,' and became the northern co-ordinator of his Southern Christian Leadership Conference. (She remains firmly Christian.) She lived in Egypt, and then Ghana, as a writer and editor, looking for African roots. (She acted in the film of Roots, as well.)

Before taking up her new post as professor, in Winston-Salem, she had scarcely been back to the South, and swore she wouldn't. She went back once to see her grandmother when she was 18. She laughs at herself now, swanking round the town in her car, her hat and gloves, all California glamour and dash. She shouted at a white sales assistant who was rude to her, and her grandmother hustled her out of town that night, before the Ku Klux Klan with their guns came looking for a lynching.

She went back again in 1980 with a television crew and a national reporter. The Klan were there, surrounding the hotel in their pick-up trucks, rifles pointing out of the window. All the blacks still had guns behind their doors, lest the Klan came round. She had made Stamps, Arkansas, famous for poverty, meanness and racism, and their only famous daughter was not forgiven. 'It hadn't changed as much as I had hoped,' she says. 'Arkansas is the middle of nowhere, it has nothing going for it, and the world passes it by.'

And she is now famous in America, on account of her books. 'I'm the bestselling black female writer in the world,' she says with triumph. Her poetry too is well-read. When an autobiography is so famous, it leaves the writer as a curious walking monument, a work of art in herself, her life a public event. Yet she has none of that dried-up, hollowed-out sense of a writer who has told her stories too many times to believe them any more. She has warmth and humour, and a sense of wholeness and content that glows through a book that is only ostensibly about suffering and hardship.

7 SEPTEMBER 1984

A world away from women's liberation

Western feminism and women in the third world

SOON-YOUNG YOON

An international feminist movement united, embracing all races, raising a single voice of protest against world hunger and political oppression – is still a dream. Many western feminists are impatient to make this dream come true. As they see it, the world is on the frontiers of a feminist revolution, and it desperately needs their help.

At international conferences, these women bring their own gospel of how to liberate women. They pound the platforms to defend third world women's rights to end female circumcision, domestic violence and rape. They are trying to build the foundations for a movement they know can change human history.

But in Mexico City and Copenhagen, many third world women rejected this leadership of the west. At the forthcoming UN Conference on the Decade for Women in Nairobi they will probably do the same. They accuse American and European feminists of being obsessed with sexual issues and of paying too little attention to poverty and national liberation. They see the western initiatives as another example of high-handed missionary zeal among the supposedly unknowing, and they resent what they see as feminist imperialism.

They do not appreciate international attention when it sensationalises patriarchal violence among Asians and Africans and ignores the greater violence of infant deaths due to hunger and wars. Third world women do understand internationalism, but only when it is based on a principle of equality. That is a lesson which has been difficult for many in the US and other western countries.

The controversy concerning female circumcision in Africa illustrates the point. Female circumcision and infibulation are forms of sexual mutilation which vary from minor cuts near the clitoris to complete removal of all external sexual parts. They are recognised as major contributors to infections, infertility and diseases such as fistula in adult women, and may account for a high percentage of infant deaths in Africa.

However, female circumcision is not a 'barbaric practice' of third world countries, alone. Until the end of the 19th century, it was also reported in Russia, England, France, and the United States. In all cases, the aims are similar – to 'control female sexuality' and enforce patriarchal custom. But the degree of mutilation as well as its meaning varies widely; in some African countries circumcision is reduced to a tiny ritual scar, and many women believe that it will ensure their fertility and sexual power.

In the last few years, female circumcision suddenly made head-lines in the western media. American and European feminists rallied around the cause, demanding that governments enforce anti-circumcision laws. Pictures of operations were widely circu-lated, petitions were signed, and Unicef speedily passed a resolu-tion of protest. African women were not pleased.

As Belkis Giorgis, a leading African expert in public health, wrote: 'The debate being waged between certain western women and African women has arisen because of the conflict between certain western women's desire to perform a civilising mission and African women's desires to define their own ways and means of struggling against oppressive structures.'

In a similar tone, Alasebu Gebre Selassie of Ethiopia, speaking in Geneva at a work group on female circumcision, said: 'I am not enthusiastic about the problem being talked about in the west. Sensationalising the subject is an insult, and it doesn't help to change the situation for women in the countryside of Ethiopia.'

The furore created in the west also gave little credit to the African women's own efforts against female circumcision; yet much is being done. The Association of African Women for Research and Development has actively condemned the practice of female circumcision. In 1979, at the second regional conference on the Integration of Women in Development in Lusaka, participants passed a resolution appealing for the solidarity among all African women to combat harmful female circumcision while recognising the value of African tradition.

Projects are underway in countries such as Egypt and Ethiopia that emphasise local and national action, and participation of women's non-governmental organisations. As many African women see it, the problem must be tackled by the women in each country because they alone understand the complexities of the problem and its cultural context.

The lessons learned from this experience can also be applied to to other issues. One of these is birth control. In an effort to give third world women reproductive freedom, many feminist groups supported international programmes on family planning. Although they never actively supported coercive population control programmes, they often did not fight against them.

In some cases, working through the International Planned Parenthood Association, western feminists promoted introduction of oral contraceptives and intrauterine devices into developing countries where there were no health facilities. Not only were the priorities wrong, the pill caused severe side effects and IUDs introduced new iatrogenic diseases among malnourished rural women. Many died of complications.

Again, development resources were placed in the hands of feminists who did not understand the third world women's experiences.

Whether the issue is birth control, rape or circumcision, western feminists do not seem to understand the reluctance of third world women to 'go into the streets' to protest or even to confront the problems openly in public debates. The absence of aggressive campaigns involving masses of women is interpreted as a problem of consciousness-raising. With that comes a feeling that they should support third world women who appear to be isolated advocates of feminism in their own countries.

The truth is that third world feminists are often isolated, but this has little to do with states of consciousness; it has to do with survival. In Egypt, Nawal El-Saadawi was imprisoned for her writings advocating feminism. In India, girls may be impoverished and disinherited for open protests against dowry and arranged marriages. The consequences of confrontation must be borne by those who struggle, and these are the realities which so often escape outsiders.

The histories of women's struggles and their socio-political contexts are different, and when third world women say that they do not want to carry on their movement like 'western feminists,' they are expressing this simple truth.

Where, then, is the role of international sisterhood? Many third world women have been radicalised to such a point that they no longer believe it is possible. They are also wrong. Just as third world women are not a single, homogeneous group, neither is there such a thing as western feminism – it is a false target. There are many sisters to be allied with among progressive groups in the west and minority women of colour living in the advanced industrial countries.

But some things will also have to change. A lead has been taken by Danish feminists working within international development agencies. For example, Kirsten Jorgensen, a consultant for Danida (the Danish International Development Agency), has acted on behalf of third world women by ensuring that the development aid money is channeled into women's programmes and that policies encourage third world women's participation and self-reliance.

As for an ideological unity, western feminists must acknowledge that 'political issues' such as the racism in South Africa and human rights in South Korea are feminist issues and that they have priority over others such as lesbian rights. An international list of feminist issues would show many common interests among women in all countries, such as the struggle against domestic violence. And disadvantaged women in the west rightfully see themselves as members of a third world.

The problem is the unequal distribution of power and resources, for this has allowed a few to set the feminist agenda for the many. Third world women have recognised this, and demand a more equal share of both so that they can fight for their own causes, as they experience them, and as they wish to have them known. In their own movement, American and European feminists would surely ask for nothing less.

2 OCTOBER 1984

Analysis of the political, social and economic progress of women

BARBARA CASTLE

Let me make a confession – I've never been good at being a feminist. I haven't had time. From my earliest years I always had one single-minded ambition: to be an MP. And I never had the slightest doubt that I would make as good a one as any man.

Of course I met the usual obstacles women meet – and they were even worse in the 1940s than they are now. I remember one political colleague (a man of course) saying to me all those years ago: 'Of course I think you should be in parliament, but unfortunately women won't vote for women.' The typical alibi of the threatened male. (Incidentally, I never lost an election in 34 years).

I was helped to my fulfilment by two lucky breaks. The first was the war, which swept Labour to power with a huge majority. Never before or since have Labour candidates had a better chance.

Even so I needed my second break. Blackburn, for which I had been nominated, was a double-member constituency, so the delegates who assembled for the selection conference (predominantly male) had two votes. They were able to indulge their instinctive preference for a man and yet have a vote in hand for the fiery young redhead who had made such a rousing speech.

Without these two flukes, my parliamentary career might never have been launched.

Since then my attitude to what they call women's questions has been ambivalent. Frankly, I found them a bit tedious. I was absorbed for years with the challenge of being an MP and later a cabinet minister. I loved it and was fulfilled by it and found it hard to understand why more women did not come forward to claim the same fulfilment.

It took a bit of time to realise that this was a samurai attitude and I am not by nature a samurai. I am a socialist because I want to help dig people out of the rubble in which life has engulfed so many of them like a terrorist bomb. In disaster we all act collectively. I believe in collective action all the time.

So over the years I have changed my view. It is just not good enough for some women to make their way to the top and then for us to say that the doors are open to all of us. They are not. Indeed, in some ways we are going backwards.

We may have a woman prime minister, but there are today only 23 women in the House of Commons, six fewer than at our highest peak in 1964. It is still the exception rather than the rule for women to get to the top in industry. There are over 9 million women at work, at least one-third of them in trade unions, but there are still only six women members of the general council of the TUC out of 50, and they are nominated under a quota system. And in spite of the Equal Pay Act and the Equal Opportunities Commission, most women are still coralled in the low paid jobs.

So tokenism has not got women very far. Indeed, Margaret Thatcher's behaviour as the first woman prime minister has made matters worse. It is not only that she has not allowed any other woman into her cabinet. She has cut back ruthlessly on the services that liberate women from some of their traditional domestic servitudes – home helps for the elderly, day centres, nursery schools, NHS community hospitals, help for the mentally handicapped; the list is endless. She is even devaluing child benefit, of which I was the proud midwife and which was intended to be the mother's wage.

It is as though she wants to dissociate herself from her own sex. A few weeks ago she had to choose two new British members of the European Commission – that civil service-cum-policy initiator of the EEC where they like to prate about the need for sex equality. So far the member states have not managed to appoint a single woman out of the 14 commissioners. There are hundreds of women in Britain who could do the job better than most of the existing commissioners. This was Mrs Thatcher's chance to get the balance right. But she chose two males.

The moral therefore is becoming obvious. A few women, with a lot of luck, have managed to achieve what they wanted to, but women as a sex are still undervalued and underused. And they cannot rely on their luckier sisters to bail them out.

Like all exploited groups they must learn to help themselves. No one else will unless they do. If that is feminism, I am now a feminist.

But I am still restive about the forms that traditional feminism takes. It seems to chase the psychological frills rather than the economic fundamentals. For God's sake, what does it matter whether, when a woman presides over a meeting, she is called a chairman or a chairperson? I never want to be described as anything so hideous. When I am called a chairman I feel that I am capturing a citadel, not surrendering one.

Where women fail is the assertion of the power they already have. To begin with, they wield more votes than men. If women, who constitute 52% of the electorate, end up only having 4% of the membership of the House of Commons, whose fault is it?

Of course, we all know the prejudices that block women's way, but if women mobilise to resist those prejudices, they can break them down. My career is proof of that. I should never have appeared before that selection conference in Blackburn in 1944 if the women's section of the local Labour party had not threatened to stop doing the party's political chores unless they had a woman on the shortlist. They won.

And think of the power of women's votes. There are enough of them to make any government tremble if they organise that power behind demands to protect their interests. I would like to see our woman prime minister presented with a woman's charter in defence of the social services which set women free to fulfil themselves in the round.

It is astonishing to me that Mrs Thatcher, who has tried to relaunch the 'back to the kitchen' morality to justify her cuts in public expenditure, has not roused the united anger of women who refuse to pick up the responsibilities that any decent society should shoulder collectively.

Or take industry. Here again, women workers play a key role in keeping the show on the road – at cut prices. Why do women put up with it? The simple answer is that a lot of them won't join trade unions.

When I rushed the Equal Pay Act through parliament in 1970, I knew it was far from perfect. I just wanted to get something on the statute book to pave the way for later refinements. But I also said at the time that legislation can only ever provide an opportunity; it can never be the substitute for personal involvement by women themselves. I remember telling a press conference: 'It is no part of my job as minister to make it unnecessary for women to join trade unions.' I have never been paternalist. (Or should I say 'maternalist'? I don't give a damn.)

In current history there are two vivid examples of organised women's power. The first is the Greenham women, about whom I don't need to say any more. The extent of their success in using woman power on behalf of a key woman's objective – peace – is to be found in the macho-male. I salute their peaceful dedication to their opposition to the aggression-cult of our society.

The second example is the miners' wives. Arthur Scargill would never have got away with his macho trade union policies if the women had not joined in. They did so in defence of the sort of aim with which the least aggressive members of our society can identify themselves; the need to provide the jobs which preserve, not only family life, but whole communities.

So I believe in the multi-group society – richness in freedom to express diversity. And because women are an identifiable group, whose needs and potentialities are neglected, and too often scorned, I am on their side.

18 DECEMBER 1984

We have as much right as anyone to dine out

CAROLYNE SHAKESPEARE COOPER

Andrew Lloyd Webber, you've got a lot to answer for. I must admit, I never really liked your shows that much anyway. I mean Evita had some agreeable tunes, and Cats packed a choreographic wallop. Newest on the scene is Starlight Express, the show that gives you everything: musical banality teamed with choreographic fluff, mediocre talent teamed with enormous egos, sexism teamed with racism.

In Starlight Express, the one and only black female is Belle, the

Sleeping Car. She is past her prime, has fallen upon hard times and bemoans the fact that her customers now show her little tenderness: instead, they just 'walk in and start undressing'. It is extremely disturbing to find that in this country black women are pushed into these categories in real life, without social status, family background or even education being considered. For the uninformed, I regret to tell you that the categories are as follows: whores, former whores, possible whores.

It is sad, sickening even, that we could be constantly portrayed this way without question or disapproval. It is frightening to think of all those white faces in that darkened theatre who saw and silently accepted a damning stereotype without raising a middle-class eyebrow. And it is surprising that in 1984, with all the strides that supposedly have been made towards bridging the cultural gap, just how often and how continuously we face this sort of harassment and how constricting it can be on one's life.

In the days before liberation and singles bars, any woman that went out by herself was considered 'fast; loose; looking for action'. Our male counterparts have now become more accustomed to our independence. However, it is primarily white females who are applauded for making headway in a male-dominated world. Few black women receive such an accolade, the prevailing trend of thought being that her achievements were more easily realised because she, like all stereotypical black women, is of inferior intelligence and her inherent easy virtue is the real key to her success.

I don't mean millions of white Britons watch Moira Stewart or Maggie Nelson (you do recognise their names, don't you?) reporting the news and wonder whom they slept with to gain their lofty positions. They represent part of the new breed of 'superwoman' who are more image than substance. Their celebrity status sets them apart from the likes of you and me.

What I do mean is your reaction to the well-groomed, self-assured black woman having dinner by herself. If you decide that she's there for any reasons other than hunger and a serious commitment not to cook, then it's about time you realised your own fears and prejudices. We do have as much right as anyone to dine out.

And what about those two young girls looking into that shop window? Can you honestly be so narrow-minded as to assume that they're there for the purpose of drawing attention to themselves and not merely to admire the latest styles? It is through your repeated errors in judgment, your incessant yet silent cry for us to explain our every move, your insistence that we prove ourselves to your satisfaction, that bigotry remains in full flower.

I spoke with 67 black women from all walks of life. Of that number, 43 of them confided with me that they felt that they had been sexually harrassed more so because of their complexion than their actual sex. I interviewed a 19-year-old clerical worker whose boss assumed that she was 'available' and also assumed that she would accept his advances. When she declined she was told bluntly: 'All niggers are hot blooded, you all fuck like rabbits. What have you got to be so dammed proud of?' He then offered her money.

Presumably your theory is that since we're all sex-crazed simpletons, it's a natural, expected step for black women to make sex a profession or at least use it to balance out the uneven hand that nature supposedly dealt us. It's hard to believe that this egregious typecasting is still practised; but it is, religiously so.

Allison, who is 29 years old, engaged to be married and working as a computer operator, told me of this incident. Walking up Holland Park Road on the way home from work, she passed two young white males, one of whom quite loudly and deliberately said 'whore'. 'I was shocked. I was beyond shocked – and hurt, I spent many hours thinking that it was something that I had done, that it was somehow my fault, something I provoked. But I couldn't find a reason. There is no real reason for behaviour like that. Perhaps they just hated women, all woman – but I do feel they would probably have ignored a white girl walking home after a hard day at the office.'

Karen was in a pub talking with a white female friend. Her friend, Marion, is 45 and manages an art gallery. Karen is 24 and works in a restaurant. 'Marion and I were sitting at the bar talking about paintings, I think. This couple came in; thirtyish, trendyish, middle class with aspirations. They were friends of Marion's and we talked together for an hour, maybe longer.

'The next time I saw Marion she informed me that her friends had said that I was on the game. These people, that I have never seen before in my life, had taken one look at an average black girl, no, average person, wearing no make-up, old jeans and a tatty jumper and decided that she had to be a prostitute. I was very hurt by this. I cried about it. I just kept thinking, "What have I done to deserve this?"'

Upon leaving a West End wine bar after lunching with friends, Kim's taxi-driver automatically thought that she, like his taxi, was for hire and started offering her money. When Rachael arrived at her flat in Knightsbridge, her taxi-driver bade her to 'Be lucky'. 'It was obvious to me that he could not believe that a black woman could afford a flat in that part of town and that I must be going to meet someone. It's sick, isn't it?'

Deborah was sitting upstairs on a number 88 bus. She had two bags of shopping with her and in her own words 'probably looked more harried than handsome'. A middle-aged white male sat down next to her, started chatting her up and tried to proposition her.

It would be so comforting to think that these are all isolated coincidences. It would be reassuring to feel that there really is racial harmony worldwide, that men and woman regard each other as equals; that we've allayed our fears and gotten on with the business of life. Perhaps if these women had not all been black and had not all been insulted in the same way, if they hadn't all had people trying to drag them down to what is seen as a normal and acceptable level for black females, these occurrences could be taken as more sexism than racism. However, the ignorance of their harassers is prominent, their presumptiveness, incriminating. Together, these attitudes breed the way Hitler bred antisemitism, the way Reagan breeds the Red Scare.

April told me that after putting off the advances of a young man at work, he returned to his friends and said, 'Well, it's going cheap if any of you want it.' In another incident, Carol told me that a 'notoriously gossipy neighbour thought she'd do me a favour by telling me that she had heard that I had had "every man in the area". My boyfriend and I moved here two years ago and haven't ever been apart. I can't believe the ridiculous lies that some people come up with.'

Grace recounted how she happened to bump into a white male neighbour. 'This man, this moron, introduced me to his son who was visiting from South Africa, put my hand into his son's, said, "Get on with it", and walked away.'

Just now, miners who want to work have had to move away from their homes due to gross intimidation. They got tired of cowering in fear. Asian families in the East End still worry about going out at night. We, as black women, are cowering in another way – we are afraid – yes, afraid to mix socially with our non-black colleagues from work or our neighbours for fear that outside that small circle, we will be taken to be whores, moral delinquents, 'easy', or perhaps the operative word is 'easier', or simply socially substandard. These beliefs are clung to and unconciously practiced just as much as Benny Hill's silly, sexist views of women are privately held as truths.

The danger lies in those who perpetuate these myths. Most do this out of ignorance. They know no black people or at best very few, and find this form of character assassination 'comforting'. It allows them a type of superiority so that they'll never see the truth – that we're all equal. Others maintain this train of thought because they would like to believe that there is an entire race given to sloth and hedonism. These accusers are secretly envious of what they see as a life free of conventional moral restraints.

Angi told me: 'A 45- to 50-year-old white woman saw me having a drink with my elderly white boss and said loudly, "Of course she's on the game". Her jealousy was written all over her face – her jealousy of what she thought was going on.'

Many white males like to believe in black promiscuity simply because of the 'forbidden fruit' theory, ie all black woman are very sexually active; mother told me not to; what would my friends, family, mates at work say. 'I had a black girlfriend at one time,' Mike explained to me, 'and all I ever heard from the lads was "Cor, Mike, how can you handle that? Don't think I could. Bet she's a goer."' It's easy to denigrate that which you secretly long for but don't have the courage to obtain.

However, these perpetrators of myths are neither horned beasts nor raving sociopaths. It could be your managing director at work, the barman at your local, the customer you sell insurance to, or even your MP.

There is no clear-cut answer, no obvious solution to this dilemma. The most I can do is offer a suggestion: that you, our persecutors, our self-appointed judges and juries, our character analysts, our slanderers, finally realise that we are all the same, for better or worse. Any one black person has as many distinctive qualities as well as faults as any one white person. As women, we struggled for years to get the vote, to be granted equal pay, to be able to choose whether we want careers, marriages, or both. As black women, we're struggling even harder for the most basic social acceptance and human respect. It's not an easy battle, but it beats hiding.

2 APRIL 1985

The double struggle

Black women and the fight against racism

CHINYELU ONWURAH

It is common to hear white women speak of 'the global sisterhood of the Oppressed', the universality of male dominance being a bonding link between the women of the world, regardless of their race, and if we could but overcome the physical and cultural distances between us a united force would be formed. So do we in Britain, where the distance between black and white is much reduced, see something of that unity of purpose?

No. White women, when they consider the plight of their beleaguered sisters across the oceans, so often forget, ignore or totally misconstrue the state of black women in Britain. They drown us in pity, suffocate us with patronage or inflame us with their ignorance. This is the result of an almost unavoidable lack of comprehension.

As one black student put it: 'They cannot understand, they cannot have our experiences.' White women know no more of what it is like to be black and female than black men. Though they may overflow with sympathy, awareness, empathy and the like, this does not constitute knowledge, and sympathy without comprehension turns ignorance into hypocrisy.

Much mainstream white feminism is guilty of racism by exclusion. Its aim is the emancipation of women but its one means is the eradication of sexism, so relegating the oppression of black women to the status of 'somebody else's problem'. When sexism is no more, women will not be liberated because black women will still be oppressed.

Mainstream feminism accepts the priorities of the white middle classes to the detriment of black women who are oppressed by both racism and sexism. Black women have a double struggle – they know they cannot win it on their own but are reluctant to trust their needs to white female or black male priorities.

Indeed, to many black women it seems as if they are being asked to give priority to their own oppression, to fight it piecemeal instead of struggling against the whole, to compromise long-term objectives for short-term gain. To some this presents no conflict, to others it is out of the question. A major fallacy in white thinking is to expect black women to speak with one voice as a uniform oppressed mass. They pick on one black woman, say 'OK, so what's it like to be black?' and expect the definitive answer, as racism allows no individuality with inferior races. But, though black women are united in their desire to fight oppression, the priorities, the tactics and the strategy all vary. Black women have differing experiences of oppression, they become aware of racism and sexism at different times and in different ways.

During childhood, racism might not be so noticeable if there are enough of you around: 'Growing up in a black community, sexism is what you come across first,' said Alison Licorish from London. 'Our school was half black, half white, so there were always enough black kids to look after each other, and when you're a child you don't relate what's happening on TV to yourself. When you leave home, or try and get a job, then it hits you.'

But if you're in a minority from the word go, it hits you earlier and your sex can help strengthen the blow: 'There were only a few black kids at our school,' said Christeena Williams, a fashion designer from Reading, 'so we got a lot of "abuse". I remember being called a "wog" for the first time when I was really young, it hurt, but because I was a girl it hurt more, I couldn't fight back, I had no defences.'

For black women who grow up to live and work in the liberal, middle-class world where racism has been brushed under the carpet, or abolished by order of committee, sexism can be a greater part of their daily lives, as Angie Ngozi, a film student from St Martins College, London, explained: 'Men will still make sexist remarks in the street or undress you with their eyes, but few will shout "nigger" though they might mutter it under their breath. If you walk any lonely street after dark, you're a woman first and foremost, your race doesn't matter, unless, of course, it's in the East End.

'I think if black women had to choose, we'd all choose to end racism before sexism but it would be more for black men than for us because black men are just as sexist as white men. Black women have to look out for themselves.'

Cheryl Turner, a receptionist from Hammersmith, is less prepared to openly criticise black men: 'They get enough stick from white people without us joining in. Though I agree with a lot of what white women say about sexism and women's rights, etc – I don't see why women should always do the washing up – when you get down to it, we're fighting white people for our rights.'

And indeed, at times it does seem slightly absurd to be fighting for the right not to do the washing up when there are people out there who want to kill us. Of course, I realise that feminism is about much wider issues than domestic chores, but in Britain at least, sexism threatens our level of existence, racism attacks our right to exist.

It is therefore not surprising that many black women consider racism the greater evil. Shirley Skerritt is a black woman activist, and ex-editor of a black newspaper, Staunch. She is very certain of her own priorities. 'In the west the relationship between black men and women is distorted because of white oppression, but even if it could be proved that black men are sexist, the struggle against racism would take priority.'

The white women's movement, most especially the separatist section of it, is in conflict with black women over this. As has been said before, they see their main preoccupation as sexism, and will rarely allow other issues to compete with it.

Shirley Skerritt again: 'Because of their history, black women have wider aims than white middle-class women, black women are accustomed to belonging to a broader culture. For this reason, they raise issues which are relevant to all women, but because they're being raised by blacks, white women say "Oh, they're black issues", and put them to one side.'

This is not to imply that black women cannot work productively with white women. Icilian Francis is a black woman community worker, co-opted onto the mainly white GLC Women's Committee. She says she now has no problems in working as part of a multiracial group. 'There is a lot of ground which needs to be covered in order to bring black and white together harmoniously, and this includes ensuring tolerance and understanding on both sides.'

But for many black women tolerance and understanding are fast running out in the absence of a relevant response. Black women are not prepared to be eternal martyrs in the cause of global sisterhood. In the end, racism is a white problem because it is a white disease. Black people may suffer the effects, but white people are the carriers; the pity, the sympathy and guilt expended by white women as if on a dying relative, is misplaced. They ought to look to themselves.

Postscript

I wrote this when I was 19, just moved to London to study engineering and, if I am honest, missing the blunt, practical, northern working-class politics with which I grew up. *Reading it now, it is a testament to how things have moved on – the 'equalities agenda', as we call it, is broader and less polarised. I believe a lot of that is thanks to the work of the Labour party, in opposition and in power. There is still a long way to go, but I don't think black women are asked to choose any more. Or perhaps it's just that no one's asking me – I'd be interested to know if my experience in the 80s resonates with young black women today.*

Chinyelu Onwurah MP

30 SEPTEMBER 1987

Beloved people

Interview with Toni Morrison

REGINA NADELSON

Beloved, Toni Morrison's new novel, is crammed to the margins with the rich prose for which she is known. More important, it has such persuasive characters of such size you hate to let them go. So does Toni Morrison, who said over lunch in New York recently that she has, in fact, ideas of keeping at least some of them alive in subsequent books.

There are Sethe and Denver, Baby Suggs and especially Paul D, the novel's hero, of whom she writes: 'For a man with an immobile face, it was amazing how ready it was to smile or blaze or be sorry with you. As though all you had to do was get his attention and right away he produced the feeling you were feeling.'

Set in southern Ohio around 1873, the 'condition' of her novel, as Toni Morrison says 'is slavery. The story a reclamation process'. The characters are mostly ex-slaves, most of whom have made impossible escapes from and, sometimes, to unspeakable terrors.

Indeed, Morrison, one of America's most distinguished black writers, has said of her own family, who migrated from the south around the turn of the century: 'Their eyes were terrible made bearable only by the frequency of their laughter.'

Like many of Morrison's previous novels – The Bluest Eye, Sula, Song of Solomon and Tar Baby, Beloved is laced with myth and ritual and haunted by ghosts, but then, Morrison has always been on intimate terms with the supernatural. Even as a child, her parents told her thrilling ghost stories.

But it is myth made wonderfully specific by the language and the detail – an old lady's passion for colour (in a piece of fabric, a pink tongue), a life-giving weapon against the harsh Ohio skies; the buckets of blackberries that became pies that became a feast for a whole town; a small child who liked the burned bottom of the bread.

'It was a book which required painstaking research,' said Morrison. 'Because there were almost no pictures. The tools, the everyday things – you had to use the language in such a way it had the effect of being concrete.'

Beloved is, literally, a big book and full of life. Nothing about it is tiny; there is none of the static prose that seems to have had life and colour sucked from it by some dainty proto-modern fiction designer. Far better Morrison's lush style, even the excesses.

And, like her book, Morrison is a large woman. Her presence is powerful and authoritative, kindly and sharp, funny and despairing. I suspect she doesn't suffer fools gladly but she laughs a lot and says she thinks the most important human quality is 'joie de vivre'. She said: 'You don't win by giving in to tragedy. You don't crown it. You are on the throne. You negotiate the relationships. You take the power into your own hands.'

What strikes you about Toni Morrison is how much you want her to like you – it's a feeling confirmed by other women I know who've met her. I mentioned that, years ago, she reviewed a book I wrote. It was a lousy review. She laughed. 'Oh dear, I'm so sorry. But it was a dreadful book.' And it was. And I laughed too.

Maybe her authority comes from the way Morrison, whose fiction has always addressed the politics of race and sex, writes about women. In the way she 'tracks the whole process of the way women love and of their self subterfuge. Who, you ask,' said Morrison, 'who is the woman who is also me? Who are the women you respect?'

What also strikes you about Morrison is that she seems to be an optimist, a woman who is cheerful by nature. 'I always was,' she said.

She was born in 1931 in Lorain, Ohio, a steel mill town on Lake Erie. Toni Morrison's family on both sides were migrants who, like many black people, were sharecroppers who lost their land in the south and went into the mines and mills of the north.

Life was lived at the edge but, by 1949, Morrison's father had achieved a measure of stability and, a 'bright child', she went to Howard University.

At America's most distinguished black university, she expected to take part in intellectual exchange with brilliant black students. Morrison discovered that life for young women at Howard, like life in the rest of America in the early 50s, was about buying clothes, going to parties and getting married. 'It was also,' she has written in some biographical notes, 'about being cool, loving Sarah Vaughan and the Modern Jazz Quartet'. Morrison went on: 'I giggled a lot, wise-cracked and tried to be with it – having no notion of what "it" was.'

Washington DC was at that time a segregated city, but Morrison said: 'Thinking on it now I suppose I was backward, but I never longed for social integration with white people. For a place to pee when shopping, yes, but I was prey to the racism of my years in

Lorain where the only truly interesting people to me were the black people.'

By the time she graduated, she had failed to secure the birthright of every American girl – a husband – so instead she enrolled in a post-graduate English course at Cornell.

A few years later, she did marry – a Jamaican architect with whom she had two sons, Harold and Slade, now 25 and 21.

It was at Howard again, however, where she returned to teach, that Toni Morrison began to write. A short story about a little black girl who longs for beautiful blue eyes became her first novel, The Bluest Eye. The writing helped sustain her when she divorced and had small children to care for, kids who, she's noted, 'provided the requirements I had not had since I left home. The children needed discipline, order, common sense, expertise, invention, constancy, affection, humour, truth, honesty, perception and a sense of reality ... When I veered toward romanticism, they got constipated. When I got bitten by the world, they grew two perfect teeth.'

Eventually, Morrison left teaching. A small textbook firm where she worked moved to New York and she went with it. Within a few years, she had become a senior editor at Random House and had great influence on a generation of black women writers such as Toni Cade Bambara, Alice Walker and Angela Davis.

Of the 60s, Morrison said: 'It was the music, after all, that carried us. But no one, either in film or fiction, has really nailed the 60s, not if you discount dreck like The Big Chill.'

Students today are far more passive, she said. 'My younger son (an architecture student at Berkeley) couldn't find anyone who would march against apartheid ... except one Jewish friend from New York.'

Toni Morrison writes full time in a former boathouse on the Hudson River, just upstate from New York City. She does not miss publishing. 'I always supposed parties were fun,' she said. 'Publishing parties never were.'

Over the years, Morrison's novels have achieved increasing critical acclaim and popular success and Tar Baby is being made into a movie. Roland Joffe was, for a time, to direct it. There were even rumours Marlon Brando would come out of retirement to star in it. Engaging in some Hollywood gossip, Morrison said she's now keen the film should be made by Willie Rameau, the young Paris-based director from Martinique.

We returned to Beloved. A book Morrison is so protective of 'for the first time in years I read the advance reviews in Publishers Weekly.' A few weeks later, the novel was reviewed in The New York Times by Michiko Kakutani (the best respected critic in town) who wrote 'it is as magical as it is upsetting. This is a dazzling novel.'

As a christening present, it has been reported, Toni Morrison gave the novelist Mary Gordon's daughter The Arabian Nights. The inscription read: 'Here are some stories a woman made up and told in order to save her life.'

19 MAY 1988

Behind the Lines: Ironing in the soul

Twenty years on, what has really changed for women? Germaine Greer praises motherhood. Her guests beg to differ

POLLY TOYNBEE

Jill Tweedie came with me to see Germaine Greer, because we happened to meet that morning, and, it being May 1988, I thought the three of us might ruminate on the last 20 years.

The sun was shining for the first time in weeks and Germaine's lunch and her country garden, as well as her conversation, were enticing. 'We cannot miss this historic meeting,' she said with a dry irony when I phoned her to ask if Jill could come too, and I thought, too late, that perhaps it might be a dreadful mistake. I don't think it was.

Germaine was in the kitchen making chapatis. In the stone-flagged dining room an exquisite summer lunch lay on the table, with a cold bottle of white wine on a sunflower yellow cloth. There were curried potatoes, chick peas, broad bean salad, guacamole, and some other grain or pulse I couldn't put a name to. During lunch, we talk about the non-emergence of this elusive New Woman – the awfulness of little timid girls and young women, as feminine as ever, mincing, speaking in baby voices, and acting helpless. There are as many about as ever there were, because it's still what men want.

Inevitably we run straight into dangerous waters. The Alton bill is fresh in mind. We recall the potty madness of some of the demos at the time of the 1967 Abortion Act, marching down the street yelling: 'What do we want? Abortion! When do we want it? Now!' As if abortions were ice creams or Christmas bonuses.

And then Germaine harks back to some of her Sex and Destiny themes. She really seems to think most women desire children most of the time. Abortion wouldn't be necessary in a society that supported and cherished its women and children, she asserts. Every pregnant woman wants her child, if only society made it easy for her. Jill says that sounds just like a Life or SPUC argument. Bearing and bringing up a child is a great burden, and not all women want all their pregnancies, not even in the most perfect society.

Germaine is indignant. It's society's fault. She has, after all, taken in mothers and children, tried to take her share of that burden in her time. She has many godchildren for whom she has played this role. She continues in praise of motherhood. 'Every moment of that child's life should be precious, treasured. Not a moment wasted.' I am stricken with guilt and anxiety. Have I enjoyed my children enough? Am I letting those precious moments slip by? Jill looks distressed. We argue back that life isn't like that. How can you possibly treasure every moment? And children just aren't utterly treasurable every minute of every day, not in real life.

After lunch, sitting on the grass in her garden, we watch her ginger cat, Christopher, stalking in her beautiful flower beds (amongst other things, she is a gardening expert). She is besotted by her pets, talking to them, cajoling them, completely admiring. Christopher plods past, the sort of cat that looks as if it is wearing furry flares. As we talk, Christopher catches a small furry animal. Jill shouts out in horror, telling Germaine to stop him quickly. The cat continues to maul the animal, letting it creep away, then pouncing again. Jill is now almost in pain herself watching the suffering of the creature, while Germaine (the vegetarian) is laughing with pride and delight at the cleverness of her cat.

I just watch, having not much instinctive liking for either cat or rodent. 'It's a poor vole!' Jill says. 'No it's not, it's a rat,' says Germaine. Then the thing, whatever it is, suddenly makes a wild rush at us where we sit on the lawn, and dives straight under my skirt, and I get up and scream loudly. The others roar with laughter, and Jill is allowed to shoo the cat off until the vole/rat has escaped into a bush. As we continue the conversation, however, I notice the cat quietly catching the vole again and eating it all, except for its face.

About this time it occurs to Germaine that I have not interviewed her properly, or indeed at all, about her book, published next week, which was supposed to be the point of this meeting. Jill wanders off to chat with some of the waifs and strays currently residing with Germaine – generous host to various passers-through, she always has a collection of the wounded.

The book is daunting, and mysteriously titled Kissing the Rod: An Anthology of 17th-Century Women's Verse, a mighty academic tome (at an academic price). Finding 17th-century poetry anyway difficult – all that dum-de-dum rhyme jars in the modern ear – I need some persuading that this is a book I want to read. Especially when Germaine says she doesn't consider most of the poems of great value. And, on reading the introduction, and the notes on each poet, it becomes clear how difficult it is to know who wrote many of them anyway, because women often wrote anonymously. They were abominably abused, and rewritten by their publishers, who spiced up their poems, and presented them as titillation, signed by 'A Woman of Quality', 'A Lady of Honour' or some such coy come-on.

However, under Dr Greer's excellent tuition, I begin to see the point of this lengthy exercise. There were certain kinds of poems that only women wrote, the best written and circulated privately. They were often written as therapy, as moral lessons, as occasions for fortitude, often on the advice of pastors and doctors. Here are collected certain favourite themes, poems written in farewell to husbands by pregnant women who expected, and often received, the worst from childbed. Poems written to surviving children by their mothers on their deathbeds. Poems written about dead children by their grieving mothers, struggling to find religious consolation in unbearable suffering. Some are mad and morbid, others overwhelmingly moving. Like this of Mary Carey's written on the death of yet another child: 'I only now desire of my sweet God/ the reason why he tooke in hand his rodd?/ What he doth spy what is the thinge amisse/ I faine would learne whilst I ye rod do kisse:/ Methinks I heare God's voyce, this is thy sinne?/ And conscience justifies ye same within / Thou often dost present me with dead frute/ Why should not my returns, thy presents sute:/ Dead dutys prayers praises thou dost bring,/ Affections dead dead hart in every thinge.'

The book is not a pointless dredging up of unknown work, simply because it is by women. It shows a different strain in women's writing, and the strain they had in writing at all – most of them semi-educated, discouraged, and the respectable ones certainly not permitted to publish.

The book is also another reminder of the many splendours of Germaine Greer, her extraordinary diverse skills and enthusiasms: writing (academic or controversial), cooking, gardening, and above all talking. Her talking is a performance arc of stories and ideas, turning the obvious inside out, taking nothing for granted, not even what she herself said five minutes ago.

So in these post-Aids days, now she decries sexual liberation (sounds as dated as a bust bodice). She looks at what it has done to women. They can't say no, they are enslaved again, a pointless, meaningless and now dangerous coupling, she says. Her berating of sex is as fierce as was her celebration. Look at the abandoned wives. What did they get in exchange for their security? And Jill and I agree.

But what shocks me in those cuttings is the gallons of vitriol that have been poured upon her over the years. Such fear and loathing, such 'I told you so' whenever anything bad happens to her. Such outlandish praise: 'The profile of a Garbo, the rump of a show-jumper' is followed by such detestation. Now she can't have babies, this high priestess of sex, they gloat over her tragedy. 'The Loneliness of the Liberated Lady' when she admits (she always 'admits' everything) that maybe she misses having a family after all.

Small minds, small spirits affronted by the sheer size and magnetism of the woman. It doesn't help that she's never been a joiner (neither have Jill or I). Never part of The Movement – whatever or wherever it might be. She lammed into the Greenham women, laid about the more frightful manifestations of Women's Lib in its day, which made her few friends. Like Gloria Steinem, she is beautiful, and above all a star. That is contrary to the orthodoxy of the true faith, which says such self-promotion is patriarchal, hierarchical, and unsisterly. (Neither Jill nor Germaine could hide in a crowd of sisters if they tried.)

We end where we began. Twenty years have delivered little to women, we agree. Plus ça change – it's all on the surface, except for a handful of super-educated lucky women at the top. For the rest, life may actually be worse.

None of us is optimistic about things getting better. None of us offers prescriptions or solutions. I do not know if it is because we are 20 years older and wiser and sadder or whether the cause is really nearly hopeless. But we had an exceedingly enjoyable afternoon talking about it.

29 DECEMBER 1988

Handbag and rule

Mrs Thatcher has never conceded one jot of her female identity. Yet in 1988, as in all the years of her reign, she's not been slow in using it to swat an aberrant male or two

BRENDA POLAN

There will be, in 1989, a great deal of brooding upon the Thatcher decade. Some will rejoice. Others will complain. Whether triumphant in tone or regretful, there will be analysis and punditry aplenty as the central conundrum of the 80s is addressed: did she merely answer the need of the times or did she shape them?

One such collection of head-scratchings is currently being compiled by Channel 4 and Hugo Young. Among the political, economic and intellectual heavies, I was called upon to pronounce not just on Mrs Thatcher's significantly evolving personal style of dress but on what fashion, bellwether of society's needs and preoccupations, had signified during the decade. They chose to have me say it in the most beautiful shrine to consumerism in London – Joseph's new emporium in the old Conran building in Fulham Road. In a Belgravia traffic jam, three thoughts: that those clothes that had served as my props were not her sort of clothes – they had too much wit and self-mockery about them; that the Thatcherite boom had started to fizzle for the country's fashion retailers more than a year ago and was well on the way to a whimper; that recent psephology had proved, despite the seductive charm of the hegemonic project theory, that the electorate is not Thatcherite. It elects her by refusing to vote against her. It's like a mass fatalism. She cannot, like Kali, be denied.

The 80s have given us many female icons, most transient, most pretty pallid, the stuff of brief adolescent imitation from Annie Lennox through Madonna to Kylie Minogue. But out of the decade (and out of Britain) have come three graven images with a magical power – power to inspire passionate adherence and excessive loathing, power to boost magazine circulations and telly ratings, power to evoke some aspect of the female or some yearning which is present to a lesser or suppressed degree in all women. The prime minister is one; Diana, Princess of Wales is another; and the third is the soap opera bitch goddess, Joan Collins. But the greatest of these is Margaret Thatcher.

Margaret Thatcher's femaleness is bound, in the coming months, to be found a factor in her achievements. Don't we all, whatever our reservations about her policies, simply adore the idea of foreign politicians (male) and recalcitrant members of her own party (mostly male) being handbagged? However awesome the results of a handbagging, male commentators rather like to snigger, implying that, as the instrument is ridiculous, its consequences may not be taken seriously.

Women snigger too. But for different reasons. For us the handbag is not a negative, silly, female symbol. (Let's leave out, since it's a long, unsettled argument, the assertion by certain costume historians that, just as the man's necktie is a phallic symbol, the woman's enclosing, secure handbag is a womb symbol.) On a simpler level the handbag symbolises organisation, preparedness, control over our immediate environment. It contains what we are likely to need: to pay our way, to gain access to car and home, to make a phone call, to summon assistance, to repair our appearance, to darn our tights, to plaster a scratch, to open a chance bottle, to change a crucial plug, to cure a headache or dyspepsia. And few of us, at some time or another, have not employed its leaden weight, at the end of a sturdy shoulder strap, as a weapon. Something similar did for Goliath.

With magnificent overtones of Edith Evans, a handbagging smacks of matriarchal power and female revenge. And just because the prime minister exhibits little sisterly solidarity and no empathy at all for the female subjects – sorry, members of the electorate – her policies constrain and deprive, it does not mean that she's not in the way of a little private revenge on the sex which doubtless, in the early years at least, patronised and circumscribed her. Did she ever make them sorry? It is devoutly to be hoped that they lived long enough.

Long enough not only to be sorry but to reflect upon the part they played in shaping this nemesis. For the anger and self-righteousness that fuels her are emotions which not only women but all outsiders can understand. Once inside, the outsider is eternally vulnerable to the suspicion that, somehow, they have brought the outside in with them and the inside remains somewhere else. So the effort and the anger and the need to prove and punish, bully and manipulate never abate.

Margaret Thatcher is one of the most manipulatory of women – a technique she has honed over the last decade. She does it with her version of charm (close cousin to a sweat-inducing brain-washing) alternating with those displays of controlled wrath. She handles people, grasping a hand, an elbow or a shoulder, and then, that strange, strained half-smile in place, she locks eyes and urges intensely. With men she uses her body in ways which are flirta-tious, almost sexually provocative. It's why the Spitting Image man's business suit is so inappropriate. There's nothing butch about this Lady – but, of course, the chaps who make the puppets enjoy the implication that a woman in charge is perverse, against nature, a jumped-up aberration. It's not unlike the familiar conclu-sion of the man whose sexual advances you reject: 'You must be a lesbian, there's no other explanation.'

'It's noticeable,' she said in 1982, 'that many of the suffragettes were very womanly.' She has never conceded one jot of her very female identity. In fact, her insistence on her culinary skills, her homey giving of a wartime recipe on the radio just before Christmas both comforts other women (yes, that's the way it is for us, however demanding the job we do) and alienates them. Isn't her need to be Superwoman a betrayal? No male prime minister would feel the need to scrub the potatoes – or to claim to. But producing a midnight platter of fried eggs and bacon for her advisors rein-forces her giving, protective mother self-image – the nanny-knows-best part of her personality.

Of course, Margaret Thatcher did have presentation problems in the early years. All three of our 80s icons have grown into their image. For Mrs Thatcher there was no precedent; she had to work it out for herself. As she rose through the Tory ranks, unthreat-ening middle-class frumpery was essential for acceptance. It did not alert the men to a maverick. The only way in which she stood out from the crowd was that her hair tended to be slightly too yellow and her make up a touch too heavy.

When she became prime minister and the groomers lowered her voice, ash-blonded her hair and toned down her make up, she did waver a little, opting for strict dress-for-success suits as advocated by American 'wardrobe engineers', feminised by pussycat bows on her blouses. She looked like the headmistress of a private girls' school.

The mature Thatcher style is fine-tuned: the skin glows (HRT according to rumour but happiness does it, too); the good bone structure shows; the clothes are breathtakingly chic. The cut of them is severe, dramatic, intimidatingly elegant – the materials are rich, opulent, very expensive. In the chill of a Polish autumn she resembled a 19th-century empress, dazzling her beholders with the luxury of her presence. And, in the language of dress, luxury has usually indicated power and the intentional emphasising of the gap between the powerful and the powerless. You have to be confident, secure and, yes, arrogant and rather unimaginative to indulge in luxurious dress.

Her critics and probably even her adherents will concede her those last two qualities and they are the chinks in the iron armour that could, one day, bring her down. It is the confidence and the sense of being completely secure, not just in her position and her right to it but in her sense of purpose and its rightness which makes her irresistible and her image so powerful – especially for women.

She revels in the kind of power of which the rest can only daydream vengefully. Watch her, reported one awed political science student, as she steps, full of suppressed excitement, towards the dispatch box. She wets her lips like a glamour model readying herself for an erotic rendezvous with the camera.

Times find the icons they need. The need creates them. Somehow, society in the 80s needed a self-righteous disciplinarian, a leader with an unwavering sense of purpose, the hard-edged sense of purpose, fuelled by the certainty that They are up to something dirty behind your back that only an outsider can have. It got a matriarch rampant who frightens the boys and secretly thrills the girls. It, too, may live to be sorry.

18 APRIL 1989

An everyday guide to misogyny

Women-haters are not freaks or outcasts, says the novelist Joan Smith, but ordinary men

ANGELA NEUSTATTER

Joan Smith, novelist and journalist, had a busy time at parties while writing her latest book. At one, over dinner, she was explaining to an artist her views on the meaning of the Yorkshire Ripper's mutilation of women. Three days later she received a letter from him saying: 'Your constant references to castration in the course of the evening were clearly an attempt to unsettle me.' Joan's husband pointed out that she had not mentioned castration but had taken a feminist stance on the use of male sexual power over women.

At a literary event in Oxford, she was asked by a middle-aged man to talk about her latest book. As she began he interrupted her in honeyed tones: 'Oh, darling, why bother? I have slept with thousands of women and I can tell you they don't want to know about that sort of thing.' When Joan insisted that she and plenty she knew did, indeed, feel the need to understand the forces of male hostility in society, his tone changed and within minutes he began to shout: 'You are demented – you're mad. Take this woman away from me.'

Over the six months she was writing, it was commonplace, she says, for a man, overhearing her talking about the book, to butt in with: 'What's the opposite of a misogynist? A feminist, ho ho ho.'

It is not, of course, surprising that a book that states that fear and loathing of women by men is alive and well in Britain in 1989, should cause some upset, particularly when the message is delivered by an eloquent, firm-of-stance woman who has the temerity to declare publicly that misogyny is not about freaks and outcasts but about men everywhere. Men have spoken and written much about man-hating women in response to the activities of feminists, but it is apparently something quite different when the reverse picture is put into frame. And Joan observes with a smile of some satisfaction: 'The responses did much to prove my point.'

The genesis of Misogynies (Faber) was the trial of Peter Sutcliffe, the Yorkshire Ripper, which Joan covered for a Sunday newspaper. She watched the exclusively male group of police officers handling the case, devising theories about the killer which rested on his hatred of prostitutes and women of easy virtue. It was the obdurate belief that the Ripper had a morally punitive philosophy in his killings which prevented them from taking note of the 'almost perfect likeness of Sutcliffe' given by a 14-year-old schoolgirl who had suffered a Ripper-like attack.

In one chapter she explores how precepts and prejudices prevented the Ripper being found much earlier and she recalls: 'I remember having terrible nightmares during the trial, feeling that the police were misunderstanding things badly because they insisted that Sutcliffe had a moral stand. To me it was clear his crimes expressed a simple, virulent loathing of the female which did not need fancy explanations like those arrived at by the police.

The thing is that most people in the book are not what ordinary people would describe as outcasts, they are ordinary men. That was why it was important to end up with the Ripper. Because what is important about him is that he is not different it's only a question of degree.

'I don't go along with the idea that all men are rapists or that they are the product of Original Sin, rather that we have a culture which supports and encourages misogyny and what we have to face is that a sizeable number of men hold very strange and perverted views about women.'

The point is made most chillingly in the chapter dealing with a pamphlet, Gambler's Song Book, described as the 'thoughts, songs and games' of a group of USAF bomber pilots at the Upper Heyford air base in Oxfordshire. They centre on sex and war, intimately linked, and some verses revile those women who arouse men's lust: 'A sloppy blowjob in a taxicab/ A c . . t that's covered with syphilitic scabs/ These foolish things remind me of you'.

Also brought to attention are the male judiciary, notably the judge who, faced with Nicholas Boyce, who had chopped up his wife, dumped parts of her body around town and boiled up her skin and bones, accepted a verdict of manslaughter and reassured him that he had been driven to this by a wife who was a nag.

Joan Smith analyses attitudes in literature and the other arts, indicting, for instance, Brian de Palma's films and others of a genre which markets female fear, offering, as a fun evening out, a vision of women victims to the violence of male predators.

As to real-life victims, there's Marilyn Monroe (and her legions of imitators) who chose to be a childlike sex symbol in order to win desperately craved affection and security and who learned that she would be unacceptable in any other guise. Dying, the author maintains, was the only logical step: 'She would have been unacceptable as an ageing sex symbol who would now be as old as the Queen.'

Taking the irresistible quote from one Anglican curate that: 'You might as well ordain a pot of anchovy paste as a woman,' the writer charts the devastating loathing demonstrated towards women by men of the Church since earliest times – Odo (AD879–942) declared: 'To embrace a woman is to embrace a sack of manure' while Dr Graham Leonard, the Bishop of London, said in 1985: 'It's not an accident that when God became "man" He chose to be a male. There's no doubt that He could have chosen to be a woman if He'd wanted to.'

And there is wit: the chapter 'A Visit from the Gasman', written as a play, describes a real-life visit made to Joan and her husband, Francis Wheen, in which the gasman did not acknowledge her presence in the room and directed to Francis the answer to every suggestion or question she made.

This book appears just a couple of months before A Misogynist's Source Book (Jonathan Cape), Fidelis Morgan's collection of sayings about women by men through the ages, suggesting that there is certain urgency abroad around the subject.

Both authors point out that women can also be misogynists, siding with men in their abuses and antipathies to other women, hoping to be accepted as honorary men. But they are primarily interested in male antipathy to women, in how men's fear of women's sexuality and their power underlies just about every aspect of our culture. Joan Smith says: 'We live in circumstances which not only restrict our freedom but physically threaten us if we step out of line: in this culture, the penalty for being a woman is sometimes death. Yet it is extraordinarily unacknowledged. I think sometimes you have to define a problem before you start to find a solution and for years and years I've felt as though I live in occupied territory. My interest is in finding a way of constructing a path out of that territory.'

25 October 1989

Awful wedded wives

What's the matter with married women? And why do we put up with them?

Monica Furlong

When Jill comes to supper the same thing always happens. She arrives, presents me with a bottle of wine or some flowers, we embrace, she sits down with a drink while I make the salad, and then she says: 'Would you mind if I just rang Jack?'

Jack is her husband and I know, because she has told me, that he dropped her at the station no more than five hours ago to do a little London shopping en route to seeing me. Now she rings him, and with a voice vibrant with concern and a generous sprinkling of 'darlings', she checks up that yellow fever has not afflicted Berkshire in the course of the afternoon or that a tornado has not suddenly whipped him from her side.

Jenny has a different quirk. When the two of us have wined and dined and are just settling into the sort of satisfying conversation that we both used to enjoy in our single days, she will suddenly look at her watch and say: 'I ought to be going.'

'Surely not?' I say. It's nine o'clock and it takes her less than an hour to drive home.

'Well, you see,' coyly, 'George likes to be able to tell me about His Day.' George is her husband.

Blodwen, a writer friend, has had a row with her publisher, and rings me up for sympathy and/or advice. I am lavish with sympathy, believing as an article of faith that all publishers treat authors abominably, but gradually I get around to the advice.

'Why not get your agent to write?' I say.

'No need for that,' she says with pride, the Welsh rising in her voice. 'Owen Glendower has written and told the chairman where he gets off.' Owen Glendower is her husband.

I ask you. What is the matter with married people, and why do the rest of us put up with their nonsense? I am not theoretically against marriage, though when I announced at the age of eight that my ambition was to be a widow, I suspect I saw quite deeply into my own, easily bored, nature. I think, however, that if the married expect continued kindness, or even tolerance, from those of us without their particular orientation, then they need better manners or a deviousness that seems beyond their weak imaginations.

Take Jill, for instance. Whenever I visit them, it is perfectly obvious that Jill finds Jack vastly irritating and she is often quite rude to him. So what suddenly makes him so lovable that she cannot live for another few hours without speaking to him? I have a strong suspicion that Jill, the poor old-fashioned thing, is rather enjoying the fact that she is married and I am not. She is far too well-bred to boast about the cost of her carpet or her car, but she does like the feeling that in this respect she has something that I don't have, and in case I am in any doubt of her superior status, any evening alone with me begins with her little two-hander.

Jenny, too, is up to something. There is guilt, of course, for enjoying an evening without George (one of the things that seriously puts me off marriage is the way married people always seem to be half inebriated with guilt) – but apart from that there is the need to establish that she Has Someone who needs her. Unlike, she imagines, we know who. So, cheery on my wine and replete with my food, she leaves me (supposedly lonely) in mid-evening so that George does not miss the ritual of describing His Day.

It was Jenny who said to me once, dramatically: 'It will be terrible when George dies.' I murmured something tactless about life alone being rather splendid, at which she cried: 'Oh, but you're used to it!'

The effrontery of this robbed me of speech, though I was quicker off the mark when Blodwen described Owen Glendower's misplaced fit of gallantry. I recalled the friend who whenever her cleaner didn't clean the bath properly, or left dirt behind the taps in the sink, used to sigh: 'Of course, I don't care, but it does make Henry so cross.' I fear the comparison was lost on Blodwen, who is not a feminist.

What gets me about all this married smugness is how out of date it is. I suppose there still are women who are longing to get married and are deeply envious of the married state, but I don't know them, and I certainly don't share their yearnings. The single state is, in my view, a rich and varied one, in which it is perfectly possible to give and receive love as well as other delightful pleasures. So that I am fast losing patience at being forced to be a witness in a round of Look How Happily Married We Are, which feels rather like compulsory games at school. I wonder how one gets a note excusing oneself.

Now that I come to think of it, though, there is one married couple I know who would inspire in me the odd twinge of envy if they did not always make me so very welcome and so very much part of their (American) family that envy seems beside the point. They do show a lot of interest in each other, and sometimes they work through the traumas of The Day, but at any suggestion that they are happily married, they blanch and shudder and promptly deny it. 'Oh, you've no idea how awful it is sometimes!' they cry, quickly changing the subject. Now, if I'm any judge, that's happily married, the best we poor human creatures can do in that department. It's quite inspiring.

1990s

I have a modest proposal. It will probably bring the FBI to my door. But I think that Hillary should shoot Bill and then President Gore should pardon her.

Andrea Dworkin

A meeting of two worlds

Lifting the veil on Islamic feminists in the west

MADELEINE BUNTING

Shrouded in a veil, destined for an arranged marriage and the immutable role of wife and mother: these are the perceptions of the Muslim woman's lot. Western women believe such customs will wither away with the advance of education and prosperity and progress just as they have done in the Christian west.

Sheila, Nighat and Rashida disagree. Education and experience of western society have recharged rather than undermined their commitment to Islam. They have a cluster of science degrees between them and all have careers. They do not claim to be typical Muslim women. What makes them interesting is that they are both well-educated and pious.

As devout Muslims, they look to the Koran for the word of God and the Prophet Muhammad for the answer to every question. They argue that the poor standing of women associated with Islam is a cultural accretion that has no grounding in the Koran. On the contrary, they claim the true Islam is pledged to equality between the sexes, an equality that respects inherent differences between men and women.

As a result, Islam is both more sophisticated and more realistic, they claim, than western feminism in its understanding of women and in the organisation of heterosexual relationships. They say that Islam has provided them with the self-confidence to assert themselves as women in their own community, and in the almost exclusively male biology and chemistry departments where they took their degrees.

Rashida, a biology teacher, says she struggled in a repressive Asian culture until she discovered the true Islam. 'I confused Islam and Asian; they are not the same. I feel as if I have had to fight all the way. People said to me, "Sit back, you're a girl" and my parents told me not to go to school. If I hadn't discovered Islam, I would have become westernised.'

Sheila, who has a chemistry PhD and works as an industrial chemist, has found all the feminism she needs in Islam. 'Some people call me a Muslim feminist, but there's no need to import a western concept; I am simply a Muslim.' The bell rings for the end of lessons at the Muslim girls' school in Bradford where Nighat is headteacher. There is the healthy clatter of children rushing to get home but, before each girl leaves, she pulls a long, gauzy hijab (veil) over her head for the walk home.

Women's clothing has become a much frequented battleground between western and Muslim women, with the hijab and the miniskirt seized upon as symbols of oppression. Rashida wears a hijab, but sometimes wishes she wore the chador (a full-length cloak). 'When men give me lustful looks, I want to be covered. I never want to be seen only as a sexual object – it is degrading. Western dress excites and frustrates men – it is designed to excite them – why?'

Sheila has struggled with the hijab issue and admits to still feeling very confused. 'The Koran doesn't say anything about women covering their heads: it tells men and women to dress modestly. I went through a phase of thinking, why should a woman cover herself up? Why not the man? Men should learn to control themselves. But my feelings have changed after experiencing the everyday sexual harassment women face in this country.'

She now wears the hijab outside but not at work. 'I am breaking new ground as a woman chemist already. Can I really be expected to pioneer as both a woman and a Muslim?' she asks defensively.

Careers bring women into contact with men and thus threaten a central tenet of Islam: segregation of the sexes and arranged marriages. 'It is wrong for men and women to mix: it is natural for them to be attracted to each other and that can lead to serious crimes which are terrible for society,' says Rashida, adding, 'God makes rules to protect us from ourselves not to bind us, but to free us from tyranny.'

On a visit to Pakistan when she was 18, Rashida fell in love with a cousin and, despite fierce family opposition, married him. The marriage has now broken up: 'My emotions over-rode me. My family objected because they did not think he was suitable: he wasn't educated and couldn't speak English. If I'd married in the truly Islamic way, arranged by my parents, the marriage would have had a better chance.' She is now entitled, as a divorcee, to contract her own marriage, but finds the idea of going out to look for her own husband abhorrent.

Rashida and Nighat argue that an arranged marriage is more 'rational': emotions are powerful and wayward, an unreliable basis for a marriage, a family and ultimately a society. 'Parents are protective and they have seen more of the world. When choosing a husband they will know his family, financial affairs, social habits, promotion chances – these details do matter,' says Nighat, who married her cousin as arranged by her parents, and adds, 'Love only grows as you live together, you can't suddenly fall in love with someone – anyone can impress you for a few hours.'

Saba Khalid is an English convert to Islam of 20 years' standing. Six months ago she persuaded her husband to take a second wife: a friend who is a single parent with four children. According to the Koran, a man is allowed to take a maximum of four wives – the Prophet himself had 10.

Saba believes she has found everything in Islam that she tried to find in drugs and free love: 'We tried in the 60s to challenge the underlying competitiveness between women. Things went wrong: it was a brave but very reckless era.' She argues that polygamy has challenged the possessiveness of having a husband, and feels the nuclear family should not exclude single mothers from financial and emotional support.

Men and women have inherent differences that feminists refuse to recognise, explains Saba. Polygamy within the Islamic framework allows the expression of difference and the fulfilment of each partner. 'You don't discover a man's sexuality until you let him go – until then, you project a female sexuality on to him. Polygamy has improved my relationship with my husband: a man is more attractive if he is free. Now I have the best of both worlds: security and freedom.'

'Men have a lot of psychological muscle power which goes flabby or wimpish if it is not used. Shouldering responsibility is good for them. A woman, on the other hand, after the emotional demands of rearing children, hasn't got the space for more than one man.'

Saba admits it has been a painful experience. She describes it as jihad (holy war) on the ego. 'Sometimes it has felt like something has been dragged out of you. I have had to learn to contain my demands on my husband but then women do tend to be very demanding, ruthlessly so.'

Man is the breadwinner, woman cares for the children, commands the Koran, but Nighat and Rashida think a career is acceptable, as long as it does not prevent the fulfilment of responsibilities to one's children. Rashida claims that, unlike western women, she has had a choice. 'I would have been respected whether I stayed at home to look after my children or went to work.'

'Look at the farce of women doing menial jobs,' says Sheila, 'serving men, such as secretaries, while other people bring up their babies in a creche. Women feel of worth in this society only if their work earns them money.'

The mother holds a position of enormous respect in Islam. 'The heavens lie under your mother's feet,' quotes Nighat. Rashida quotes the hadith (saying) in which the Prophet was asked who was the person most worthy of affection: 'Three times the Prophet answered "your mother"; only on the fourth occasion did he add, "your father".' There are, however, some hadiths and chapters of the Koran that Muslim women are hard put to explain. They have been used to justify highly discriminatory customs and a vibrant strand of misogyny in the Muslim world. For example, the Koran says you need two female witnesses in business transactions where one male will suffice; in rape cases you need four male witnesses and eight female witnesses; and men are 'to a degree superior' to women. There is a hadith that says the majority of people in hell are women hanging (significantly) by their hair.

Rashida refuses to answer the specific. 'You can't pick bits out of the Koran and ask what they mean. Islam is like a jigsaw puzzle: if you pick out one piece it may seem unjust.'

Saba believes the Koran's injunctions are based on the differences between men and women. 'Men can detach themselves from their feelings, but women cannot because of the child-rearing role. For legal matters and business matters, it is important to be detached.'

Sheila claims that the requirement for twice as many female witnesses gives them added protection in numbers.

Such explanations may seem far-reached – their defence is to point out similar examples in the Testaments: St Paul was no champion of women. Rashida feels Christianity is more denigrating of women and she was horrified to hear that the pain of labour was God's punishment on all women for Eve's temptation of Adam. 'If I'd believed that, I'd never have had a child. We believe labour is the woman's jihad, struggling in the way of Allah. If a woman dies in childbirth, her reward is to become a martyr and go to heaven.'

They dismiss western women's criticisms of Islam as either

ignorant or prejudiced. Their attitudes to western women range from admiration to pity. Rabina and Bushira, pupils at the Muslim girls' school, say they respect Mrs Thatcher, while Rashida feels western women are exploited for their bodies and that their needs for children and emotional stability are denied. She says women in Islam are spoilt in comparison. 'Men don't commit themselves: they will leave if they find someone better. Women tell me they don't really want to have sex but they are worried they will lose the guy if they say no.'

Nighat was reticent, feeling it 'inappropriate' to comment. 'Our perceptions of western women come from the poor communities we have lived among. They always seem drunk, abusive. We've met few ladies like yourself.'

Saba was the most critical. She spoke contemptuously of the freedom western society claims to espouse and of which Salman Rushdie and Fay Weldon write – it offers no choices, she says. But, looking back, she is grateful to the feminist movement in the 60s for the confidence it gave her in her own rationality – a rationality she denies women can display in business transactions.

Every quotation is countered with another that supports their belief that emancipation of women was a matter close to the Prophet's heart. They refer to his wives, much-respected figures in Islam: the 46-year-old divorcee businesswoman he married at the age of 23, and Aisha, who became a great stateswoman in the early years of Islam.

'Fourteen hundred years ago, women were liberated. They got inheritance rights, the right to keep their own earnings, the right to divorce and keep their own surname,' says Nighat. By implication, the west is only just catching up.

24 AUGUST 1991

My daughter begged me: Don't die

In her first interview in Holloway, Sara Thornton talks about her life sentence for killing her violent husband and why she stopped her hunger strike for her child's sake

DUNCAN CAMPBELL

She had had a 30p haircut, a letter from Angela Rumbold, and half a fish finger. It had already been quite a day. After nearly three weeks on hunger strike in Holloway prison in protest against a life sentence for killing her violent husband, Sara Thornton was contemplating her future.

Wearing a red top and black trousers and looking remarkably alert, she explained why she had embarked on the hunger strike. 'It was a revolt, because I felt so isolated,' she said, speaking in what is best described as a trans-Pacific accent, located somewhere between Coventry and the Gilbert and Ellice islands. Angered by the suspended sentence given, shortly after she had lost her appeal, to a man who had killed his 'nagging' wife, she had seen no other option.

She ended her hunger strike after a visit from her daughter, Luise, aged 12.

'I had had hundreds of letters from people asking me not to go ahead with it, but they were just pieces of paper. Seeing her saying she did not want me to die crystallised it for me. Also, I felt that as long as I was on hunger strike I was not trusting the people who were supporting me, and letting them help.'

At the same time, there was a kind of regret: 'I felt – you're weak, you're a wimp.' She would not embark on another one. 'It would be too much like moral blackmail to threaten to go on hunger strike every time the Home Office doesn't do something.'

Sara had just received a letter from the Home Office minister Angela Rumbold. It was two pages long, explaining with some sympathy why the home secretary felt unable to intervene, and apologising for what Rumbold felt would be disappointing news. She ended the letter by saying that 'the home secretary will consider very carefully any fresh evidence'.

That 'fresh evidence' may be from experts in alcoholism – from which Sara's husband, Malcolm, suffered – and would argue that the spouse of an alcoholic may be driven to act in ways that seem inconceivable to the sober world.

But she is anxious that Malcolm should not be portrayed as an evil thug.

'I get upset when I see him described as a "violent brute", because when he was not drinking he was a lovely man. He was very funny, had a great sense of humour, and was extremely intelligent – he taught himself Arabic while he was working in Saudi Arabia. When he was sober he never hit me once.'

But as his drinking got worse, so did his violence.

'He drank anything: beer – Carlsberg Special Brew, in particular – red wine, whisky. He used to try and hide it by injecting vodka into oranges when he was working [in the record shop he ran]. He would say "Look, I'm being really healthy, I'm eating oranges." There would be oranges sucked dry all over the shop. He injected them with a syringe I got for injecting brandy into the Christmas pudding on our first Christmas together.

'The benders would start at Friday lunchtime and go on for the whole weekend, but once he had his shop he could drink the whole time because he wasn't employed by anyone. It was Jekyll and Hyde. Or, as they say in Coventry – street angel, home devil.

'One thing people ask is: "Why didn't you leave him?" It's difficult to explain, but I felt guilty. I felt that his drinking was my fault. That if I was sexier or quieter or a better wife he wouldn't need to drink. I wanted a home for Luise. And I worried that he would commit suicide.

'I do feel tremendous guilt about my daughter, guilt that I stayed because I thought having a home was best for her and that would help with her dyslexia. I do feel guilt about that.'

Some of Malcolm's relatives have criticised her, blaming her for not walking out, saying that Malcolm was planning to divorce her anyway.

'I don't think anything is to be gained from slagging matches,' she says, studying newspaper cuttings in which Malcolm's relatives accuse her of being the provocative one and where his first wife says he was 'silly, not violent' when drunk. 'He never mentioned divorce. Malcolm's family are very aware of what happened.'

She was still weak, she said. Her first meal had been a tuna fish sandwich, and she had had half a fish finger yesterday. She was aware of some of the media coverage of her case, although she does not see the television news.

'It's either Neighbours or Home and Away, and I get out-voted. Anyway, the other girls say, quite rightly, that if I want to hear the news I can get it on the radio, and Home and Away and Neighbours are a very important part of life in here.'

Sara is reading Joan Smith's book, Misogynies. 'Brilliant, particularly the chapter on "My Learned Friends". Reading it, I realised that if Malcolm had killed me, all the things that were said about me in court would have been used in his defence – that I nagged him, hid his drink, that sort of thing.'

The campaign to free her is being led by George Delf, a writer and researcher whom she met when he came to visit her in Durham jail and on whom she clearly dotes. He believes that a combination of public support and legal argument, including a plea for a royal pardon, should be pursued.

'I am not sure about a royal pardon,' she says. 'Because I did kill Malcolm, I did stab him. You ask yourself – do I deserve a pardon? But one thing I am determined about is that if it comes to another appeal I will speak for myself.'

A fellow inmate had given her a very snappy 30p haircut that morning, and she had attempted some exercises – she was known as Jane Fonda at her previous prison, Bullwood Hall, because of her aerobics.

In a black plastic bag given to her by a solicitous prison officer, there were hundreds of letters of support. 'Men write apologising on behalf of men, there are old people, young people, dozens of stories of violence that mirror mine.'

Sara Thornton spoke almost in bafflement about the night she killed her husband: 'I cooked a meal afterwards. I didn't believe it. I was in shock. I wanted to take a photograph of him.'

She may now try to put some of her thoughts on paper. It has been a strange, free-wheeling life: born in Nuneaton 35 years ago, she grew up in the Gilbert Islands and Fiji, where her father was in the colonial service. She returned to this country when a great aunt died and her father inherited an estate in Cumberland. She ran away to Germany, returning to train as a nursery nurse, to please her ill mother, who died of a brain haemorrhage when Sara was 19.

After that she worked at Pontin's and in telephone sales in Manchester. Her first husband, Helmut, was German. They married in Denmark. Luise was conceived in Marseilles and born in Brussels. She separated from her husband in Venezuela.

Back in England she met Malcolm, a former policeman and security adviser, who had two broken marriages behind him. They found a brief happiness.

Now, a relationship that began amiably in a Warwickshire pub and ended in bloody tragedy is being examined in detail by lawyers and leader writers, feminists and civil servants.

Over the weekend, she will be staying in the hospital wing, perhaps watching the video of Pretty Woman that the Sunday People, who are backing her case, have sent in for her. The many women in Holloway jailed for prostitution offences will doubtless watch that fairytale of a Californian hooker with a wry smile. Sara Thornton must wait to see whether her own strange tale has a happy ending, and how long she has to deal with a hunger for something much less tangible than fish fingers.

30 MAY 1992

The Gender Agenda

She makes Martin Scorsese look laid back and Joan Rivers look polite. She's aroused the fury of feminists, and the venom of the American academic establishment. She's Professor Camille Paglia and she's also very funny

SUZANNE MOORE

'I am for strong women and strong men: not strong women and castrated men like you've got right now. Not these men who go all sensitive and say, "Oh excuse me, can I touch your left breast?" This is bullshit. I was inspired by the authentic spirit of feminism of the 20s and 30s, by Katharine Hepburn and Amelia Earhart, women who demanded equal rights, equal opportunities, to be taken seriously as human beings.

'But right now feminism has just become this whining "Oh nasty men you did this to me." I think many of these women are depressive, OK? So now you get these women's studies programmes that deny the greatness of male artists. They don't even have the category of greatness because hierarchy is like a dirty word, OK. They say that greatness is a projection, a value judgment about a bunch of Dead White Males. These namby-pamby, wishy-washy little twits cannot even admit how great Michelangelo was. These people know nothing about art. Now everything is great. So they go that some quilt made by some woman in Kansas is as important an object as the Sistine Chapel. Give me a break. I mean Puh-lease.'

This rap is being delivered by Camille Paglia, Professor of Humanities at the University of the Arts in Philadelphia, author of a big book called Sexual Personae: Art and Decadence from Nefertiti to Emily Dickinson. I am in her office adorned with Madonna posters and stickers that proclaim 'I don't have PMS – I am a Natural Bitch' and this fireball of a woman is talking in a manner which makes Martin Scorsese look laid back and Joan Rivers polite. She is on permanent fast forward and she is right in my face. But that's the reason I am here. Professor Paglia is in a lot of people's faces at the moment.

She is in the face of the American academic establishment. 'Is there intellectual life in America? At present, the answer is not. In the summer-camp mentality of American universities, the ferocity of genuine intellectual debate would just seem like spoiling everyone's fun.' She is in the face of political correctness, not only proposing the abolition of all literary conferences, the engine that drives the Ivy League crowd ('drab uncultivated philistines'), but also by her refusal to toe the party line on issues such as date rape and sexual harassment.

But mostly she is in the face of feminism and this is what has propelled her from out of her leafy little college and into the mainstream of the American media. Paglia had been on the Today show the day I met her, she had already done Donahue and been featured in everything from the New York Times, to Spin, Esquire, New Republic and Rolling Stone.

So how has a 44-year-old academic who has written a book which is primarily a work of literary criticism become a media princess? Why do people care whether Professor Paglia posed with whips outside a porn store for a San Francisco magazine? Or that she called Naomi Wolf 'a pampered yuppie twit'? Or that she spent much of her childhood in drag dressed as a Roman soldier or a toreador: 'I guess in modern-day terms I had a massive gender dysfunction. I now realise I was a pioneer. I just wanted to be what girls are allowed to be now – brash, athletic and outspoken but I had these two big problems. Was I male or female? And was I gay or straight?'

Yet it is not simply her outspoken 'eccentricities' that have made the media sit up and beg but the fact that what she is saying seems to be striking enough of a chord not only to put her book in the bestseller lists but to pack out lectures everywhere she goes. Her enemies regard her as the bete noire of feminism, an intolerable presence whose snide attacks on just about every other feminist thinker come from little more than a twisted need for revenge against what she sees as the feminist establishment. For Susan Faludi, author of Backlash, Paglia is herself part of the backlash – 'the one new self-proclaimed "feminist" theoretician that the press did pluck from obscurity was actually an embittered anti-feminist academic'. Faludi, according to Paglia, is sincere but 'hopelessly deluded' having swallowed whole the Women's Studies Progamme she learnt at Harvard. 'If you want to see how atrocious education is in the Ivy League, look no further than these women – Faludi and Wolf.'

Paglia doesn't have any time for backlash theories. 'There is a backlash but it is against this kind of ideology. When I speak out against it I am called anti-feminist but that's not true.' Paglia is not interested in the 'kiss-ass yuppies, the sex-phobic moonies' who have taken over the Women's Studies Programmes and continues to proffer her soundbites to the media, who gobble them up ravenously. Anita Hill was not a feminist heroine. 'You cannot just call your friends and complain and whinge to them and 10 years later make a big issue out of it. She missed the boat.' Date rape is just something dreamt up by neurotic middle-class white girls. 'People are saying that we have to reform men so that a girl can dress in Madonna's brassiere and have 11 tequila shots and go to his room and still not get raped. Are these people out of their minds?'

Such carelessly incendiary and offensive statements have brought the righteous anger of the feminist establishment down on Paglia's head. She is talked of as a woman-hating, neo-conservative, an attention-grabbing harpy who is betraying womankind. She is the face of the Backlash itself. Teresa Ebert, of the State University of New York, admits that for a long time she wasn't taken seriously. 'But her attacks are part of Ronald Reagan's and Margaret Thatcher's conservatism.' Helen Vendeer at Harvard says that Paglia 'lives in hyperbole. It is a level of discourse appropriate to politics, sermons, headlines.' And of course talk shows, which Paglia adores. When I ask if she is looking forward to coming to England, she replies: 'I have cable TV. I have 35 channels. Why would I want to go anywhere?'

Paglia, however, thrives on criticism. Hers is not the finessed critique required of the intellectual elite. It is rough and tumble, rude, crude and very, very personal. 'Marilyn French said that I hated the female body. What crap. That woman is a good example of someone who is filled with buried resentment. She is incompetent. You see, all these women married men, they allowed men to dominate their lives and suddenly the men dump them. I never made this mistake, my anger towards men is absolutely clear, overt – I have never allowed men to push me around. That's why all these women are sulking "I could have been a contender." Look at Gloria Steinem's record with men – it's horrible.'

She complains that many of those who dismiss her have never read her work. They are also wrong to categorise her as neo-conservative. And she is right. Paglia's significance is precisely that she is not classifiable in any simple left/right terms. She may be inflammatory and anti-feminist in some of her views but she is not simply so. She may by flying in the face of PC orthodoxies with her outrageous opinions but it is difficult to underestimate how stifling the PC debate has become in America. If Paglia attacks the feminists' orthodoxy it is because the feminist orthodoxy has left itself open to attack and that it continues in a myopic fashion to categorise any challenge to itself as inherently rightwing. Paglia's views are actually as uncomfortable to the right as they are to the left.

While I disagree with much of what Paglia says, I also find her a much-needed antidote to the last batch of recently imported American feminism. The appalling wholesomeness, the bland rationality and complete lack of humour of much American feminism personified by people like Naomi Wolf, is exactly what Paglia is railing against. Sex in Paglia's terms is a deep, dark, dirty, violent business. The complexities around an issue such as date rape or pornography are ones far beyond the reach of the committee.

Her real position – 'I am a 60s libertarian' – seems beyond the grasp of many of her critics. 'I believe the state has no business interfering with anything in private life. I support sodomy, abortion, prostitution, the legalisation of drugs and suicide. These liberals that criticise me – they don't know what a radical looks like. The idea of the tenured radical is bullshit – there is not a single leftist anywhere in the establishment. Look, I have written seven hundred pages on paganism and sado-masochism and they call me a neo-conservative. It's ridiculous.'

It is ridiculous because in the midst of all this hype, hysteria and hypocrisy, the book itself gets lost. A massive book written in

1981, it was the first half of a two-part work. Having been rejected by several prestigious publishers, it finally came out in 1990. During this time Paglia was barefoot in the wilderness, living on nothing and finding it difficult to get a job anywhere. This may explain some of her attitudes to the establishment. She later tells me, 'I'm Italian. We invented the vendetta.' This is Paglia, the driven intellectual who doesn't even have a soft chair in the house, who was prepared by the Catholic church for the monastic life of the true scholar. The book was rejected, she says with her engaging egotism, because 'it is a whole new system of thought'. She had resigned herself to the fact that she would have to wait until she was dead, until she was famous, but she never gave up the faith.

The book itself presents a far more measured attack against current feminist thinking than any of her loony-tune outbursts. Much contemporary feminism differentiates between biological sex and socially constructed gender in order to show how so many of what are perceived to be natural differences between men and women are in fact culturally created. This has been absolutely crucial in arguing for the possibility of reconstructing ourselves and our relationships anew. Paglia argues on the other hand that the sexes are fundamentally different, that sex and nature are brutal pagan forces that cannot be contained by culture and which continually threaten to disrupt civilisation. The historical identification of women with nature is not a man-made myth but a reality.

Actually these ideas are not new at all, having surfaced everywhere from Freud to goddess-worshipping radical feminism. What Paglia emphasises though is the duality of Nature. She embraces Nature as both cruel and ugly, as well as the Wordsworthian chocolate box version beloved by the west. Nature is primarily a force to be struggled against. 'Everything great that humanity has done has been by shaking our fists in the face of Nature. But one must take Nature into account.'

As women, however, are really little bits of Nature themselves, they don't have to struggle against it as much as men who have in the process created the whole of western culture. 'Men created the whole of civilisation, let's just admit it, OK?' While one may profoundly disagree with Paglia's thesis, one cannot deny the epic sweep of the book. Yet, as with all analyses of this kind, women's power resides in the spiritual, sexual, mythical world while men get on with the real world. In such a world it is difficult if not impossible to imagine how anything might change, how the day-to-day lives of women could be improved and as such it is a deeply pessimistic and conservative message.

However, some of what Paglia addresses in her work cannot be so easily dismissed. The whole book sets up a dialogue between the Appollonian desire for order in society against the ever-present Dionysian forces. Against thinkers like Rousseau and Wordsworth, for instance, she lines up De Sade, Nietzsche and Blake. In this context her grudge against contemporary feminism begins to make more sense.

Feminism is closer to Rousseau than to his critic De Sade, in its belief in the innate goodness of humanity and in the importance of social conditioning. Yet Paglia sees in this tradition a denial of Nature, of the darkness of sexuality and aggression. For Paglia feminism has made the mistake of following Rousseauan thought by viewing everything bad as coming from outside itself whether from 'men, the media or patriarchy'. Instead she asserts: 'We are not naturally good. I'm saying, like Freud, like Nietzsche, like De Sade, like the Catholic church, that our propensity for violence is inherent.'

The main battleground on which this war is waged is sexuality itself and so out of this confusion step the various 'sexual personae' that she celebrates thoughout history – from beautiful boys, to lesbian vampires, to femme fatales, to the 'hermaphrodite Heathcliff'. Along the way she manages to discuss everything from the cunnilingual nature of raw clams to the links between Byron and Elvis Presley in what she describes as 'the first female epic'. Yet while Paglia sees herself as absolutely unique, as a lone voyager, she is not the only woman to challenge the bland niceties of feminist thinking. Paglia needs 'the feminist' to argue against as much as 'the feminists' need patriarchy. She does not or will not recognise the diversity of the reality of modern-day feminism. From our own Angela Carter to Pat Califia, purveyor of lesbian SM fantasies, to the new mood in gay clubs where women are also in drag, there has been a move towards exploring both the darker side of sex and what the writer Simon Watney describes as 'psychic masculinity'.

Yet Paglia's fundamental insistence on the difference between men and women is, she argues, borne out not only by research but by her own experiences, of herself, of men, and of hormones. There has been no female Mozart because there has been no female Jack the Ripper. When I mention Germaine Greer's book on women artists (The Obstacle Race) she gets really excited. 'Look, she says that there have been no great women artists because you don't get great art from mutilated egos. What level of dementia is that woman in? The greatest art has always come from mutilated egos. It's not that women are inherently less creative but they don't have that kind of obsessiveness that produces great art. You have this maniacal egomania, you mutilate your social life, all your personal relationships for what you are doing. Look at me. I am a deviation from the human norm.'

So, what about babies, Camille? 'Katharine Hepburn and I agree. You can't have it all. Having a baby changes you physically. I've seen it on talk shows. You get all these beautiful, intelligent, ambitious actresses. Suddenly they have babies and they are sitting there going "I now see the world in a completely different way. I'm not so important, it's my child that is important." How did that happen? HORMONES,' she shrieks. 'Look at Chrissie Hynde, this fabulous dominatrix singing "Fuck off". Suddenly she is in a video holding a baby. What happened?'

Hormones count for a lot in Paglia's world. Nature rears its ugly head yet again. They account for the attraction between the sexes. 'That's why sex with men is so hot. You get the best sex from men actually if you pretend you are not so dominant. It's so easy to make men wilt – if feminists don't realise that, they are stupid. What I see is a worldwide conspiracy by women to protect men from the knowledge of their own limitations. Men are very, very simple beings. They just want approval and attention, you pat them on the head and they go off and conquer the North Pole. But they are desperate. They are exiles from the world of intimacy. The life of men is one of anxiety, they constantly fear the shadow of women over them. Their confidence is utterly frail, they need daily maintenance.' Would you do that, Camille? 'No way. I'm not a nurse.' Indeed, the inscription she wants on her tombstone is: 'She served no man'.

That Paglia should venture into Robert Bly and the Men's Movement territory is intriguing, but she sees herself as doing for women what Bly is doing for men – 'recovering the history of the gender'. But Paglia's main identification is with gay men – like her idol Madonna she cites her two biggest influences as homosexual men and the Catholic church. For her, the gay man is an intensely romantic, aestheticised figure flying in the face of nature. She even sees her friends who have died of Aids as romantic heroes. 'They rejected the comfortable, prudent life of heterosexuality, they lived short, passionate lives. They lived for beauty.'

She also talks sadly of the end of her social life: 'The gay men of my generation went wild after Stonewall. I saw the doors closed in my face – I lost my social life when the bathhouse scene started. I tried to get into an orgy room once. I was in drag but I'm small and couldn't pass.'

This image of Paglia, the self-proclaimed fag-hag locked out of the orgy with her own 'miserable sex-life', may be the key to her own peculiar sexual persona. She would, one feels, rather be a gay man, than to be what she is. Having been an open lesbian all her life, she describes other lesbians as 'intellectually and sexually inert'. She now calls herself bisexual because 'I couldn't find anyone to sleep with me. Women don't want sex. They want to get together and talk about their mothers and play volleyball and cuddle, cuddle, cuddle.'

We start talking about lunch. I imagine somehow that Paglia will be a carnivore. 'Yeah, sure, steak for lunch and dinner sometimes.' She gets into a tirade about Foucault before we go. 'That wimp Foucault. He wrote about power. But the world of Foucault is a world without Hitler. He never did anything in his life. I am a person of action. I punch and kick people. I've been doing it all my life so my attitude to the law is that you need people like me, OK? If there were no laws I'd be completely out of control. It's the Italian way of bringing people up. It's like No, No, No, because we realise that human lust is completely unbridled, the desire for revenge is completely unbridled. My attitude is like kill.' From this she goes in for a far more sustained and serious attack on the school of deconstruction which ends with: 'It is meaningless in this country. We have no high culture to deconstruct. Our problem in this culture is regression not repression.'

As we step out into the bright sunshine, everyone is nice and friendly to the professor. This fast-talking little woman is clearly well liked. Later on, her childhood friend, the writer Bruce Benderson, tells me that underneath her ferocious exterior 'she has this real user-friendly side. People don't see it but she is really funny.' She is really funny, but he also says something that explains why she is an important figure in American cultural life at the moment. 'You have to understand that both the left and right in this country are anti-libidinal. Camille is absolutely pro-libidinal, that's why we've been friends all these years.'

We go to eat and she points out her dimples, saying that she really wants to look like Keith Richards from the Rolling Stones. Rock'n'roll and the cinema are the great forms of the second half of the 20th century. 'And I live fully in both of them,' she says. She makes me laugh, this woman, but there is still one thing left to ask her. Do you ever doubt yourself, Camille? 'No, I am an Aries. I am like Bette Davis, Joan Crawford. It's the first sign of the zodiac and let me tell you the ego structure of the Aries is incredibly powerful. My earliest memories were of this incredible ego. Like I said when I was talking at Harvard, "Who is the better role model for women – Gloria Steinem and Kate Millett with their self-esteem problems or me?" I have no self-esteem problems.'

20 JANUARY 1993

Ordinary madness

Thousands of abused women testify to systematic rape in Bosnia. But the Serbian army is not made up of proven sex offenders, they are 'regular guys'. Are, then, all men potential rapists?

CATHERINE BENNETT

'They said they'd kill me if I didn't.' This is not a rape victim speaking, it's a rapist. The man is a deserter from the Serbian forces. The people who were going to kill him if he didn't rape two teenage girls were his fellow soldiers. His story, together with statements from other penitent rapists, is part of the evidence that rape in Bosnia is not sporadic but systematic, organised rather than adventitious.

An EC mission has estimated that 20,000 women have been the victims of 'organised rape' in Bosnia, while Muslim and Croat sources claim that the incidence is much higher – 50,000 women raped, more than 30,000 women impregnated. Uncorroborated, one-sided, and publicised by a desperate people, the figures must be received with scepticism. But, whatever the figures, the collective testimony of the women who have been sexually abused in this war still challenges the assumption that rape is the preserve of a criminal minority.

It certainly tells us something about conditions in former Yugoslavia. But does it also, as women's groups are now asserting, tell us something about the men we live with here? All men? Or is concerted rape radically different from random rape? At Amnesty International (which has yet to find any proof that sexual abuse is an instrument rather than a corollary of war in the Balkans), Helena Harbraken's opinion of rape in Bosnia is not dissimilar to Lucrece's reaction after rape by Tarquin: 'O opportunity, thy guilt is great! . . . Thou sets the wolf where he the lamb may get'.

'It's just because the occasion is there,' says Harbraken, who works on Amnesty's Yugoslavia research team. 'Rape happens in every war, and it's happening in this war . . . the occasion is there, the women are there, they are seen as either victims or as an extension of the enemy.'

Susan Brownmiller, whose Against Our Will, published in 1975, is still the fullest inquiry into rape, describes the fate of women in war as 'double objectification'. In peacetime, women are raped because they are objectified. In war they are raped because they are further dehumanised as enemies. 'The penis can be used as a weapon,' she says. 'In warfare it becomes another weapon.'

Men, she recites, raped in the first world war, then raped in the second. Americans raped in Vietnam; in the First Crusade even pilgrims raped. All that's different now are the outraged, if inconsistent reactions of feminists and women's groups.

To Harbraken, the emphasis and speculation about rape in Bosnia – as if it were something weird and unprecedented – is not only uneven but unhelpful. 'I think men never need an excuse to rape, and if you say they rape because it's an order you take all the power out of that first statement, and you're saying actually they don't want to rape, and in general they're really good, brave guys.'

Brownmiller also suggests that the current concern over rape-strategy is peripheral, something that has been alleged before by the stricken or defeated. 'My point has always been that you don't need orchestration, or commands from on high when you have a young soldier with a gun. You don't need any orders to rape.'

You do, however, need men who are capable of doing it. 'First,' Brownmiller says, 'they're adrenaline-rushed; second, in Bosnia the Serbian fighters are irregulars, they're not part of an official army. Every army has rules of conduct in warfare, and we know that rape is outlawed in the terms of the Geneva Convention — but what is the authority that's going to court martial these guys? There is no authority there, so they have permission to rape, the way they have permission to kill.'

But the Serbian forces are not carefully composed of proven sex offenders. It's an army of regular guys, not former victims of sex abuse, or sufferers from disinhibiting brain abnormalities – types of men who are likely to rape in peacetime. Isn't it curious that the granting of permission should instantly turn common soldiers, 'ordinary Joes' as Brownmiller calls them in her book, into rapists? 'Don't you feel that a lot of people are confused about sex?' Brownmiller replies, easily. 'And particularly if you think of women as property, as property belonging to someone else, in this case the enemy. So you're destroying the enemy by raping the enemy's women.'

For rape is an effective instrument of war – an act which at once demoralises and humiliates the enemy, defiles his property, and deters him from propagating his own people through the bodies of violated females, and hence assists in crushing a people. Rape and its concomitant, forced prostitution, also offer sexual bonuses for victorious troops.

'There are certain situations where women are taken because there is a belief that when men are deprived of a regular release of their hormones, or sexual drive, then this builds up and may create disorder among the troops,' says Dr Gillian Mezey, a forensic psychiatrist who has worked with rapists and victims. 'There's a sort of myth about this biological sexual drive that needs to be satisfied.'

Still widely considered, like pillage, to be one of the routine, if mildly regrettable facts of war, rape has never been assiduously reported, rarely defined as a war crime. Innocent men have not thought it sufficiently grave, guilty men have kept quiet, women have been too ashamed or too powerless to prosecute their tormentors and find help for themselves. Even now, sympathy for Bosnian victims of rape has competed for publicity with the excitement generated by an uncovenanted consignment of white, adoptable babies.

'It's ignored, it's forgotten, and I think that's a factor in perpetuating the whole notion of rape being OK in wartime,' says Dr Joan Giller, a gynaecologist who treated women in Uganda's Luwero Triangle, where, she estimates, tens of thousands of women were raped by government troops in the early 80s.

'Women were very reluctant even to admit to it – this was maybe six, seven, or eight years after the event, and they were still having serious problems because of it, and yet hadn't talked to one another, hadn't talked to their spouses. Quite a percentage of them hadn't had a relationship with a man since the rape . . . so many women denied it, then once you started to talk about it they came forward.'

Now, in Zagreb, Slavenka Drakulic, a Croatian writer and feminist, is interviewing Bosnian rape victims and discovering the same patterns of shame, concealment, reluctant disclosure. Her questioning of these women reflects a common female incomprehension that 'ordinary' men can rape. 'I asked one woman who was raped by four men: "Were they drunk? Did they look abnormal? How did they look?" She said: "No, no, they were perfectly normal men, if you were to meet them in the street you wouldn't say that they are rapists."'

Drakulic's conclusion is disheartening, unattractive, but maybe inevitable after such evidence: all men are potential rapists. 'I'm very unhappy to say that, I really am – but what can you conclude?' she says. 'How can they do it under the conditions? How can they do it when a gun is pointed at their head? You would say they cannot, they cannot do it if a woman is revolting against it, and screaming – but they do it! It's amazing. Do you have any other opinion, that men are not potential rapists?'

Well, naturally, we have the opinions of indignant men, who say that they would be incapable of forcing themselves on a woman. 'I'd say 50% are capable of it,' guesses Robert Bly, the author of Iron John, a story that tells men to rediscover the 'wild, hairy man' within. So what stops the 50% like him? 'They're not the type,' Bly says. 'They would be the ones who are expressing emotion and doing art.'

Even in wartime? In 1971, one Vietnam veteran told a conference on war crimes how he saw seven friends from his company, all 'basically nice people', rape a young Vietnamese girl. 'I just couldn't figure out what was going on to make people like this do it. It was just part of the everyday routine, you know.'

'Probably the most useful way to look at it is as some form of continuum,' says Carol Sellars, principal clinical psychologist at Broadmoor. 'What stops most men is social sanction and a sense of the sequel to what would happen in peacetime.' One might, however, say the same about the continuum from shouting at your children to beating them up. Most parents do the first, few do the second. Any continuum can be declared.

But Sellars cites American studies of undergraduates in which a healthy majority said they would commit a rape if they thought they could get away with it. 'It's quite disturbing,' she says. 'I think you've got to look at the culture, particularly at things like films and literature, one of the problems is that it's always portrayed first and foremost as a sexual act, which it isn't.'

Then what is it? 'If you actually talk to rapists, in most cases it's about two things. One is about asserting domination and humiliating the victim, and sexual degradation is seen as the ultimate form of degradation. The other is to do with asserting masculinity, which again is essentially about domination and aggression, not really about true sexuality, if you think of sexuality as an expression of warm feeling and closeness, and all these other things which women would more commonly tend to associate with it.'

And this, perhaps, is the most perplexing thing about rape, in war or peace – that men should choose sex, the most intimate act, as a vehicle for aggression. If male Bosnian Serbs hate female Bosnian Muslims, how can they tolerate this proximity? How can they generate sexual excitement, spontaneously or to order?

'Men can respond in a physiologically sexual way if they are highly aroused, and some men can be highly aroused in the middle of combat, and they can be highly aroused by aggression,' says Mezey. 'I think that sexuality and aggression are closely linked and when you get into a situation where you're operating at the extremes of the aggressive drive in a way it doesn't seem surprising to me that that sort of level of arousal can become misinterpreted or misperceived by the men concerned as sexual.'

Other women, unaccustomed to the company of rapists, can find the link between sex and aggression inexplicable. 'I've no idea – how can men go and have sex with prostitutes? I don't understand any of that,' says Leonora Lloyd, co-ordinator for the National Abortion Campaign, and one of a women's coalition which believes that a sex strike by British women on International Women's Day would demonstrate solidarity with their Bosnian sisters.

'It happened to me,' Lloyd adds. 'Some man broke into my home, and I was there, so I was raped. There was no attraction there, how could there be? I don't understand that, this was about five years ago, and I still don't understand it.'

Andrea Dworkin has a theory. Rape happens, she thinks, because we live in cultures that promote hatred of women, that purvey debased images of women – and despite the best efforts of polemicists like herself, nothing has changed. 'One feels a terrible sense of failure, because certainly there's more rape now than there was before. It does make one feel incredibly ineffectual.'

So can anything be done to deter men – the actual or potential rapists among them – from associating sex and aggression, from using their penises as weapons? Perhaps it's just biology, a bestial instinct. 'No, because animals don't rape,' says Sellars. 'I think we're moving in the right direction, very slowly, by educating men into not feeling they have to be dominant to be men, not feeling that sexuality is the only way in which they can prove themselves, being more aware of their emotional side, encouraging a less instrumental approach to sex.'

'Our society needs to be made more motherly,' suggests Stevie Davies, a novelist who has written about men, sex and militarism. 'The maternal values of care and sustenance and so on should be directed more and more towards those who need them desperately – the males.'

Oh no it shouldn't, retorts Bly. Hairy men believe in a firm hand. 'The greatest worry we have is around young men, and if we do not find a way to provide more fathering, the young men are going to burn down the cities, and they are already doing it in Los Angeles. I think in Bosnia you have a situation where many of these are unfathered children too, the fathers they do have are rabid nationalists, and you're seeing a lack of repression on a massive scale.'

Having seen the aftermath, Mezey reacted with 'disbelief and depression, a sense that people do not learn from history. In another sense sadly they do learn, because many of the actions you see repeated in wars are activities and abuses that have been learned . . . there's this interesting kind of victim-to-victimiser cycle that you see being played out.'

And what does it say about men? 'I don't want to condemn all men, no matter what the evidence might be,' Mezey says. Stereotyping is for rapists: 'This is what rapists do about women – say that all women are the same, they're sluts, or whores, only after one thing.'

Brownmiller stands by the central assertion of Against Our Will, that rape is 'a conscious process of intimidation whereby all men keep all women in a state of fear.' That doesn't mean all men are rapists 'but rape is the weapon by which women learn they are distinguished from men, particularly in warfare'.

What will using this weapon mean to these men? Sellars predicts 'horrendous guilt' for many of them. But this scarcely compares with the misery of their victims. 'It's appalling,' she says. 'It actually, in many ways, is more destructive than murder, because although the life is left for that person, for a significant percentage, their lives are literally never the same again.'

14 December 1994

Feminist under a fatwa

The Bangladeshi writer Taslima Nasrin has been forced into exile with a price on her head. Her crime, she says, is trying to free her countrywomen from slavery

Linda Grant

Taslima Nasrin is smoking a cigarette, though not very well and it doesn't look as if she inhales. It looks, in fact, like something of an affectation. When I draw attention to the cigarette she is annoyed. 'All the journalists ask me about this,' she says. 'They all write about it and they do not write about my campaign.'

This is hardly fair. While Nasrin's name is not as well known as Salman Rushdie's, many have heard of her as the feminist who has provoked a fatwa against her in Bangladesh. The smoking operates as a symbol: it is forbidden for women to smoke in her country.

'If a woman smokes in the road, people will stone her,' she points out. 'I will stop because it is injurious to health. Drink is also forbidden but the men do it. When women are oppressed, they call it tradition.'

Nearly two years ago Nasrin published a novel called Lajja (Shame). It described the fate of a Hindu family in Bangladesh who were attacked by a Muslim mob in the riots of 1992, after an Indian mosque was destroyed by Hindu extremists. Five months after the book came out, it was banned by the government on the grounds that it might 'create misunderstanding and mistrust'. Two months after the ban, a group of Islamic fundamentalists held a public meeting that accused her of offending the religious sentiments of Muslims and offered a bounty of 50,000 taka to anyone who would kill her.

The fatwa provoked massive riots in the capital, demands for her public hanging and the bizarre threat of releasing 10,000 snakes to symbolise her infamy. Unfortunately the matter was compounded earlier this year when, in an interview with an English-language newspaper published in Calcutta, she was quoted as saying that she advocated a revision of Islamic law. By July the crisis had escalated to two-day public strikes and protest marches to demand her death, and ultimately, a warrant for her arrest. The day it was issued she went into hiding. Finally in August, she managed to escape from the country, having been invited to take up exile in Sweden.

This interview, which has been organised by Pen, the international writers' committee, is taking place in a safe house, the location of which is not revealed until the last moment, provoking a scramble to bus and tube to get there on time. Nasrin enters the kitchen in a red, gold and green sari, pours herself a cup of tea and lights up. She has been interviewed all morning and she is tired and possibly tense. Her English is adequate but not fluent.

Asked if she would like to go to lunch after the interview, she says she would prefer to visit a book shop. A long discussion takes place between the representative of Pen and the owner of the house about the likelihood of her being identified on the street.

I ask her how she felt about leaving her home country, about being in involuntary exile. 'I left because I thought that if I wanted to continue my fight I should be alive,' she says. 'I never thought I would survive. I thought they would kill me. Every day 20,000 people were demonstrating that I should be killed. The government wanted me in jail but even that was not safe because I could be killed in jail.'

Since her departure, her parents' house has been attacked and her father, like Nasrin a doctor, has lost his patients – 'they have been isolated in society'. After the arrest warrant was issued, her sister, a botanist, was advised by her boss not to come back to the office.

The crucial aspect of Nasrin's case is that it has provoked demands for the introduction of a blasphemy law similar to that which operates in Pakistan, and which carries a mandatory death penalty. Initially, after its long war with Pakistan, Bangladesh was established as a secular state and was regarded as a liberal bulwark in the Indian subcontinent, but in 1988 a version of Islamic law replaced the earlier constitution.

The existing prohibition on 'giving offence' is a 100-year-old carry-over from colonial days, a British import. Fundamentalists argue that, since Britain has its own blasphemy laws, why should Bangladesh be regarded as savage for wanting to introduce one? Yes, but what kind of blasphemy law have we got? The last person to go to prison for it did so in 1923. The most recent case took place nearly 20 years ago, involving the prosecution of Gay News.

The problem Nasrin faces is that she is that increasing impossibility in the subcontinent: a liberal humanist. I point out that when one argues with Muslim fundamentalists against fatwas and the like, they counter that humanism is an import from the west. We are mired in post-modern cultural difference and can never agree.

'Humanism is not western or eastern or southern or northern,' she declares. 'It is just humanism. They protest against me but I am surprised that they don't protest against inequality and injustice. What I have done is protested against the system which is against women. I have seen that, in the name of tradition, society wants to keep women in ignorance and slavery.'

Brought up in a middle-class family, Nasrin escaped the ignorance, illiteracy and virtual slavery of many poor women. She trained as a doctor, married first a poet and then a journalist. The first committed suicide, the second she will not discuss but they are now divorced. How was her life any different from a woman doctor in the west? How was her freedom diminished?

'I realised from childhood that women were treated as child-bearing machines or decorations, not human beings,' she says. 'Oppression does not mean that I am beaten by my husband, that I have to stop my studies. But I feel oppression by society. Yes it is true that I am a doctor and I have had a few opportunities to become educated, but the patriarchal system is equally applicable to educated women and poor, illiterate women. And the religious system is also equally applicable.'

Her next novel will be about a Muslim woman whose family forbids her to study and will follow her as she tries to get an education and hence her economic freedom. Another wearying aspect of dialogue with Muslim men is their hot insistence that they respect women far more than western men: look at the way they will not allow them to be sullied by the male gaze, they contend, how they protect them by keeping them indoors.

Critics of Nasrin have pointed out that plenty of Bangladeshi women have careers. Feminism has made its mark. It is, of course, the essence of all systems of power to point to the freedoms you allow the oppressed. 'It's true that many women are educated in Bangladesh but it is not a proper education because they stop work when they marry,' she argues. 'They always have a guardian: father, husband, brother. It's one kind of torture to treat a woman as a doll. They keep the doll in a very good place, but it's not real respect. This system keeps women as a decoration or sexual commodity.'

Like Rushdie, Nasrin is accused of having brought trouble on her own head, that she could have predicted the response that would follow the publication of the book and she would have been better off remaining silent. She believes that there are large numbers of progressives in Bangladesh but they deliberately keep silent. 'When I write I never think of what will happen,' she says. 'As a human being I should tell the truth.'

The problem of her exile is that there is no opposition party at home which would campaign for her release and whose return to power could remove the charges against her, apart from the small and marginalised socialists. 'It is very strange for me to live in Sweden but what can I do? I have no alternative. We have lost our hope in any political party.'

Both the main parties in Bangladesh rely for their support on fundamentalists and the court case against her (which will begin in absentia in January), was about satisfying the fundamentalists.

Meanwhile, in obscure villages, women are being killed as a result of fatwas all the time, she says. Aid work has targeted them for help and in doing so has made them vulnerable to men jealous of their little freedoms. If a Pakistan-style blasphemy law is introduced, the accused will have to establish they are completely innocent to avoid execution. When judges are lenient, the released defendant still has to face the mob. Now she is in Sweden one hopes that she will stop smoking. As a gesture of defiance it has served its purpose. Feminists and humanists need her alive and well to go on defying the fatwa.

23 November 1995

The princess and the pain

Forget the future of the monarchy, divorce, the constitution. The most important thing Diana did in her Panorama interview was to give countless silent women a voice

BEATRIX CAMPBELL

If Princess Diana's words seem 'extremely paranoid' – Nicholas Soames' verdict – then let's remember what Diana said about the establishment for which he spoke: she is their enemy. We believed her because what she revealed was how they made her mad, and how they represent her mutiny as madness.

Never before on British television has an aristocratic woman been so eloquent about pain as protest.

The reason we believed her was that behind her are thousands of women sent to the tower, to the asylum, to the attic, to solitary confinement. The drama of self-destruction unmasks the impossibility of protest. The establishment has been locking up women for centuries. It's what they do.

The confidence that they'll go quietly is confirmed by the bumbling megalomania of Charles' marriage. He thought he could get away with it. He thought he could love another while scouring the shires of England for a seemly virgin, a girl who would give him sons and secure his mission as a man who wanted to be king. He found an uneducated young woman who, these days, could only come from either the poor or the rich – the only classes for whom gender is destiny.

The monarchy, lest we forget, is the most atavistic monument to patriarchy. The aristocracy disinherit their girls and demand that they deliver boys. Diana and Charles and the royal family must be the only people in Britain these days who care whether their babies are boys or girls.

Diana's interview did, at least, protect her pride and his reputation when she allowed her own version of his liaison dangereuse with Camilla Parker Bowles to synchronise with his. We think we know better, however. There were always three of them in that marriage. He always deceived her.

But unbeknown to her, his life was her destiny. When her disappointment about something so simple – lack of love – demanded sympathy, not to mention some strategic imagination, she was rewarded with 'treatment'. If not the tower, then the isolation ward.

Her description of bulimia as a survival mechanism was arresting. It became her only means of protest – a survival strategy to which the palace reacted not with care but with contempt. A spokesperson for the Northern Initiative on Women and Eating heard an echo in Diana's unprecedented – for a royal – description: she said what other women have said, 'seeing it almost as a friend in the middle of traumatic isolation. She said what lots of women in our groups say. And it is so different from the way psychiatrists describe it, as a symptom of a personality disorder.'

She was hurt. Her survival has depended upon calling attention to her pain and to the perpetrators. Some saw it as soap. Some saw it as a woman scorned. Many feminists saw her suffering as a symptom of her exile.

The establishment saw it as an attack on the establishment. They were right.

To tell your story is the most dangerous thing you can do. Modern movements of survivors, from Siberia to Sloane Square, have redeemed their pain from the psychiatric wards, via the fridge and the phone, the samizdat and the secret services, and transformed it into public, political discourse. Her triumph was her testimony: by bearing witness, she broke the vow of silence that is the perpetrator's secret weapon. We were all witnesses. But to speak does not make you safe.

Princess Diana has been seen as a weak woman. Now she is describing herself as a survivor, and locating herself among a long line of women, ill-treated and even ill, whose rebellions have, until now, been quelled. She has used her power – not her beauty, but her stamina and strength – to call her class to account, and has revealed how the establishment fears that power like an exocet.

Diana is no revolutionary, she is no Rosa Luxemburg. But never before has a woman in her position articulated mass pain. The result is that she has mobilised an army of supporters, and the palace has been forced to show some respect for the impact of her words.

Remarkably, there is still no republican movement in Britain with the wit to reunite public and private. The political system has not made the link between sex and power. It has failed to register one of the great themes of our time: the behaviour of men within marriages. The greatest danger Princess Diana's speech poses to the establishment is the impact on ordinary people of this future king being called to account as a man.

21 DECEMBER 1995

Yea, though I walk through the valley of discrimination

Three years ago, the church took a bold, brave step towards reversing Christianity's 2,000 years of patriarchy. Being at the forefront of such change was always going to be hard

MADELEINE BUNTING

There are now more than 1,500 female priests in the Church of England, there's a sitcom every Sunday night about a female priest and in January, the first woman is likely to be appointed archdeacon, marking another step up the church hierarchy. This is the story that female priests happily tell. The much-predicted mass exodus from the church has not happened, and to everyone's relief the majority of parishes have accepted women at the altar far more calmly than anyone had dared hope. One could be forgiven for concluding that the battle for female priests was now a subject only for the history books. But you would be wrong.

There is another side to the story, which female priests are reluctant to tell. The report last week of the female priest who received vicious hate-mail offered a glimpse. The battle has shifted from the national stage down to the grassroots into the parishes and the individual lives of clergywomen. The newly ordained women are struggling to cope with the structures of a male-dominated institution. Many are desperately anxious to prove themselves, grateful for being allowed the opportunity to do so, and above all apologetic for the 'trouble' they have caused the church.

The anxiety to please, the gratitude, the apologetic attitude make them reluctant to talk of the difficulties of being a tiny minority (they make up just over 13% of clergy). Female priests are not by and large radical feminists and there are plenty of stoics among them. Ask how it's all going and female priests and their supporters are brightly, determinedly positive. Only when pressed do they admit their concerns as one female curate said: 'It is unfair but then, as my children say, life is unfair.'

The problem is that any complaints play directly into the hands of the opponents of female priests, who are showing undimmed determination. Last month, 3,000 of them gathered for a dramatic show of strength at a service in St Paul's Cathedral, and the Rt Rev Edwin Barnes, one of the 'flying bishops' appointed to look after those parishes who object to female priests, provoked a furore by announcing a campaign to repeal the 1992 legislation. He described the General Synod vote as 'wrong and silly' and claimed that 'women's ordination simply isn't working. The women are not happy and are saying so publicly. They're not getting promotions and are not being appointed as priests.'

Bishop Barnes' comments were astutely manipulative: if women complain, it's proof that their ordination isn't working.

So female priests put great emphasis on doing the job well in the hope that they will win their critics round. The danger, fears Vivienne Faull, vice-provost of Coventry Cathedral, is burn-out. Many days, she works from 7.30am until 10pm.

'The perception is that if you do something well, you're just doing the job, if you do something badly, it's because you're a woman. As women, you feel responsible to each other and so most women are working enormously hard. The question for many of us is how long can we carry on like this before handing on to the next generation? Will we maintain our vigour?'

Female priests frequently have to deal with some form of hostility. At its crudest, it is hate-mail – Faull gets about half a dozen pieces a year, ranging from the abusive to the pornographic – and at its most formal, the parish opts for the jurisdiction of a flying bishop. Nearly 900 parishes (one in 16) have made their opposition clear, claims the conservative pressure group, Forward in Faith. But parishes can also indicate a gender preference more informally. The treatment of female priests in different dioceses varies considerably. Opponents of female priests have been appointed to two of the most senior jobs in the church this year – Richard Chartres as Bishop of London and David Hope as Archbishop of York. What many women priests find difficult is that opposition to them is sanctioned by church legislation.

'After the vote, everyone was feeling very generous and the Act of Synod was passed overwhelmingly – yet it enshrines discrimination against women. It gives legitimacy to people who are opposed – people who are not even trying to get along with those in favour of women priests. Bishop Barnes was appointed to look after opponents, not to campaign to reverse the decision. His comments were deeply offensive. The church is taking time to catch up with the nice decision it took three years ago. But 20 years down the line it will be overwhelmingly accepted,' says Christina Rees, spokesperson of the Ministry of Women (formerly the Movement for the Ordination of Women, which decided it should change its name rather than close down).

Judith Rose is likely to be appointed the first female archdeacon early in the New Year, thus making her the most senior woman cleric in the church. She takes a brisk, businesslike attitude. 'I haven't met opposition and I don't expect to,' she says. 'For the most part, I'm accepted for who I am. Unfortunately, because we are women, some things are not easy, but other people have other limitations.'

Even she admits, however, that 'the church has built into its structures discrimination against women and to some extent I do resent that. It's a compromise and it may be the best we can do at this time, even though I don't like it.'

Current discrimination and the legacy of the long and vituperative battle for women's ordination have been internalised by many female priests, according to Rose. 'I've been in ministry for 30 years,' she points out, 'and for the majority of that time, I've not been allowed to be a priest. That's not an affirming experience. So there has been a tendency to apologise – for being around, for causing trouble for the church, for even having a vocation to the priesthood. The alternative to apologising is aggression. Neither is a very good quality for positions of responsibility.'

There are other problems hampering the career development of female priests. If a job specifies a certain number of years of experience as a priest, women obviously won't qualify. Only 61 out of the 6,158 incumbents (vicars and rectors with freehold) are women, although the number has trebled in a year. What is more worrying is that a much larger proportion of women to men are opting for unpaid priesthood. In part, this is explained by the backlog from the long wait for legislation – many women by the time of their ordination were past the 45-year-old threshold, so were no longer eligible for stipendiary ministry. But the numbers currently in training also show a dramatic disproportion of women to men applying for non-stipendiary ministry. Women priests could find themselves on the fringes of the church in an extension of their traditional role of voluntary workforce. As one female priest admits: 'We do have to ask ourselves, who is the church paying?'

Some will be happy to remain on the fringes, Faull says. Being a full-time female priest can be hard and lonely. 'The biggest problem is that of male clergy trying to sideline female priest colleagues,' Rees says. 'Sometimes going into clergy chapter [meetings of half a dozen local clergy] can feel like going into an old boys' club.'

What makes their position even lonelier is losing some of that heady solidarity that kept female priests going through the campaign.

'The institution is masculinising,' Faull says. 'It's what we feared, that we would have to play the same games as the men. We can push out the boundaries so far but we can't do it all. The next generation will have to take over.'

Three years ago, the church took a bold, brave step towards reversing Christianity's 2,000 years of patriarchy. Being at the forefront of such change was always going to be difficult, particularly given the problematic compromises the church adopted to maintain unity. Female priests place great faith in time smoothing out the wrinkles, but there are rocky times still ahead as the pressure groups continue to force the pace. At General Synod last month, many signed a private member's motion to discuss female bishops (currently banned) and a debate is likely next year. The issue is seen as a crucial test of the church's commitment to women's ministry: are they to be leading and governing the church in the next century or will they remain second-rate priests?

Significantly, opponents also signed up to the motion, hoping to force a showdown – the church's compromise could still break down. Further embarrassment will follow in 1998 at the Lambeth Conference when all the bishops of the Anglican Communion worldwide gather in Canterbury. There will be female bishops from America, Canada and New Zealand, but not, of course, from England.

9 OCTOBER 1997

Chamber of horrors

This week, the government announced it will take action against opposition MPs who make sexist comments in the Commons. A PC fuss about nothing?

ANNE PERKINS

'I don't want to comment,' says one of the female MPs who has prompted government whips to start monitoring harassment by Tory backbenchers. 'They are very rude people. I can take it,' she adds defiantly – and unconvincingly.

It is not hard to make the charge of political incorrectness against Tory backbenchers. It fits so easily with the hoary image of large, middle-aged men in three-piece suits. Unreconstructed, inadequate public schoolboys. These are the chaps whose chairman, Sir Archie Hamilton says – on the record – that the role of women in the party is making jam.

They hotly deny harassing Labour women, however. 'Absolute ********!' complains a prime suspect. 'I like girls. It's not my nature to be beastly to them.' Emma Nicholson, now a Liberal Democrat peer, nevertheless finds it all too easy to believe. 'As a Tory MP, I was sickened by the abuse hurled at opposition women.

They used words I have never heard in social circles.' She won't be specific. 'Suggesting they were prostitutes.'

It is, it seems, all a question of how you react. The former education secretary Gillian Shephard said it was 'all absolute rubbish'. What, she's never heard terrible things? 'Of course I've heard terrible things, but they should have heard what I heard at the NUT.' According to Labour whips, half a dozen of Labour's 101 female MPs have complained of harassment in the chamber. One of the whips, Jane Kennedy, says she has not experienced it personally: 'But most of us understand that the chamber is very, very tough. They don't take prisoners. They are trying to throw you off balance.'

The complaints began after some of the new intake, anxious not to fluff, read out their questions instead of pretending they had occurred spontaneously in the light of the debate. This is frowned upon in a chamber where form is preserved long after it has ceased to serve any function at all. Other MPs then gleefully shout: 'Reading!' 'I think Labour women do get an unfair barracking occasionally,' one Tory MP admits. 'But it's just as much from their own side as ours.'

The Commons is a notoriously woman-unfriendly place. Linda McDougall, who is married to the Labour MP Austin Mitchell, has been interviewing the new intake for a TV documentary series to be shown in the New Year. 'Most women don't like the chamber,' she says. 'They get worried by it. It's the confrontation they find difficult.' There are plenty of men who have also found it all but overwhelming. Being a woman simply opens up one more line of attack.

Most Tory women claim not to notice. The former education minister Cheryl Gillan, who now speaks on trade for the Tories, says of course speaking in the chamber is intimidating and adds that she thinks the new women may be in too much of a hurry to impress. 'One of the best pieces of advice I got was not to rush. Sit and listen. They've only had six months. Oh, and don't have a sense of humour bypass.'

Labour women don't think it's a joke. Another, who also prefers not to be named, says: 'If you're none too confident, having a Tory MP stand in front of you, eyeing you up and down before pronouncing on your appearance, is not very funny.'

Ignore it, say the men. Like the celebrated Dame Elaine Kellett-Bowman, now retired, who sat for years immediately behind Sir Edward Heath, delivering a quiet but steady flow of criticism ('Entirely of a factual nature,' she insists) whenever he spoke. She says that in her 27 years in the House, she suffered no harassment at all. This is extraordinary: ask anyone else and they remember that whenever she rose to speak, Labour MPs opposite would howl in what they thought was a hilarious imitation of her voice. She never faltered. It now seems she didn't even hear.

And of course you can always wallop it back. As one Tory woman said yesterday, on her way to tackle Sir Archie Hamilton on the question of Tory women's role: 'He's the one who keeps his brain under his seat.'

24 OCTOBER 1997

Pro-lifers have lost but won't give up

DECCA AITKENHEAD

The students at a pro-choice meeting in Oxford last week weren't entirely sure what to call it. Is it a celebration? we wondered. A commemoration? We thought about it, and none of us seemed able to decide.

The Abortion Act reaches its 30th anniversary next Tuesday. It is being honoured by the various pro-choice groups with the publication of writings by campaigners, doctors, politicians and women who have had abortions. The pro-lifers of SPUC, the Society for the Protection of the Unborn Child, have opted for lobbing flowers off Westminster Bridge in protest – a characteristic enough gesture, which does not appear to be exciting too much interest. The date looks like passing by quietly – and for most of those who support legal abortion, the very modesty of the commemorations confirms the success of the act. The argument is won.

There is a considerable temptation to go along with this view. Everyone you know who wants an abortion gets one, one way or another. Abortion 'on demand' hardly seems worth fussing about, sounding as it does a bit like a pedantic flap over semantics. The only vaguely interesting stuff these days seems to be scientific questions about when a foetus becomes viable outside the womb, which abortion procedures are unacceptably grisly, etc. But no one takes fanatics shaking plastic foetuses very seriously any more. And a gaggle of folk tossing tulips off a bridge are unlikely to raise the alarm. But the danger lies in assuming that this is all pro-life gets up to, and that the anti-abortion lobby is as unsophisticated and ill-fated as ever.

Thirty years ago, campaigners against the Abortion Act were perfectly candid about their objections. It was not the foetus but the family which was their concern – how could we allow this affront to motherhood, and what would become of traditional family life? At a time when feminism was gathering force, this proved an ill-advised approach, and once the act was passed, the argument moved on to one that shrieked 'Abortion means murder!' Sadly for pro-lifers, this line did them little good either, and every assault on the 67 act was as unsuccessful as the last. By last summer, anti-abortion campaigning in Britain was looking like a lonely and slightly laughable preoccupation. But in the past 18 months we have seen a sustained, and altogether more sophisticated pro-life strategy – so sophisticated, in fact, that it it is not always obvious where the attack is coming from, or leading to.

Last summer there was an outcry over the destruction of 3,300 frozen embryos – this was presented as 'infanticide'. We had a media frenzy over the selective abortion of a healthy twin, and noisy disgust at a gynaecologist who admitted that, hours after conducting an abortion, he had simply 'forgotten all about it'. Life and SPUC rustled round raising money for the mother of the twin, to help 'persuade' her to keep it. Likewise, they joyfully endorsed Mandy Allwood's rather surprising attempt to give birth to a litter of eight.

We also began hearing about cases in the States where mothers who smoked while pregnant, or 'ate what they liked', were prosecuted for 'prenatal child neglect'. We heard a new phrase, the 'maternal environment' – used, as one commentator observed, 'to describe women as more or less passive spectators in their own pregnancies'. Concern spread about 'designer babies' and doctors playing God. And we saw the media suddenly start to take the 'rights of the foetus' very seriously – only, it began talking of the 'rights of the unborn child' instead.

Was this a spontaneous public outburst of anxiety about technology-gone-mad? Perhaps. An alternative explanation is this: that the pro-life lobby has wised up and identified new and, in media-speak, sexy issues, which get us all talking and thinking about the foetus again. From there, it does not take a genius (which is fortunate, given the calibre of the average anti-abortion campaigner) to work the argument back round to an assault on the law which allows women to abort – or 'murder' – that foetus.

Pro-choice supporters have tended to react to each of these issues on its individual terms. The arguments are time-consuming, knotted, and largely distracting – late term abortions, for example, account for less than 0.05% of all terminations, yet the debate about time limits occupies an inordinate amount of time and energy – all of which suits the pro-life lobby very well. For as long as supporters of abortion are tied up in the tangle of each detail, they are distracted from pointing out the fundamental argument: that the decision over any unwanted pregnancy should lie only with the mother.

If you were to sit down with someone entirely ignorant of the history of abortion in Britain, and tell them the story of the past 50 years, I think they would find it surprising. The principle that abortion is not murder but a legitimate procedure was accepted in law 30 years ago. Public support for that law has increased steadily ever since. Almost 5 million women have benefitted from that law – 40% of women will have an abortion at some point in their life. And yet the debate on the agenda is all about limiting abortion – rather than making sense of the odd law we have that allows it.

'Abortion on demand' is a strangely off-putting phrase. It sounds faintly truculent. But what we have instead is abortion by deceit – one where women are required to pretend to be having a nervous breakdown, and doctors are required to pretend to believe them. If you are middle class, and understand the rules, and realise that if your doctor is disinclined to collude in the pantomime, you can simply take your cheque book down to the nearest clinic, then the whole thing is fine. It really is just a question of semantics. But if you don't understand the system, and your doctor doesn't feel like playing it, it becomes a question of being forced to go through a pregnancy you do not want. When people speak indulgently of our charmingly British fudge of a law, perhaps they forget this.

'I am a bit sad,' writes a founder of the Birth Control Trust, in their booklet to mark the anniversary, 'that my own children are not involved in our sort of campaigning . . . You have to keep going, otherwise you will be overwhelmed by the waves coming back.'

This is something the pro-life lobby plainly understand, and absent-minded supporters of abortion would do well to remember.

29 JANUARY 1998

Dear Bill and Hillary

The whole world is talking about it, but what do American women really think of the presidential affair?

ANDREA DWORKIN

Monica Lewinsky is in a terrible, terrible mess. She's being threatened by a very mean special prosecutor who has unlimited powers. And he plays hard ball. She has my sympathy. Of everyone who is a player in this game, she is the one who is going to be destroyed by it.

We are talking about a man who, in a predatory way, is using women, particularly young women. In this case, a woman who was working as an intern, for no money, because of her devotion to the Democratic party and to him. In an alcove next to the Oval Office, he simply unzips his pants and she sexually services him.

Bill Clinton's fixation on oral sex – non-reciprocal oral sex – consistently puts women in states of submission to him. It's the most fetishistic, heartless, cold sexual exchange that one could imagine.

People are characterising this as a sexual scandal, but it's an abuse-of-power scandal. It corroborates what both Paula Jones and Gennifer Flowers have said, and it's a disaster for this particular young woman, Monica. I think there probably are many more of them, but I don't know how many will come forward. Whoever steps into this is stepping not just into public spectacle, but on to a legal landmine. And it is a very hard thing for someone who is

20, 21, to find herself in the middle of all this, subpoenaed to talk about her sex life.

The second issue that concerns me is what Hillary Clinton is doing, which I think is appalling. She is covering up for a man who has a history of exploiting women. If there is one thing being a feminist has to mean it's that you don't do that. You don't use your intellect and your creativity to protect a man's exploitation of other women. She's done it before and she's doing it again.

Ever since she went to the White House as First Lady, her life has been going down the tubes. She had to give up her profession and she's been the staunch wife standing by her husband, no matter what vile things he does to humiliate her. It's pathetic. She should pack her bags and leave.

Women of Hillary's age – my age – have a responsibility not to let the men who are our peers exploit and destroy younger women. It breaks my heart to see Hillary on television. It's a performance and as such it's a lie. Whatever kind of deal they made in their marriage, I don't believe it included the public humiliation of her. And this has to be the most towering humiliation of all.

I had great hopes for her at the beginning. I thought: 'How wonderful – a feminist in the White House. She's so smart.' But I have not understood the choices she's made and I have not been able to respect them. In protecting her husband, she is betraying younger women.

Maybe it was different 20 years ago. Maybe it looked different to her when Bill was fooling around in Arkansas. She had her job and her child, perhaps she didn't care. But now this is a man, her husband, the president, being sexually serviced by a 21-year-old woman – in her house.

It's impossible to believe that she, and everyone who works in the White House, doesn't feel utterly betrayed by him. They really thought he had stopped all this. They thought he was a creep before – even Monica calls him a creep – but when he became president, they thought he knew he couldn't get away with it any more.

There is a strain of misogyny in him, though. People say it has nothing to do with the way he makes social policy, but I think it does. These things are connected. There are plenty of women who are simply expendable to him – clearly the White House interns are.

As for the conspiracy theory, I just don't believe it. Yes, there are rightwing people who hate the Clintons, but to think there's a conspiracy would mean somehow the right wing planted the young woman in Clinton's office to entice him into sexual acts.

I have a modest proposal. It will probably bring the FBI to my door. But I think that Hillary should shoot Bill and then President Gore should pardon her.

The silence from other feminists in this country is deafening. There's no outcry against Clinton, there's no outcry against Hillary for fronting for him. I think a lot of feminists are very distressed and disappointed in him, but they don't want to say so publicly because many of them are connected to the Democratic party. It's a problem. It was a problem when Bill Clinton threw poor women off welfare and used pregnant teenage girls as scapegoats as if they were causing the economic problems of our country. Clinton has good policies for middle-class women, but I don't think he has good policies for poor women.

Male politicians' policies in respect of women are important, but sexual harassment is an issue, too. You don't say it's OK for the leader of your country to be having his cock sucked, by someone half his age, while he is in the people's house. Yes, the law says that if both parties are consenting, it's not sexual harassment and it's not illegal. As far as we know, Monica was consenting, but I believe Clinton is culpable because I think he's guilty of exploitation. I care about how men in public life treat women. Clinton shows a real callousness in what he was doing to someone who was just about his daughter's age.

He may not have to resign, but I think he should and I think he will.

I don't want him as my president. I think he's toast, I think he's done, I think he's outta there. And I'm glad about that. Most of my feminist colleagues won't be. They feel he's a good president and the country's in good shape, they feel he's a good guy. Yeah, he just did this one little thing that was wrong, but he's really a nice guy. Au revoir, Slick Willy.

2 FEBRUARY 1998

All white now

Take a closer look at the picture painted in the press of Britain's New Feminism. See any black women?

Heidi Safia Mirza

I despair. The debate surrounding the state of New British Feminism makes me aware that one thing has not changed: new or not, British feminism is still self-confidently all white. It is as if the political lessons of the past (when black women were excluded), the change in the global economy (with international movement of people) and the shifts in consumption and identity and sexuality (young women wear short skirts) have made no impact. With their self-indulgent, in-crowd, middle-class perspectives, women in the public eye still jealously debate if the older or younger generation, or American or British feminists, have 'got it right'.

But New Feminism is not just the voices of Natasha Walter, Melissa Benn and Kate Figes, who make up the new and latest feminist media babes. There are other new voices out there who never get a look-in as they are not part of the powerful and privileged media brat pack: the hidden voices of black women who live in another world – a world far more representative of what is Britain today.

The terrain for feminist struggle has changed. Slowly and silently, under the very nose of old and new white feminism, a generation of ethnically diverse women have grown up here and now wish to be heard in the struggle for equality.

This is not about educating white feminists to become better feminists. It is about the way women have changed to become strategic players in the ways we are represented and defined. It is about the struggle we as women face every day to define who we are when the world keeps on telling us what we should think and feel.

The battle for women's equality is no longer simply waged in women's meetings in old, cold halls or even at middle-class dinner parties over a glass of wine. The battle for power has shifted to new sites of struggle. It is now waged on our bodies and in our language, the way we speak and are spoken about.

In the book Black British Feminism (a new collection of essays by ethnically and racially diverse women), we tell stories about our hidden world, scarred by cultural imperialism, masculine domination and feminine exclusion. We tell of the way harmful myths – such as that of the single, unmarried, Black Superwoman, like Diane Abbott – undermine any real attempt to make black women's conditions better. We tell of the way we are eroticised and exoticised as objects of desire – Naomi Campbell, Iman – until we ourselves do not know the 'truth' about who we are. Mixed-race women talk about the pain of invisibility because they do not fit into any convenient ethnic monitoring or cultural categories. Southall Black Sisters reveal the way the law makes cultural assumptions that perpetuate violence against women.

Thirty years ago, when our parents had just arrived on the shores of Britain as postcolonial migrants, we were not powerful enough to write about our experiences. Now, educated here and with a new sense of belonging and self-confidence, this generation of women challenges all that has gone before. The media image of angry black women can no longer be used to undermine the credibility of the feminist agenda.

Black British Feminism is not just for black women, it is not about guilt-tripping white women, it is not about simply celebrating 'our difference'. It is about shifting the old power lines of what feminism could and should be about now that we approach the millennium.

If white media feminism (old and new) is being paraded as the role model of feminism now, it is no wonder that you hear young women like the Spice Girls saying they are not feminists. If feminism does not incorporate their experience, it will be rejected. If feminism does not appeal to the mass of young black and white women, then surely something is wrong with it? But New British Feminism is not the only feminism. Feminism has evolved beyond any traditional recognition. It belongs to a generation of new and 'different' women; it does not have to be confrontational and overtly politicised. It is time feminism changed its meaning to embrace all our differences.

Get a life, girls

What's missing from women's lives is interests other than men

Elizabeth Wurtzel

In late June, Time magazine ran a cover story illustrated with the faces of Susan B Anthony, Betty Friedan and Gloria Steinem, pictured in grave, grainy black and white. Next to the likeness of this right-eous triumvirate was a colour photograph of Calista Flockhart AKA Ally McBeal, above the red-lettered, alarmist question: Is feminism dead? The article went on to decry almost all feminists under 50 (or maybe 60), complaining that none of us is serious enough and all of us dwell on our personal problems too much.

What the Time story failed to note was the simple tedium of so much that currently engages feminism, with its echo chamber of conversation and its Mobius strip of writings that leave civilian women running for Bridget Jones' Diary and The Rules, craving anything that actually reflects The Way We Live Now. Can we really continue much longer to discuss the usual date rape and sexual harassment matters that have vexed us all for so long? And when might we cease to debate the collective of sociosexual concerns that can be summed up by the question of whether, in the guise of girl power, the Spice Girls really might be nothing more than boy toys (a query Madonna was meant to have answered over a decade ago)? What feminism must do, to revitalise itself and help make women into fully fledged creatures ecstatically engaged in life, is, quite simply, to encourage and engender fanaticism in us all. It must show women how to be complete nutcases, crazily committed to ideas, ideology, interests – anything. It must teach women how to be bonkers about something other than men (or a man because, let's face it, we tend to get obsessive and insane about one man at a time, pathetically investing one twerpy under-six-footer with the power and fury of Atlas having a bad hair day).

If you think this sounds patronising, if you believe, like the moronic Time writer, that 'few women alive haven't dwelled on relationships . . . but most manage to concern themselves with other things too', turn your attention to what are known as women's magazines. Of course, as Cynthia Heimel once pointed out, they should rightly be called men's magazines, as they are devoted wholly to the acquiring, nurturing and pleasing of Mr Dreamboat.

But before I elaborate on this point about the pursuit of interests as an end to inequality, let's consider the arguments that the feminist agenda ought to deal with more serious injustices and whatnot, which of course it should. Well, sort of. For starters, consider this grim fact, sad but true: in the US, women earn 76 cents for every man's dollar. For all the outrage this figure should summon – of course, it is up from 59 cents in 1980 – it is still just a number, a dry statistic furnished by the Bureau of Labor. Most people don't even know what it means. How is it measured? Is it referring to comparable work, to pink collar v blue? Or are we talking a female attorney's salary pitted against a man's? Is the disparity a result of women preferring to teach and nurse, while men like to engineer and lift large objects, and are the former less remunerative because they are perceived as women's work or for more democratic causes of supply and demand? See there: there's the mire one gets quagged into by examining the inequities upon which feminism's fight was predicated long ago. We are left with this feeling that something is wrong, but after all these years of picketing and placards, we don't quite know what to make of this

76 cents business, we don't know what we can do except continue to agitate and get uppity. And it starts to seem like a better idea to talk about . . . dating etiquette. Or the politics of fashion. Or the goddess in every woman. Or mascara: friend or foe? I don't think this is necessarily a bad thing. These are often the things I like talking about and the important part is that we are talking, the conversation goes on. That's precisely right: after a prolonged latency period, women's rights are a hot topic again, such that even fictional characters whose feminist character is of dubious merit, like Bridget Jones and Ally McBeal, still refer to Susan Faludi's Backlash as their benchmark.

But where women's agenda is concerned, it ought to be clear by now that we cannot live on bread alone – that, in fact, the focus on legislation and logistics, at the expense of leisure, has cost us in the long run. The point of this whole sexual revolution was to give women fuller lives: it was not so they could grimly labour to earn only three-quarters what men do, then come home to nothing but housework and screaming children. If women had the kinds of consuming passions men seem to, that they will not allow a single fucking thing to get in the way of – be it watching sports or drinking with the boys – women would do more to assert their own rights. By, for instance, filing a complaint when the boss says: 'Hey, baby, nice butt.' Because, worthy as it is to call the sleaze on his sexually harassing behaviour, it is not fun. In fact, it is probably a tedious, tiresome procedure, which is why so many women don't bother. But insisting upon doing something you love, no matter what – well, that makes a woman a creature of enjoyment and indulgence and, frankly, a certain kind of liberating self-sufficiency. It is empowering to say no, but it is a great deal more pleasurable to say yes – and to have things to say yes to besides some man.

That aside, I would argue that a woman is more likely to put the kibosh on her manhandling, leering boss if she has lots of things she likes to do because there is something about loving life and yourself and your enthusiasms too much that makes it hard to put up with any idiot's crap. And the people most likely to be in possession of joie de vivre are people who have insane interests, consuming passions, constant sources of enjoyment that do not depend on the approval of others.

'Be drunken, always. That is the point, nothing else matters,' wrote Charles Baudelaire. 'Drunken with what? With wine, with poetry or with virtue, as you please. But be drunken.' And women must learn what is meant by these lines, what it means to be besotted with something other than some useless bloke.

I've a feeling this point has been made many times before. Even in the much-maligned The Rules, the authoresses suggest their readers take up hobbies, study French, play bridge, all to seem busy to the men they meet and date, all to seem not-desperate to the boyfriends they hope to convert to fiances and eventually husbands. That's fine: if men are the only incentive women can come up with to develop passionate lives, so be it. But I'm suggesting something slightly better: I'm suggesting women follow this course because it is fun and it will make us all happy. I'm saying life will be more enjoyable. I'm saying we should do these things for their own sakes.

While so many feminists, among others, object to Ally McBeal because she thinks too much about boys, that doesn't bother me because, well, give us a break, all of us single people are preoccupied with mating and dating. (Our mums were right: if we'd all just married young, we'd be getting a lot more done.) Nor do I care that she wears thigh-high skirt-suits to court – I think we can all agree that it is preferable to allow Giorgio Armani or Calvin Klein to dictate hemline length than ceding the business to Germaine Greer or the National Organization of Women.

No, the trouble with McBeal is that she is an alleged Harvard law grad working at an enlightened firm of young smarties and yet, frankly, she does not seem so smart. McBeal and her colleagues simply lack intellectual engagement. They talk about boys, personal gripes, contraception, introspection, but never do they express passions for anything else. McBeal's art class leads her to dating the male model who poses nude – but not much else about it seems to hold her interest. Besides these useless attempts at adult education, is there anything outside the courtroom or the bedroom? Does McBeal love renting Hitchcock movies? Getting clam sandwiches at Revere Beach? Going to Red Sox games? Is there nothing besides men and the trouble she gets into because of men? Now, it is true, of course, that men spend much time and effort building bodies and salaries just to please us. But men also do plenty that not only fails to please us but actually rather annoys us as we find ourselves left behind. Sports spectatorship is surely the most alienating thing, but men don't mind, apparently, disappearing into the television and leaving behind women and the world at large.

I have no doubt my delight in spending three hours roaming the cosmetic department of Boots is far more beautiful. I mention this last personal passion because I truly believe make-up, along with fashion, is hardly a harmful fascination. Even Naomi Wolf now concedes that lipstick is not the enemy. And I do think one can enjoy indulging in beauty for its own sake, as pleasure pace pleasure, boy bait not an issue at all.

In excess, however, such concern is not merely vain but dangerously narcissistic – which is the same problem of obsessing over some man. You may think you are thinking about him, but really you are thinking about yourself via him, which is not only ugly and unhealthy, but also a hellish path to an ugly and unhealthy relationship. This is how women get themselves into trouble. Women who have better things to do than be obsessive stay out of trouble.

13 FEBRUARY 1999

The power of one

Talk shows made Oprah Winfrey rich and famous. But now she's having second thoughts. Maybe talking is not enough

MAYA JAGGI

It's her birthday, and Oprah Winfrey is singing lustily in the bathroom of her hotel suite on London's Park Lane, sounding a homely note amid the ostentatious glamour. She's in town to promote Beloved, a film she has nurtured for 10 years, and which she also produced and starred in, and is catching the evening flight back to Chicago and the studio she owns. 'To make up for the two days I wasn't there, instead of doing six shows next week, I've got nine,' she says. 'Soooo, I stay pretty busy.'

Birthday revels evidently take a back seat for America's Queen of Talk, though, at 45, you'd think she has much to sing about. The daily Oprah Winfrey Show has ruled daytime chat for all of its 14 years on air, and has won 32 Emmy awards in the process. With 33 million viewers a week in the US, where it appears on 206 channels, and is syndicated to 132 countries (including Britain's Sky One at 10am every weekday), her brand of sometimes gushing confessional therapy brushed aside last year's challenge from the low-brow king of studio brawls, Jerry Springer. Winfrey is now signed up to host and produce the show until at least the end of 2000. With an estimated personal fortune of £550m, she is the first woman to head the Forbes list of top-40 richest entertainers, and last year pushed Steven Spielberg down into second place as the most powerful person in showbiz in Entertainment Weekly's annual survey – again, she was the first woman, let alone the first African-American, to get there.

Yet, there are signs she has become disillusioned with the talk show genre: that she will get off the 200-shows-a-year treadmill when her current contract runs out – that she will develop other forms of television that 'can make a difference'. She has talked before about giving up her talk show, however, and her present disillusion may have as much to do with the disappointing reaction in America to her 'beloved' Beloved as despair at the sensationalist direction rival shows are heading.

Winfrey's influence reaches far beyond showbiz. The US National Child Protection Act is known as 'Oprah's Law', after President Clinton signed it in her presence in 1993. Her monthly on-air book club – launched in 1996 'to get America reading again' – has made her the most influential bookseller in the US, and her choices overnight bestsellers. In fact, her word carries weight whatever the subject: US beef prices plummeted to a ten-year low, dubbed the 'Oprah crash', after her show on BSE – 'It has stopped me cold from eating another hamburger,' she told the nation – and her subsequent court victory last February after Texas cattlemen issued a 'veggie libel' writ against her showed that she is now far freer than politicians to speak her mind.

Lying on the sofa and nursing an outsize mug of tea, Winfrey is funny, given to impersonations and dramatised anecdotes, much like the Baptist orator she seemed destined to be as a child. Yet she is in sombre, if defiant, mood. Beloved – based on the Pulitzer prize-winning novel by the 1993 Nobel laureate, Toni Morrison, and directed by Oscar-winning Jonathan Demme, of The Silence of the Lambs and Philadelphia fame – opened in the US last October. Despite a lavish $53m budget from Disney's Touchstone Studio, an additional $30m for marketing – Winfrey graced a dozen magazine covers, including Time and Vogue – good reviews and the undoubted power of the film, its box office returns were dismal: Beloved reached only No 5 on its opening weekend, making a paltry $8m. After a month, it had grossed only $21m.

This tepid response has provoked gloom among African-American film-makers, not least because Beloved follows in the wake of Steven Spielberg's slave-ship mutiny yarn, Amistad, which grossed only $44m the year before. The fear is that if neither Spielberg nor Winfrey can draw the crowds, then studios will now balk at funding serious dramas not just about slavery, but also any whose themes touch on race or that feature black characters, even. Winfrey, whose daytime presence has been a hugely influential force in assailing racial barriers in the US, finds the reception to what she terms her Schindler's List 'very sad and very disappointing. I will never do another film about slavery,' she says flatly. 'I won't try to touch race again in this form, because people just aren't ready to hear it.'

She bought the film rights for Beloved after reading the novel in one sitting when it came out in 1987. That same evening, she says, lacking Morrison's phone number, she rang the author's local fire department asking them to pass on a message that she wanted to talk. As Morrison has recalled, 'She said, "I'm going in my pocketbook and write a cheque." It reminded me of myself: a single black woman who said, "I'm doing this, it's going to be hard for me, but that's beside the point." She was deadly serious.'

Dedicated to the '60 million and more' slaves, the novel marks the beginning of Morrison's trilogy on African-Americans and their descendants who fled north following emancipation in 1865 – to Ohio in Beloved, to Harlem in Jazz (1992) and to Oklahoma in Paradise (1997). Spanning the pre civil war era right through to the 70s, the trilogy traces their tortuous roads to freedom and the persistent psychological aftermath of enslavement. Based on a true-life fragment of a runaway slave named Margaret Garner, who tried to kill her children rather than see them recaptured, Beloved is set in the 1870s, with pre-war flash-backs to the 'Sweet Home' Kentucky plantation from which Sethe, the Garner figure, escapes – only to be haunted by the past and the choices to which it drives her. Unlike Amistad's grand stab at history – with its dubious thrust that one mutiny sounded slavery's death knell in the land of the free – Beloved's focus is on how individual characters felt and struggled, remembered and tried to forget.

'Never before had I read a book that allowed me to feel the experience of slavery and reconstruction so personally,' says Winfrey. 'It was the realisation that reconstruction was not so much a physical experience as a spiritual and psychological one. Each person in that period had to reconstruct their very being. You had to figure out, what is your soul. Who are you as a free man, as a free woman, with free will? How do you begin again to construct your life? That just fascinated me.

'Sethe's courage was demonstrated a million times and more by many men and women who managed to cross over to the other side, from slavery to freedom. The relevance in terms of my own life is that I am a descendant of slaves. And to come from no voice, no power – economically or otherwise – and to be able to achieve what I've been able to achieve means that only my own personal vision holds me back, that anything's possible.'

Winfrey was born in Mississippi on January 29, 1954, her name accidentally transposed on the register from the Biblical Orpah. Her parents were unmarried, and she spent the first six years of her life on her maternal grandmother's farm near the segregated town of Kosciusko. Her memories of childhood are mixed. 'I grew up not feeling loved,' she says. 'My greatest emotion of that time is feeling alone, but I felt special because I was such a good reader. I'd read and recite on cue, any time anybody passed by. In church people would say, "Whoooo, this child sure can read, this child is smart." So, all of my feelings of value and of being loved and appreciated came not from being nurtured by my grandmother or feeling loved by my mother, but from being able to read and perform.'

At six, she moved to Milwaukee, Wisconsin, to live with her mother, Vernita, and step-siblings. 'I'm in awe of the patience I see from real mothers.' She tells of recently watching her godchild being soothed by its mother: 'As a child, I would have been slapped upside the head, number one. Would not even have been allowed to feel cranky. I wasn't allowed to feel what I felt. I even remember getting whippings where I would cry, then be whipped some more for crying, and then, if I would pout afterwards, get whipped again – "How dare you sit there and pout." Well, you just beat me, and I'm now supposed to express no anger or emotion or feeling about the fact that I was beat?'

She has described the writer Maya Angelou as her mother in another life – they even acted together as a mother and grandmother in a television film, There Are No Children Here, set in the Chicago projects. 'I call her my mother sister friend, because she's all of that to me. If I'm in trouble, she would be the first person I'd call.' Angelou's trauma of being raped as a child, described in I Know Why The Caged Bird Sings (1970), mirrored Winfrey's own sexual abuse by family and friends between nine and 14. 'When I first read The Caged Bird, that's the first time I'd ever heard of something like that happening to another person. Maya was the woman who offered me a sense of hope and belief in myself.'

At 14, and headed for juvenile delinquency (her mother sent her to a juvenile hall where she was turned away for 'lack of beds'), Winfrey went to live in Nashville, Tennessee, with her father, Vernon, who 'turned my life around'. She won a scholarship to Tennessee State University for her oratory skills, and was crowned Miss Black Tennessee. 'I entered a lot of contests: first, I was Miss Fire Prevention, just as a lark, a sport, because I was the first black kid who ever entered – prior to the year I won it, you had to have red hair. And I won beauty pageants, not because I was the most attractive, but because I could always win on the question-and-answer period.'

At 19, she became Nashville's first black TV news anchor, and went on to read the six o'clock news in Baltimore, until she was 'demoted' to a morning chat show, People Are Talking. Then, in 1984, she moved to Chicago to take over an ailing talk show, AM Chicago, and within a month had knocked the legendary Phil Donohue off the top of the ratings. Renamed The Oprah Winfrey Show (and quickly syndicated nationwide), the show's success coincided with the 1985 release of Spielberg's The Color Purple (based on Alice Walker's 1982 novel), for which Winfrey was Oscar-nominated as best supporting actress for her portrayal of Sofia, the pugnacious foil to Whoopi Goldberg's put-upon Celie, who punches out her husband when he tries to beat her ('Girl child ain't safe in a family of mens').

That same year, Winfrey founded her own studios, Harpo (Oprah spelt backwards), and three years later set up Harpo Productions. She now owns not only her show and the studio that records it, but some 2m share options in its distributor, King World – 'Oprah reports to nobody but God,' one of her staff once said. It would be a tremendous wrench – and not least financially – if she did indeed end the show.

Winfrey has been described as the first person on US television to look like her viewers, and her call to soul-baring, seen in some circles as ushering in the therapy culture, has had cross-racial appeal among the women who are its chief audience (they send most of the 15,000 letters she gets each week). The show was saved from voyeurism not only by Winfrey's talents for listening and exuding sympathy, but by her broadcasting her own problems: she dieted publicly (famously, she once came on stage pushing a wheelbarrow of lard to illustrate her – temporary – weight loss), she revealed her rape at the age of nine and the infant death of her premature baby at 14, she told of losing her brother and friends to Aids and, in 1992, she announced her wedding to the former basketball pro Stedman Graham – which then failed to take place, although they are still together.

Yet her greatest decision, she says, was not to publish an autobiography that she had finished. 'I'm so thrilled that I didn't publish it. That was a turning-point. I was a great pleaser and, up until that time, I did everything because I wanted to make everybody happy. I was in the heart of a learning curve. I was still 237lb, and telling myself that I just liked fries. I hadn't even reckoned with why I did overeat. I stopped the book because I was cheating myself and would be cheating the reader.'

Graham was reported to have put his foot down. 'He wasn't in love with the book, but that's not the reason. He thought I told too much, but there's not one thing in that book that I haven't already told. To be honest, he thought my depiction of my mother was too hurtful.' As for writing one now, 'I honestly feel like I've said everything. On a daily basis, being on the air, 200 shows a year, I think people know me as well as they need to.'

Asked if she regrets living her life so much on air, she says, 'The only thing I ever regret is bringing up Stedman's name so much. Some people think that's some kind of longing I have to be married, but I just mention him because he's in my life, like Gayle (a close friend) is in my life, like my dogs are in my life.'

Winfrey has been moving upmarket for years, and she's taken her audience with her. Among her highly personal choices for the book club, on which the audience chats with the authors, have been Toni Morrison's Song of Solomon ('Sales were thunderous,' said Morrison. 'It sold more in three months than it had in 20 years') and Paradise, Ernest Gaines's Lesson Before Dying, Edwidge Danticat's Breath, Eyes, Memory and Ursula Hegi's Stones From the River – all of them literary novels. Harpo also produces successful television films and mini-series, such as The Women of

Brewster Place (1989), in which Winfrey herself had a part, Before Women Had Wings (1997), The Wedding (1997) and David and Lisa (1998), many of them based on books.

Mention of Jerry Springer – who is said in some quarters to have shunted Winfrey towards respectability by cornering the moral low ground – elicits a steely but voluble scorn. 'Jerry has absolutely no influence on me whatsoever. I've often said to my producers that you can't win any race by looking at what the other guy's doing. The moment you even take the time to look backwards is when you lose your place. The most you can do is decide who and what you want to be, and then get on with the business. I can't out-Jerry Jerry. I can only go deeper inside myself. So, the only influence, if any, that Jerry has had on me is that he's helped me to re-focus and decide more clearly who I want to be. I want to be the exact opposite of that – bi-polar. I have no judgment of it. I live in America – free country, free speech – and this time last year I was sitting in a courtroom being tried for speaking my mind, so I certainly believe in his right to do it. But it saddens me that so many people choose to see it. I think it's nothing short of vulgar. But, obviously, lots of people like vulgarity.'

While Winfrey's confessional, 'letting America know' TV was always more tutelary and reconciliatory, she admits to having had some retrospective doubts: 'You learn from your mistakes. The kind of show I was doing 14 years ago – confessional, confronta-tional television – was fine for its time. I have no regrets about exposing subjects that were once taboo (including incest, wife-battering and date rape), but I have some regrets about particular shows. We did one about adultery – a husband who cheated on his wife confessed to her that his mistress was pregnant, and his wife, the look on her face, she was so shocked, embarrassed and shamed that I started to cry for her, and I couldn't take it back because we were live. After that, I went into my producers' office and said, "That should never happen." You should not have to come on television and be publicly shamed and humiliated. The people who go on Jerry Springer, however, know what they're in for. For a lot of them, this is their 15 minutes of fame, their big, bravado moment. They don't know any better.'

Last autumn, Winfrey launched the weekly Change Your Life TV, a move from self-exposure to self-help. Though ratings have been low so far, it may well be a shrewd bid to tap the huge market for self-improvement books and videos. Make the Connection, for example, a fitness manual co-authored with her personal trainer, sold 2m copies, while her former cook, Rosie Daley, made publishing history by shifting 6m copies of In the Kitchen With Rosie. Besides giving air-time to self-help gurus such as John Gray (Men Are from Mars, Women Are from Venus), Winfrey herself has been shown meditating in a candlelit bubblebath, a move that drew particular flak from the Christian right for veering into New Age spiritualism.

It's a claim she denies. 'My aim is to get people to think about their life and how they choose to lead it. It doesn't really matter to me if you worship Buddha, Jesus or don't worship anything at all, if you meditate and say a mantra, or just sit in silence. I believe the ultimate journey is inward, and if I've learned anything in life it's that you really only have control over yourself. Complaining about what the world is doing, what your neighbours are doing, even what your husband is doing, doesn't change anything. The only change comes with your willingness, your choice, to change yourself. Some people claim that to be New Age, to me that's just life. It's common sense. And I now constantly say, because I've been so misinterpreted, "Oh, so we're supposed to meditate and everything's supposed to be better?" It's not one thing – no, meditation isn't by itself going to change your whole life. Keeping a gratitude journal for the things you already have, exercising or eating right aren't going to change your life if you still have bills to pay and a husband who doesn't love you. It's the process of looking inward, of constantly working on yourself so that you can be better for other people.'

Winfrey's philosophy that 'intention rules the world', that if you want strongly enough nothing can hold you back, is a neat adjunct to the American dream. She supplements it with philanthropy – she makes donations to numerous colleges, and founded the Angel Network to spur viewers to take up voluntary work – although her failed projects such as Families for a Better Life (with which she supported a handful of Chicago's poor, and which was ambitiously pitched at 'destroying the welfare mentality') may be a pointer to the limitations of her individual-centred approach.

Yet, while many Americans who have 'made it' seek to 'give back' to their 'own' communities, Winfrey has always been more inclusive, and more influential. 'What we do on a daily basis, just by the fact that I'm a black woman – I own the show, I own the studio from which the show is broadcast, I own the rights and so forth – speaks volumes about the possibility of what a black person, a black female, can do. I've always thought that introducing a black therapist, or a black father in a show about fathers who care for their children, showing people of different backgrounds expressing the same emotions, does more for improving race relations than, say, a show about the problems of black men. Because the point about breaking down racial barriers is to show that we're more alike than we're different, that all feelings, all pain, all joys, all sorrows, bear no colour. The reason I've been successful is because I focus on the commonality.

'An American interviewer said that he'd never have believed 14 years ago what I could possibly have in common with a white suburban mother in Oregon. Well, we want the same things. Everybody thinks it's defined in material things – "Oh, if I had a big house" – when, ultimately, what you want is contentment, a sense of fulfilment. For many people, it comes from their children, carpooling. For me, it's my career.'

Winfrey's journal of her time on the set of Beloved has been turned into a book, Journey to Beloved, with Ken Regan's sepia photographs. Stripped of her studio glamour – she lost 20lb to play the part ('Jonathan [Demme] said, "You have a fine body, but it's too big for period costume"') – she is almost unrecognisable as 'iron-eyed' Sethe, whose proud, closed heart is the antithesis of the verbose empathiser. As Toni Morrison puts it, 'Oprah cries; Sethe doesn't.'

To prepare for her role in a film that runs to almost three hours, Winfrey re-enacted part of the Underground Railroad, the perilous escape route once used by slaves fleeing the South, during which she was first blindfolded, then threatened and called 'nigger gal'. 'I'd initially done it to try to feel what it would be like running in the wilderness, not knowing how to find your way. But, out in the woods, what hit me was that the physicality was minor compared with the emotional and spiritual devastation when you know your life is owned. When I first read the book, I thought Sethe didn't have to try to kill her children, I thought there could have been some other way. But, after the Underground Railroad, once you hit that psychic space, you know slavery is a living death, because you have no free will, no choice. Sethe says, "I got my children out. It was the first time I did anything on my own, thinking for myself." Just that, what it meant for her – boy! She realised, "I can do it." Maybe that was her first sense of self-esteem.'

The film accords with Winfrey's sense of mission to spur people to an awareness that they have the freedom to shape their own lives. 'Power comes out of powerlessness,' she says. 'Look at people who had nothing but their own spirit, their own soul, to build on. They had zero, and look at the power they had. And now look at your own life, look at yourself, and feel the power. Because all our ancestors are a bridge to this moment.

'I always intellectually understood that you would have to be mighty strong to endure and withstand that constant degradation and humiliation and still call yourself a man. What it takes to do that is extraordinary, and beyond anything that any of us alive has ever had to deal with. And what Paul D [Sethe's lover] tells her, "You your best thing", is my motto for life that I try to carry to everybody on TV, to make people see that for themselves.'

Little wonder that the film's low audience has left her feeling bruised. 'After Beloved came out, white people said, "I don't want to be made to feel guilty", and black people said, "Why do we need to look at that again?" So, I feel, people are not ready. There's so much shame still attached to slavery in the States. We're in a big denial about race, and about where we've been and where we need to go. The whole country needs therapy.' Some evidence of that denial emerged last year, when DNA tests proved that Thomas Jefferson had fathered at least one child by his slave Sally Hemings. Winfrey's reaction was to bring together black and white descendants of Jefferson, but what ought to be an obvious fact of ancestry seems to have given many Americans trouble in relation to their founding fathers.

Beloved's box office troubles aside, Winfrey has also suffered some bad press of late, in a perhaps predictable backlash against the success that now distances her from her audience. Professor Patricia Williams of Columbia University, who gave the 1997 Reith lecture, senses that an 'unfair critique of Winfrey as a controlling cultural figure, a touchy-feely healer, eclipsed the movie'. But Winfrey remains defiant. Asked how the film might play abroad, she says, 'I come with no expectations. It's a ghost story, a love story, a historical saga, a spiritual odyssey, and Britain and Europe might be able to look at it for what it is, a piece of art, a masterpiece – because you don't have the ghost of American slavery. I don't say that modestly, because there's no reason to be modest. Nothing will I be as proud of as Beloved.'

In the meantime, she is putting a lot of her effort into Oxygen, a cable network co-founded by herself and aimed at women. 'It's supposed to start on January 1 2000, and we've got to hire 289 people, so trying to build a network from scratch has got me kind of busy. For the past 14 years, I've been dealing with women and their untapped economic power: they control the television sets, they control what's bought in this country and what's not. I've been interested in helping women use that power more wisely. You can do that on a daily basis if you have your own network. You can take every idea you ever had and put in on TV. Doesn't work? Take it off, try something else. You have no ratings, nobody bossing you around.'

The approach sums up Winfrey's pragmatism and willingness to take the public temperature – coupled with a genuine desire to use television as a medium for change – that are so crucial to her success. 'One article said: "'Oprah's lost the golden touch". Well, I don't think I have a golden touch, or any kind of touch. Every project, you start out and you do the work, and you hope that it's received well and that people appreciate it as you appreciate it. It's about trying to follow your own instincts. Sometimes, you're right on with the public, and sometimes you're not. I don't know anything golden about that.'

As for her plans to use her immense power as a producer, 'The whole power label is so foreign to me. I think the only power that happens is your own authentic power. And one of the things Beloved taught me was that until you own yourself, are defined by your own terms, operate from the centre of yourself, are not dictated by other people's definitions and expectations, then you are still enslaved. You're enslaved to what society thinks you should do.' Clearly, Winfrey will be making her own future.

8 November 1999

The promises feminism made, and broke

BELL HOOKS

When I walk out the door of my old tenement building, I step into a world of incredible affluence, a world that is straight and gay, hip and stylish, and increasingly all white and well-to-do. There are no signs that read White Only. Yet when I go to the deli, I am asked whose girl am I or who I work for. Or, when I ask a black woman for a bit of washing powder in the corner laundry, she tells me the lady she works for measures each cup. Her apology is laced with shame. These days, no one in the US wants to talk about class.

Long ago, anybody who wanted to make it as a writer dreamed of coming to New York City, of inhabiting spaces where great writers lived and worked. That dream was a difficult one for women to fulfil – the struggle to come to voice, to find the room of one's own, to produce, to publish. I live in Greenwich Village, where Margaret Mead, Audre Lorde, Dorothy Parker and a host of others once made their homes.

It was as a young poet struggling to find her voice that I entered the feminist movement and was swept away by the glorious revolution that promised to change our lives forever. Living here, I daily face the triumphs of feminism (one being my own presence here as a successful writer) and see its harshest failures.

The feminist movement we dreamed would change the lives of all women for the better has had little impact on the lives of masses of women. It has most positively changed the lives of well-educated women with varying degrees of class privilege. Thirty years ago, most of those women were white; today they come in varying shades. But as their class power has increased, and with it their acceptance into mainstream, male-dominated worlds, they have abandoned all concern for women who are working-class and poor.

Sometimes when I am on these streets, I feel I am in the old South, in the affluent world around me, dark-skinned nannies tend the children of the mostly white women who are 'liberated' – free to have careers, to stay out all night, to pay someone else to do the dirty work of childcare and housework.

The professional women feminism liberated are, for the most part, not interested in the disenfranchised females who must remain subordinated if they are to be free. They do not want to be reminded that we did not end patriarchy, that feminism has become more cool lifestyle than real politics. They see no connection between their fate and the lot of masses of women who daily enter the ranks of the unemployed, the poor and the disenfranchised.

We live in the country that proclaims it has given the world 'the' vision of women's liberation, yet when the white supremacist patriarchal capitalist government attacks single working-class mothers and daily dismantles welfare, the voice of feminism is barely heard. No feminist activists called for us all to take to the streets to defend the rights of working-class and poor women who are one pay cheque or welfare payment away from dire poverty and homelessness. No one wants to talk about poor women giving birth to babies they do not want and cannot support because abortions are fast becoming a luxury. Yet the state will sterilise a poor woman any time, at no cost to her. Feminism has not been looking out for these women or looking at them. Like all the poor in the United States, they are invisible.

There are more than 30 million citizens living in poverty in this nation. A vast majority are female. Yet the 'power feminism' of today ignores their plight. There is no door-to-door education that takes feminist thinking out of elite colleges and off the theory page to tell folks, especially women, what it's all about, how and where they can join, learn and transform their lives.

Most women work outside the home and inside, are paid less, do the childcare and housework, have little sexual satisfaction and stay in their place because they do not see any place else to go. Feminism promised to show them the way. That promise has not been fulfilled.

2000s

The choice, it seems, is that you can be represented by your gender or by your colour, but it is simply too much to ask for both. It feels like I'm being asked: Which would I rather lose, my sight or my hearing? And for black women it's an all too common feeling.

Hannah Pool

Trailblazer of feminism

Interview: Sheila Rowbotham, a pioneer who got lost in the 80s but is being rediscovered by a new generation

Melissa Benn

Sheila Rowbotham's study is exactly that of the absent-minded writer. There is no overt order, no stern clearing for the author at work. Every corner and shelf is stuffed to overspilling with books, papers, magazines. While most of her life has been spent scraping a living from teaching, political projects and research grants, it has in recent years become somewhat more financially and professionally settled: for the past five she has been a research fellow at Manchester University and was recently appointed as a reader. But home – in a Manchester suburb – is still the place she likes best to write, even when there are two televisions blaring.

In T-shirt and dark trousers, the trademark red hair in a neat cut, she does not look anything near her 57 years. According to one friend there is now just the touch of the grande dame: 'She is very conscious of her intellectual territory, she does not take well to being maligned.' There is something extraordinarily still, almost stubborn about her, especially when crossed. She has never developed a hard shell in relation to public life – critics have been known to receive letters literally splashed with Rowbotham's tears of anguish. But she is also giggly, loquacious, radiant.

In her youth an intensely serious sexual libertarian, a socialist with an interest in everything from religion to rock, the pretty young historian was perceived as a potent mix of Marx, Methodism and Marianne Faithfull, a mix old friends still refer to. In one early incident, Jean-Luc Godard wanted her to walk naked up and down stairs while he filmed her speaking 'words of emancipation', a request that the modest Rowbotham refused, on the characteristically prosaic grounds that her breasts were too big and floppy for 60s fashion.

She has been called the most underrated feminist of our time, a ghost at the feast of the politics she helped create. To many, it is a mystery why she is not a more famous feminist, like Germaine Greer or, to a lesser extent, Juliet Mitchell, elder stateswomen who are endlessly consulted and quarrelled with, praised and provoked. Sally Alexander, professor of modern history at Goldsmiths College, London, says: 'Sheila is not a media person, but in other ways she reminds me of Germaine Greer. Both are scholars and writers, although Greer was never part of any political movement. But they are both deeply radical.'

Like Greer and Mitchell, Rowbotham emerged in the early, heady days of women's liberation. Like them, she is a pioneer who has not merely survived but reinvented herself many times over. Rowbotham, in particular, had an enormous impact on her generation: her early books, dense texts that explored women's neglected role in radical history and the dawnings of a new consciousness, had a profound influence on the emerging movement.

And then something happened. Rowbotham didn't stop writing, but the ideologies and reference points that had both sparked and buoyed up her work slowly dissolved. Women's liberation became feminism, a quite different politics that soon splintered into a maelstrom of competing arguments and identities. Thatcherism individualised women's quest for change, gave it shoulder pads and selfishness. When the Berlin Wall came down in 1989, official socialism lost its last shred of moral and economic power, taking the elaborate critiques of unofficial, libertarian socialisms with it, at least for a while. What happened to Sheila Rowbotham was what happened to socialist feminism: both were suddenly considered unfashionable, dull. Nobody in the broadsheet-reading classes thought it relevant any longer, all this intense utopian questing after the lives and lore of the working class, especially women, this earnest desire to fit together the jigsaw of socialist and feminist aspiration.

But that Yorkshire stubbornness which refused Godard's seductive request has never disappeared. In the intervening decades, Rowbotham has carried on writing about history and politics, capitalism and change, personal and public life, in that idiosyncratic style which mixes the solidly empirical with the almost dreamily theoretical. As a result, she now stands as one of feminism's great chroniclers, an accessible writer about complex social movements and significant moments of social and economic transformation.

Her output has been prodigious. Since the late 70s she has published a long essay on feminism and socialism in Beyond the Fragments, a biography, a book of interviews, two volumes of collected essays, a play, an encyclopedic history of the birth of radical movements, and a study of modern feminism in action, as well as articles, talks, even poems. A Century of Women, her monumental history of women in Britain and America in the 20th century, was published in 1997. Promise of a Dream, a personal memoir of the politics of the 60s published this month, is her 17th book.

In the mid-90s she co-authored two books on women in the global economy, which took her to India. In Bombay she talked to unemployed textile workers establishing a new living feeding shift workers. In Gujarat she met street scavengers trying to organise cooperative rubbish collection. Street vendors, forced by police to pay them bribes, held a demonstration featuring the slogan 'Dignity and Daily Bread' – Rowbotham took it for the title of a book.

There are many ironies about Rowbotham's career. Sometimes maligned as the epitome of 70s feminism, her work has frequently failed to reach a wider audience, not because of some arcane polemicism but because of its very complexity, its attempt to connect women's struggles with changes in the economy and politics. A new generation of feminist historians and academics talk of her work with respect, but younger media feminists tend to ignore rather than dismiss her, partly because she deals with class issues rather than with popular culture. Her work was always about far more than Madonna or Margaret Thatcher.

It is hardly surprising that in The New Feminism, Natasha Walter focused on Greer, not Rowbotham, who hardly gets a mention. Greer's The Female Eunuch is full of certainties while Rowbotham's writing has, in the words of her friend Lynne Segal, 'an almost infuriating tentativeness'. She is an elaborate and poetic writer whose style works particularly well in the essay form. But lack of public attention has suited her. As a generation of academics have increasingly turned to questions of representation and identity, and a generation of female journalists investigate their own or other celebrity lives, few writers look any longer at what used to be called the bread-and-butter issues.

When future generations ask what were the campaigns and issues that occupied ordinary women in the late 20th and early 21st century, they will find the answer in Rowbotham's work. Here are the human and political tales of, among others, office workers in America, miners' wives in Britain, home workers in Bradford, cleaners in London, tenant organisers in South Wales, poor women in India. These stories now fill a unique space in our political culture.

The historian Dorothy Thompson, who has known Rowbotham since the mid-60s, says: 'She is one of the few people who has kept links with the trade union movement, with home workers, with adult education. She understands that that woman smoking quietly in the corner of the factory floor has a fight on her hands, keeping her kids in shoes. She sees her as a human being. That is why her work remains relevant, always pushing out frontiers.'

Rowbotham is nervous about Promise of a Dream. Even before its official publication, it has been attacked by Jenny Diski in the London Review of Books for its earnestness, its refusal of a mature, graceful disappointment at lost dreams. But, Rowbotham insists, she just wanted to tell it like it was: 'I got fed up with the way the 60s is misrepresented. I was on this radio discussion a few years back and either it was about revolutionary students or the Oz hippie world. But there was so much more than that. There was community and trade union politics, all the apprentices and dock workers, the kind of people I was teaching in adult education. No one talks about the working class in the 60s, but it was a ferment, all these barriers breaking down. And then there were important movements in art. It's funny now that people I knew vaguely in passing, like the artist David Medalla, have big books written about their work.'

Rowbotham was born in Harehills, Yorkshire, in 1943, the late child of elderly parents who already had a 17-year-old son, Peter. Her father, a trained engineer, sold pit motors on commission to the National Coal Board. Her mother was considerably younger than him, and was a stylish and affectionate woman who found the constraints and economic dependence of marriage difficult. 'She loved going to a big hotel and taking tea,' says Rowbotham, 'and wherever she was, a man would appear and light her cigarette.'

Rowbotham describes herself as 'a mistake. My mother had just come out of hospital after treatment for breast cancer and did not discover she was pregnant until it was too late. She tried to take quinine to get rid of me, but it didn't work.' Rowbotham loved her mother, but was forever clashing with her father, a political conservative 'who hated posh people. When people like Hugh Trevor-Roper came on television he would shout at the screen.'

At 10, Rowbotham was sent to boarding school in east Yorkshire, where she was very unhappy. But then: 'I began to read, and suddenly the words got to me and it was like a penny dropping.' A stylish and sardonic teacher called Olga introduced her to social history, taking her to look at archives where 'we could read about what people ate in the workhouse'.

Later, the teenage Rowbotham became a beat, doing her best to look the part in a big black sweater, tight skirts from Leeds C&A and lashings of eyeliner. Promise of a Dream records the agony and ecstasy of the late teens and early 20s: trips to Paris, first sexual encounters, worries about love, dependency, orgasm, clothes, hair, having the right – or left – views and attitudes.

At Oxford, she found the 'straight history' of Gibbon and Macaulay boring but was rescued by the iconoclastic historian Richard Cobb, who sent her off to meet some friends of his in Halifax. These turned out to be the historians Edward and Dorothy Thompson. They were nervous, Rowbotham records, about her arrival, fearing she was pregnant and abandoned by an older lover. Instead they found an intense young historian, keen to exchange ideas on politics and history. Dorothy Thompson remembers her as something like the comic character Tiger Tim. 'Richard Cobb used to call her that because of the red hair and because he'd seen her involved in some argument. We took to Sheila as soon as we saw her. She was very bright, inquisitive, very spirited, pretty, and charming.'

In the late 60s, Rowbotham began working on Black Dwarf, a revolutionary newspaper that attracted the likes of Tariq Ali, Robin Blackburn, Anthony Barnett and Fred Halliday. Sally Alexander met Rowbotham in 1967 at the flat of the writer and film-maker Clive Goodwin. 'My memory is of Sheila and I sitting on the floor at Clive's stuffing envelopes. She was very beautiful. She had this pale skin, large wide-apart eyes, always friendly and smiley. And she had an encyclopedic knowledge of the radical left.'

Tariq Ali persuaded her to try her hand at writing, which resulted in one of the first pieces ever written on women's liberation in this country, published in the centre of a special issue on women in Black Dwarf in early 1969. Writing the article, she says, was 'like reaching a clearing. I knew I must not write from received authorities on "women" but from my own observations and feelings. Suddenly all those scattered experiences could take a new shape.'

When, in her early 20s, her parents died, the young Rowbotham was drawn to powerful parental and intellectual mentors like the Thompsons and the magisterial historian Eric Hobsbawm, supervisor on her unfinished PhD, who has remained a friend for more than 30 years. Friendships, too, quickly became intense, and have proved remarkably long-lasting. The journalist Nigel Fountain, who lived in Rowbotham's rather chaotic Hackney house during the 70s, describes it as 'the most wonderful intellectual experience of my life. I can still see Sheila wandering in at three in the morning because she'd had an idea. The funny thing about talking to Sheila was that she made no distinction between people who were alive and people who had died 100 years ago.'

Promise of a Dream ends just before the first women's liberation conference, organised by Rowbotham and Alexander, at Ruskin College, Oxford. Rowbotham was prolific in the next few years. Women, Resistance and Revolution, Woman's Consciousness, Man's World, and Hidden From History were all written in the early 70s. It is hard, in retrospect, to appreciate how groundbreaking these works were. Woman's Consciousness, Man's World is a highly disciplined but subjective volume about love and longing, capitalism and consumption, sex and history, which moves easily from Marx and Betty Friedan to the lyrics of Cliff Richard's 'Living Doll'.

Now we accept the jumble of high and low culture, then it was an innovation. Hidden From History was clearly influenced by EP Thompson's excavation of unknown English popular movements: Rowbotham re-examined women's role in four centuries of radical history. Eric Hobsbawm says the work was pioneering. She 'mapped the ground for us', says Alexander simply.

As one of the first feminist writers, featured in the nationals, interviewed by Jill Tweedie on television about women, resistance and revolution ('the only thing my revolutionary friends who had been watching in a pub in Islington said afterwards was that my hair had looked nice and tidy'), the young Rowbotham was inevitably exposed. In her own recent memoir of early feminist activism in the United States, Susan Brownmiller records the intense pressures on these early stars. Publishers wanted them to write 'big books', or the same big book over and over again, while other women criticised them for taking all the glory.

Rowbotham says now: 'I wasn't good at being an individual star. I just didn't enjoy it. It was a strain living up to others' ideas of what I should be like. By temperament I love watching and observing.' Dorothy Thompson says: 'The marvellous thing about her is that she has never allowed herself to become a celebrity, which would have been easy for someone as intelligent and sparky as she.' Rowbotham remembers 'getting a bit tearful, having a bit of a breakdown, about my own role as an individual. But this collectivity also had a really positive side which offset all the suspicion. It was very confirming to have this sense of connection, it helped you do things you otherwise wouldn't do.'

By the late 70s, feminism was changing. Rowbotham remembers being at a socialist feminist meeting in 1976 'and someone started talking about careers'. The days of scraping by with a couple of days teaching were finally passing. Politically, feminism was breaking up, or breaking down, depending on your point of view. Lynne Segal, a long-time friend and now professor of psychology and gender studies at Birkbeck College, London, says: 'By the early 1980s, socialist feminism was no longer a sexy subject. It was considered dull. Also, anyone trying to gain an overview of what was happening was declared suspect. The new was particularity, identity and difference, particularly ethnic difference.' Segal thinks that was an important shift, but that these changes too easily led to a 'sibling war of younger sisters against the old guard, which was kind of ridiculous in relation to Sheila, who has always been on the outside. No one was less a part of the old feminist establishment.'

Rowbotham was always radical, but never a radical feminist. According to her friend John Hoyland: 'She was always very, very tough in her feminism but it was tempered by this enormous heterosexual enthusiasm.' Rowbotham also rejected any essentialist theories about masculinity or patriarchy. 'I was influenced by existentialism, so I resist fixed definitions. When you try and put something into an abstract category, you distort its living reality.'

An avowed sexual libertarian, Rowbotham has never married. There have been, instead, a series of committed but often combustible relationships with significant men of the left. Promise of a Dream gives a poignant and often hilarious account of her relationship with a young Bob Rowthorn, now professor of economics at Cambridge. Thirty years on, it is not hard to spot the incompatibility of these two young radicals. Rowthorn was a keen athlete, a ferociously abstract and logical thinker, who kept his pencils stacked tidily in a jar. As Rowbotham records: 'He was not at all interested in my obsessive analysing of emotions and relationships.'

In the 70s she lived with David Widgery, the socialist GP and writer. Widgery had guest-edited Oz, the hippie underground paper, and, says one friend, 'while Widgery had brought politics to Oz, Sheila was trying to bring cultural and feminist politics to the left. So they met somewhere in the middle.' Nigel Fountain describes the relationship as 'tempestuous . . . they did feed off each other in terms of ideas, but there were a lot of slammed doors'. When Rowbotham left to have a child by Paul Atkinson, a young community activist, Widgery, says Fountain, was devastated. Friends say he never really forgave her, right up until his sudden death in 1992.

Rowbotham says now that she chose to have a child 'with someone who in no way resembled my father, or had his anger'. When her son, Will, was born in 1977, she joined 'a group of women trying to think about their fathers. I had this little baby boy and I felt I had to understand my reaction to my father as an individual if I wasn't to pass on some of those problems to him. I had to get a more balanced relationship in my memory.' When Will was five, Atkinson got involved with someone else, and Rowbotham lived alone until the mid-90s. She now lives with Derek Clarke, an assistant head and committed trade union and community activist. Will is now 23 and works as a librarian in London.

Like many on the left in the 60s, Rowbotham had given up on the Labour party, largely over Vietnam. But Ken Livingstone's GLC offered a new chance, as she says, 'to resist Thatcherism on a wider, more organised basis'. From 1983 to 1986 she worked at the GLC economic and social policy unit, editing a popular newspaper, Jobs for a Change, with John Hoyland. The GLC, she says, was 'libertarian but practical socialism. It distresses me that it is never talked about seriously but just dismissed with a sneer. We tried to work with people on the ground, community organisers, local groups. And so much has since become common sense, like the idea that people with disabilities should have access to the tube.'

For her, personally, it was a happy period. 'It was true unalienated labour. I hate getting up in the morning, but I would be up and off to work at six on a Saturday morning. The Tories on the GLC simply couldn't understand this enthusiasm. They even thanked us for our work.' When the GLC was finally abolished, Rowbotham, supporting her young son, thought she would turn her hand to freelance journalism, 'but by that time, I was a no-no. It just got harder and harder for me in Britain.' In the late 80s she got RSI: 'I was immobilised for several months and for over a year couldn't handwrite for more than a few minutes. For two years I couldn't type on a computer.'

From the late 80s, searching for income and some political support, Rowbotham began to lecture in Canada and the United States and then did research for what she jokingly calls the 'Global GLC', the United Nations University based in Helsinki and Maastricht. From this period dates her work on new forms of economic organisation among poor women in non-European countries, Dignity and Daily Bread, and changing patterns of employment in the developing world, Women Encounter Technology. Both books were written with the academic and activist Swasti Mitter, who had read Rowbotham's work in the late 60s but did not meet her until the mid-80s.

'What I learned from Sheila is that truth lies in the detail,' says Mitter. 'You can talk about the tension between class, race and gender, but you understand it better if you convey it in the context of an individual or a community.' Mitter believes that while Rowbotham's work was tremendously important in Britain in the 60s and 70s, in the 80s and 90s it was talked about extensively in non-European countries. 'In these places feminism and socialist feminism are not only about body politics but about bread-and-butter issues,' she says. 'Women in Mexico, India and Malaysia will know about Rowbotham and her writing.'

In many ways, the publication of Promise of a Dream brings Rowbotham full circle. Politically, she says she sees a lot of similarities between the 60s and now – 'a new Labour government for the first time in a long time, this same uncritical attitude to modernisation, and a complacency about the inequalities of American-style capitalism. Class really does seem the unmentionable.' She was heartened by the anti-capitalist demonstrations in Seattle. She and her partner joined a sister demonstration in Manchester, but 'it was tiny and they all looked like schoolchildren.'

Rowbotham says she finds younger women mysterious and seemingly very confident, but is philosophical rather than disheartened by modern feminism. 'I find a lot of parallels with the 60s, where an unease about gender is expressed in cultural rather than political terms, and there's this laddish belief that we all shared that a woman can do and be anything. There's a dying down of feminism as politics. Marcuse said that women's liberation was a utopian movement and one can see elements of it still, although it is interesting how some of our original demands have been taken up and yet changed. We would never have believed, for instance, that women's refuges or women's studies courses could have taken such strong root, but they are much more disconnected now from any wider movement for social change.'

Rowbotham is finally enjoying a late flowering, a return of public appreciation. She has also benefited from the recent boom in popular history publishing. Her first editor in the early 70s was Neil Middleton at Penguin. ('Neil said that for someone who wrote so well he had never met anyone as unconfident about their work as I was.') She has returned to Penguin for her last three books.

Two women in particular have played a crucial role in her new success – her agent, Faith Evans, and her editor at Penguin, Margaret Bluman. Both recognised her political and historical significance but also saw her potential as a popular historian, an accessible writer possessing an enormous range and depth of knowledge, who could be repackaged in the best sense. 'The first review of A Century of Women that came in was by Naomi Wolf, then the hottest young feminist writer around,' recalls Bluman. 'It was the lead piece in the Times. The good reviews just kept flowing in. All this has brought Sheila in contact with a new, younger audience.'

Rowbotham is about to embark on a new study of women's theories on the organisation of work in the early 20th century. But history students still read the books from the early 70s, and the old work lives on in surprising new forms. Rowbotham tells how she was approached recently by a woman who was looking at Beyond the Fragments, written in 1979. 'She is active in the Palestine Liberation Organisation and they are trying to think anew about the connection between liberation movements and feminism. I thought that book was in the past, of no relevance now. It really pleases me that people are still finding ways to make use of my work.'

27 JULY 2000

Sisters of mercy

For 21 years, Southall Black Sisters have campaigned in defence of women jailed for killing violent men

MELISSA BENN

You wouldn't give it a second glance, this drab shop front in a silent suburban street. Press a buzzer on the side of the red door and you are in a dark but homely house, a warren of meeting rooms and offices. There are toys out for visiting children, cake in the fridge. But the curtains of the front room are permanently drawn to deter brick throwers, death threats or irate husbands with sawn-off shotguns.

Welcome to a unique institution in British radical life, black life, feminist life. This month, Southall Black Sisters celebrated their 21st anniversary. 'Oh yes,' said a friend in instant recognition. 'They save women, don't they?'

It's easy to see what she means. Over the past two decades, Southall Black Sisters have mobilised some of the most public and poignant campaigns in defence of women jailed for killing violent or abusive men. When Kiranjit Ahluwalia was released from prison in 1992, after the court agreed she had killed her violent husband in a final act of survival, she came to SBS to say thank you. She couldn't believe her eyes, says Pragna Patel. 'When she saw that we were so few, she said, how do you do it? How does an organisation with such a big persona operate on such small reserves?'

One answer is commitment, sheer hard work. Southall Black Sisters have four full-time workers, three of whom are funded by Ealing Council, the fourth by a group of charities. Their small offices are cramped, the phone rings constantly. A thousand women a year come knocking on their door, many fleeing domestic violence and the problems it throws up: homelessness, benefits, racial violence, difficulties with immigration status.

'This is no ordinary nine-to-five job,' Patel says. 'The workers are so busy dealing with women during the day, the only time they can do their paperwork and administration is in the evenings or at weekends.'

In addition Patel, who has recently completed the academic stage of a solicitor's qualification, reckons she and the other committee members give to Southall Black Sisters 'between 50% and 70% of our working time, mostly unpaid'. What motivates these women is 'a sense of belonging, of confidence, a sense that here we are our true selves'.

Patel, 39, has been involved with Southall Black Sisters since 1982, but there is a younger generation coming up now, among them Anita Johal, 30. 'I came to Southall Black Sisters because I wanted to put in a wider context what had happened to me. I had done a masters in law in relation to race and immigration, yet I had been in a violent relationship myself. That was a cruel irony, to be theoretically studying the issues and yet, in reality, facing them. This job has politicised me, no doubt.'

Southall Black Sisters emerged from the 1979 clashes between anti-racist youth and fascists in Southall, the ferment that killed the white teacher Blair Peach. Black women's groups were springing up in many cities but according to Nira Yuval-Davis, professor in gender and ethnic studies at the University of Greenwich, SBS never drowned in what was once fashionable identity politics. 'They had enough of a grounding in their own position to be open to other feminists and to work towards shared goals and visions.'

As an example of this, she cites a 1984 demonstration outside the house of a young woman driven to suicide by her violent husband. Patel recalls how, after the first ever march through Southall against domestic violence, 'we adopted the methods of the Indian women's movement, by standing silently outside. A lot of the women were disguised as they had left the area already because of domestic violence. They were incredibly brave.' A white socialist feminist academic ran the creche.

Since then, Southall Black Sisters have worked with an array of groups to secure the freedom of women like Kiranjit Ahluwalia or Zoora Shah, the non-literate Muslim woman who, in 1992, murdered the man who had waged a campaign of physical and sexual terror against her. Shah remains in prison – Rahila Gupta, a member of Southall Black Sisters since 1989, is writing a play about her.

According to Gupta: 'We have always been under attack for washing our dirty linen in public, not just from traditional conservatives but from the black left in general. We are accused of fuelling racist stereotypes.' She pauses. 'This is the big question we are always asking ourselves – how to present a public face without being considered counterproductive.'

The question was particularly pertinent in both the Rushdie and Tyson affairs. Southall Black Sisters tried to find a political way, often at great personal risk, between what they saw as white racist stereotypes and a failure in the black community to examine honestly its attitudes towards women.

But public success and a changed political climate have brought new difficulties, Patel says. 'We were used to oppositional politics under Thatcher and Major. With Blair, there's a feeling that we should seize the moment and see if we can have a positive influence on the institutions.' One of their biggest recent successes was to get the government to drop the notorious one year rule, which left women newly arrived in this country, who had fled violent marriages, with no immigration status. Now such women are allowed to stay indefinitely.

The group is also often asked to talk to senior police officers about race and domestic violence. At one seminar, Johal says: 'They had to sit and listen to us for a whole day. Wonderful!'

The price of inclusion is not always so pleasurable. Having lobbied hard to make sure the working party on forced marriages consulted a wider range of women's groups, the Southall Black Sisters member Hannana Siddiqui resigned from the working party last month in protest at its support for mediation as a viable option for women in forced marriages.

Yuval-Davis says: 'Southall Black Sisters have come to represent some kind of ideal to black feminist activists. But I don't see them as unique so much as the better expression of a wider trend, a trend of self-assertion that has taken root in both the urban centres of Britain and globally. It is the kind of politics that was evident at Beijing where often the best organised groups were not led by western white feminists.'

Think global, act local. In their own community, 21 years may not have brought respectability but they have finally brought a measure of acceptance to this extraordinary group of women. 'In the early stages,' Patel says, 'the community was much more hostile. We would be hassled in the street, called prostitutes, home-wreckers and lesbians. But the community has had to acknowledge that we exist. They may or may not like us but they can no longer deny us.'

5 FEBRUARY 2001

'When the woman in the witness box began to cry, I cried too'

Police believe David Mulcahy may be Britain's worst serial rapist – we hear from one of his victims

DIANE TAYLOR

Court No 1 at the Old Bailey is crowded. The trial of David Mulcahy for multiple rapes and murders is drawing to a close. The crimes of which this man has been accused are so grotesque that members of the jury have been visibly shaken by the details. The air prickles with anticipation about the imminent verdict.

In the public gallery, Mulcahy's friends and foes alike are breathing a little faster. He looks relaxed in the dock, scribbling furiously in an A4 notebook. With his glossy, mousy hair neatly cut, his cheap grey suit and bland face, he could easily be a middle manager from M&S.

In one corner of the gallery, a woman fixes the defendant with a stare. Jess (not her real name) is writing too. She is deeply absorbed in the trial because Mulcahy is the man to whom she says she lost her life.

Mulcahy's friend John Duffy was jailed for murder in 1988. Ten years later, he confessed to other, similar offences and implicated his old schoolfriend in many of them. On Friday, Mulcahy was given three life sentences for murdering Alison Day, 19, from east London, Dutch schoolgirl Maartje Tamboezer, 15, in Horsley, Surrey and Anne Lock, 29, at Brookmans Park, Hertfordshire. He was also convicted of seven rapes and five attempted rapes, in what was called the worst series of rapes and murders this country has ever witnessed.

Jess was raped by Mulcahy in 1983, slap bang in the middle of a rape spree the men described as 'going out hunting'. Mulcahy has not been charged with raping Jess, although she went straight to the police afterwards. A police doctor collected forensic evidence and prescribed her the morning-after pill, then she heard nothing. Four years later, police invited her to an identity parade where she picked out Mulcahy – but again she heard nothing.

When the case was reopened in 1998 following Duffy's confession, Jess thought the details of the crime against her would at last be aired in court. But in July the Crown Prosecution Service told her that in her case there was insufficient evidence for a realistic prospect of conviction. The forensic evidence from the night of the rape had not been passed on by the police. So Jess sat discreetly in the public gallery, conducting her own private cross-examination of Mulcahy.

'At first I was terribly nervous about seeing him and the first time he made eye contact, I just looked away. But I became bolder and started to stare him out. When he was questioned about identity parades, I stared really hard at him. He fumbled a bit and said that nothing significant had emerged.

'So many details of the rapes were identical to mine. When the woman in the witness box began to cry, I cried too, because I felt totally empathetic with her, even physically. The two men burned some of the women after they had killed them and soon after the jury were shown forensic evidence of charred limbs, I came out in a rash. When it came to the evidence about the murders and the box the rape victims had testified in was empty, I felt desperately sad.'

It was in July 1983 that Jess was raped. She was a gifted arts student about to complete her university degree. She was walking briskly down a south London street at around 11pm on her way to visit her boyfriend when a man asked her the time. Twenty yards further down the road, another man grabbed her from behind, placed his arm around her neck and held a knife to her back.

In a state of terror, she was dragged off the road and down on to a piece of land next to railway sidings. 'He held me against a wall, blocking me with his body. My attention was focused on the knife and all I could think of was that I was going to die. The attack was obviously premeditated and I had a sense of leaving my body. In a situation like that you can't scream and you are immobilised because your body is flooded with adrenaline.'

Instinct told her to keep talking to the man. He said to her: 'My name is Dave and I've never touched a woman before' – the same eerie remark he made to other victims. A kind of surreal small talk was established between them and at last Mulcahy loosened his grip. At this point Jess tried to escape but he came after her, more aggressive than before, and dragged her along to another piece of ground before swiftly, angrily, raping her.

Like Jess, many of the victims were dragged along the ground during the men's 'hunting' session, in a sick parody of cavemen trapping their prey.

'I know feminists say rape is about power and not about sex,' Jess says, 'but I think that's simplistic because these men objectified everything and chose their victims very carefully. And it's rubbish to say women have fantasies about rape. There was nothing erotic about that podgy, thick, dirty, beer-smelling man forcing himself on me.'

After going to the police, Jess decided she just had to get on with her life. 'I kept telling myself that I hadn't been murdered, I hadn't been mutilated, and I should just think of the whole thing as a one-night stand. I remember telling a friend about it soon afterwards in a very upbeat way, insisting chirpily that I wasn't going to be a victim.'

In terms of recovery, that was the worst possible thing to do. 'I had some very damaging therapy sessions, first with a woman who gave me internal examinations to see if I had a phobia about having things stuck up my vagina, then with a psychologist who advised me to go out and have lots of flings and take risks with sex. I now know that what I should have had was a period of bereavement, with no sex at all.'

Underestimating the impact of the rape in the early days has been very damaging for Jess and she gets angry when she sees men reading the titillating details of rape cases in the tabloids. 'Men generally don't understand that being raped takes the victim's life. Mulcahy had children. I'd have loved some but I have none because I have no partner. Although I had successful relationships with men before the rape, I have not been able to have any since.'

Jess has discovered more helpful therapies since her initial disastrous experiences and some healing has taken place, but she still feels unable to get emotionally or physically close to a man, and even has avoidance strategies to stop herself getting too close to friends, family or colleagues. She is now a successful professional but says: 'I feel maybe I would have been more successful if it hadn't been for the rape. Somehow it has held me back from going after the things I want in my career. I'm more inclined to do what others want me to do.'

It is almost as if her innermost energy is being perpetually sapped by the attack. 'If a friend phones me, I don't always return the call. I can't manage that leap of energy to make a connection with people. If I go to a party, I'm happy to dance but I don't want to talk to people I don't know. In some way all this has affected my language, too – at times I just lose words. And if I come across someone I feel is more powerful than me, I can't bear to be in the same room as them.'

Her outwardly confident, cheerful persona belies the inner desolation. 'For a while I had terrible dreams about half-dead, rotting animals. A friend of mine who had also been raped [by another man] had almost identical dreams.'

But Jess doesn't want revenge on the man who raped her. 'I feel grief rather than anger, grief for the loss of my own life, for the loss of the other victims' lives and for the outcome for the rapists. What a mess for all of us who have lost our lives.

'Even in the beginning I didn't really feel anger because I could see that this man was in a disturbed state. I have wept a lot, but particularly hearing the details of deaths and mutilations in the trial, the whole thing feels almost beyond anger. Being raped means the end of your life as you knew it before. From that moment on, things are radically different and part of that is about a lost innocence. I think that's a feeling all women who have been raped share.'

She has applied to interview Duffy and Mulcahy in jail – she wants to hear them talk about the rapes and the murders to make them real. 'I need to have that sense that these events really happened, rather than having them just a suppressed memory. Watching Duffy give evidence and confess to everything in court, I believe he really has changed. He seems to be utterly truthful and no longer has anything to lose.'

At one point, Jess's job took her inside a category A jail to work with violent offenders, including rapists. 'I stood up in front of them and said: "I'm a rape victim and I believe in forgiveness." One of the men stood up and said: "I want to say that I know I did wrong and I am sorry, I regret it and I hope I never do wrong again." One by one, all the other men stood up, too, in a strange kind of solidarity. The feeling was incredible. All of them were able to be honest about themselves in a way you only can when you have gone beyond ego. These men need to be taken out of circulation but a therapeutic environment is what they need to heal so that we, their victims, can heal too.'

1 SEPTEMBER 2001

Stitched up

What happens when a power feminist becomes a parent? For Naomi Wolf, it meant the birth of two children, rage at the way women are treated – and an explosive new book

KATHARINE VINER

When Naomi Wolf gave birth for the first time, nothing happened the way she thought it would. She arrived at the hospital at 3am, when an angry nurse sent her into the toilet to stimulate her nipples – supposed to encourage stronger contractions. Within minutes, the nurse pronounced that her cervix had not dilated enough and the baby was in distress. She was rushed to a delivery room. Hooked up to a foetal monitor, she was forced to lie on her side. Drugs were dripped into her veins to increase dilation. She was offered an epidural and, in pain, took it: her partner was not allowed to hold her, yet she was told that if she flinched while the six-inch needle was pushed into her spine, she would be paralysed for life. Everybody watched only the foetal monitor, not her. She could not feel her legs. She was told that if she didn't deliver in 24 hours, they would operate – she was terrified and her labour stopped. The surgeon cut her open – she retched as she felt a violent, numb tugging. A baby was lifted out – Wolf lay naked and freezing. She heard the surgeon say, 'I need to get this small intestine back in.' With her abdomen still split open, she was unable to hold her child. She saw the reflection of the closing-up operation in the glass doors opposite. She saw a group of people, up to their elbows in her body, 'an open cauldron of blood'.

This was no scandalous one-off, as Wolf was to discover, it was an 'ordinary bad birth', suffered by millions of American and, increasingly, British women every year. But it had a revolutionary effect on this mother. Naomi Wolf , author of the bestselling feminist book The Beauty Myth, importer of American-style power feminism, controversial adviser to Al Gore, white wedding dress-wearer, the radical feminist who looks like a beauty queen, 'the sunny, shiny face of feminism': when she gave birth, things got ugly. 'Pregnancy, birth and motherhood,' she says, unequivocally, 'have made me a more radical feminist than I have ever been.'

We meet at Woodhull, a women's retreat in upstate New York. Today, she looks like an ordinary weekending mother-of-two: her usually voluminous hair is tied up, she wears black shorts, sandals, a maroon vest that doesn't quite hide a slipping pink satin bra strap. Her eyes are the colour of her sapphire engagement ring. Her voice is silky, but she is furious. 'I feel absolutely staggered by what I discovered after giving birth,' she says. 'Birth today is like agribusiness. It's like a chicken plant: they go in, they go out.'

The scandal of the medicalisation of birth is not new; from the 1960s, activists such as Ina May Gaskin and Sheila Kitzinger have fought against the interventionist tide that sees birth as an illness, rather than part of a woman's 'wellness cycle'. But it is a scandal that has reached extraordinary proportions: in 30 years, the caesarean rate in Britain has more than trebled – one baby in five is now delivered this way. (The US figure varies from 50% for healthy, middle-class women in their 30s and 40s in private hospitals, to between 1% and 15% for those in public hospitals.) Of course, Britain is different from America in that the market does not rule healthcare – US hospitals get a $1,000 bonus for every epidural requested. But the story is absolutely relevant here, with doctors under increasing pressure to avoid litigation, a severe shortage of midwives, the increasing popularity of elective caesareans for women who are constantly told that vaginal childbirth is traumatic and terrible, and the threats of private interests entering the health service.

It is not only birth that has shocked and radicalised Wolf: it is pregnancy and motherhood, too. She claims that throughout her pregnancy she faced 'the medical establishment's sheer contempt for women's right to know', and was given misinformation, conflicting information or little information at all. Men would comment on how big she'd got. ('Nice to see you,' said one, ' . . . so much of you.') She, meanwhile, was mourning the loss of the independent, free-spirited young woman she had been and realising, as so many women do, that 'true revolution' would come about only when society had restructured itself 'radically to support babies and new parents'. In other words, the world was a liberated place for young women – until they had children, when all of that changed.

After birth, she suffered a crippling depression, which she tried to escape by walking, compulsively, around the streets at night. She noticed, very soon, that the expectations of her generation were not going to be fulfilled: high hopes of combining work and home, both partners working flexibly and sharing the childcare. She was acutely aware of a 'radical social demotion' and a sense of 'statelessness', made stark by the lack of value she felt was attached to the work of parenting. And all around she saw the egalitarian relationships of her peers collapsing into stereotypical gender roles, difficulties and rows. As she says, her politics had rebalanced around her belly.

Naomi Wolf is now 38, author of four books, mother of two children. She grew up in an 'egalitarian paradise' in the hippy Haight-Ashbury district of San Francisco, with liberal parents ('My mother was reading The Second Sex in the delivery room,' she has said). Her father was an English professor, her mother a graduate student; she has an older brother, half-sister and half-brother, the common thread being their father.

Much of what we know about her life we know from her books. At school, she had anorexia – as she wrote in The Beauty Myth (1990), 'My choices grew smaller and smaller. Beef bouillon or hot water with lemon? The bouillon had 20 – I'd take the water. The lemon had four; I could live without it. Just.' Her doctor said he could feel her spine through her stomach. The book – which was written, curiously enough, in Nicolsons Restaurant, the same Edinburgh cafe in which JK Rowling wrote the first Harry Potter – was a massive bestseller around the world, 'the most important feminist publication since The Female Eunuch', according to Germaine Greer. Wolf was accused of being derivative because many of the ideas had been rehearsed before but the accessibility of this powerful polemic undoubtedly brought to a new, younger generation feminist ideas about how 'images of female beauty [are used] as a political weapon against women's advancement'. Wolf was also accused of hypocrisy, for being the 'anti-beauty cutie' who criticised the beauty myth while employing its tools. (If she had been plain, she said, that would have been used to attack her, too.)

Her childhood was studious but, post-anorexia, she was a lively Californian teenager – after a variety of boyfriends, including one who hit her, she lost her virginity at 15. As she wrote in her 1997 book Promiscuities, 'Martin and I could have been a poster couple for the liberal ideal of responsible teen sexuality – and, paradoxically, this was reflected in the lack of drama and meaning that I felt in crossing that threshold.' Wolf won a scholarship to Yale to study English literature, a Rhodes scholarship at Oxford and then she moved to Edinburgh to live with a boyfriend, published The Beauty Myth and became a sensation.

Her books have always reflected her life; her second work, 1993's Fire With Fire, took on the subject of female power just as she was realising that she had some herself. It looked at why women became alienated from feminism in the 1980s, criticised its tendency to glorify victimhood and poked gentle fun at the right-on excesses of some kinds of American campus feminism (at one of her lectures, a student asked her whether the very act of writing a book was itself exclusionary to women who couldn't read). Her alternative was a glossy, can-do brand of 'power feminism', of pay rises, achievements and kicking ass.

She got married in 1990 to David Shipley, an 'egalitarian, nurturing man' who used to work for Bill Clinton and is now deputy national editor of the New York Times. As she wrote in Promiscuities, she wore a white wedding dress, and said it was a way of women returning once more to the times when we were 'queens of our sexuality . . . When we are swaddled in the white satin of the formal bridal gown, we take on for a few rare moments a lost sexual regalness.' All of this caused controversy, and conster- nation – even if she thought these things, was it politic to say so? But the biggest bomb was, undoubtedly, an article about abortion, 'Our Bodies, Our Souls', published in the New Republic in 1995. A pro-choice campaigner, Wolf wrote: 'Clinging to a rhetoric about abortion in which there is no life and no death, we entangle our beliefs in a series of self-delusions, fibs and evasions . . . we stand in jeopardy of losing what can only be called our souls.' Wolf claims she was trying to show that, even though abortion must be a 'legal right', individual women (herself included) may still have moral or emotional difficulties with it. And that, at its best, feminism must always be 'faithful to the truth'.

It caused a furore – critics rounded on her for her semi-religious language (our souls, the furies) and for threatening abortion rights

– and it appeared to give succour to the enemies of feminism. The Daily Mail trumpeted: 'How pregnancy turned a feminist against the sisters.' This makes her angry: 'I'd like to say to the Daily Mail that it made me more radical than ever.' So that's down to Rosa, six, and Joey, 20 months.

'I think that America and Britain hold mothers in contempt,' she says, expanding on her theme that it's not just women's bodies that are under attack, it's women's lives. 'I think there is lip service paid about how important motherhood is, but the actual labour of mothering is seen as next to cleaning restaurants. It's underpaid, undervalued, disrespected. Just look at a playground. What do playgrounds say to women? They say: "You know what, just fuck you! You haven't anywhere to change dirty diapers – fuck you, deal with it. You and your babies don't count enough for us to put in the plumbing. Are you going to sit for hours under the boiling sun? OK! Because you don't count. This work doesn't count." It's not even the physical discomfort that matters – it's the slap in the face about the status of the work you're doing.'

In the book, Wolf lays out a 'mothers' manifesto' – ranging from flexitime for mothers and fathers to turning playgrounds into 'true community centres' and founding neighbourhood 'toy banks'. There needs to be a radical mothers' movement, she says. 'Politicians feel very comfortable using mothers and children rhetorically and strategically, without actually having to answer to representatives of mothers sitting at the table.'

So why don't they have a political voice? 'Well, the first answer is that we're exhausted!' she laughs. 'But second, the most powerful interests are stacked against us. For instance, when motherhood is cast as your private problem, and the work/family conflict is seen as your lifestyle issue, and if you can't balance it, there's something wrong with you as superwoman – then that's very handy for the business lobby, which is hand-in-glove with the Blair government in your country and the Bush administration in mine.'

In a brilliant section in the book, Wolf shows how 'Machine Mom' – the 'ideal of the superfunctional mother/worker, who is able to work at top capacity up to the due date, takes one to three months off to deliver, nurture and bond, finds top-notch child-care, and returns to work' – is nothing more than a product of the market. 'Who are the beneficiaries of Machine Mom?' she asks. 'Not women, not kids.'

The third reason for mothers' lack of a political voice is ideological: 'If motherhood is defined as that which gives and gives and never says, "Help me with this", then you're a bad mom for saying, "Yo, salary!"

'I think women should have it all, and so should men,' she says. But the phrase shouldn't mean what it has come to mean. '"Having it all", as it is defined now, means working full-time and having a family – someone's going to pay the price somewhere. I think we need to evolve as a society in which men and women have balanced lives as workers, partners and parents, and a real community life. This is the big no-brainer conclusion at the beginning of the 21st century: that if you give it all to the marketplace, people become cogs in the wheel and everyone suffers.'

In the US in particular, there is a shocking level of institutionalised discrimination against mothers who want to work: the only maternity leave is unpaid, just 12 weeks – 'and even that was a 12-year struggle. Bush Sr said that if you had this, capitalism would collapse. It was one of the first things Clinton introduced in 1992.' Britain's maternity policies are, she says, 'right in the middle. They're worse than Norway, Denmark, Sweden, Italy – better than Greece, Spain. In Germany, they have three years, but it's not gender-equal. I don't support laws that say women get time off and not men, because that designates them as the caretakers.' As examples of good policy, she points to China, where both parents get six months and can choose how to allocate it, and Canada – over 90% of pay for more than a year.

Much of Wolf's analysis is a criticism of the market's role in medicine; the corrosive effect of a free-market economy on something as fundamental and necessary as healthcare. It has resonances with other recent books by feminists, such as Stiffed by Susan Faludi and No Logo by Naomi Klein, which have looked back to the anti-consumerist roots of feminism with the view that an out-of-control market harms all ordinary people, and women the most. Has Wolf turned against the market? 'Well, no, I believe in equipping women so that they're not disempowered in the market economy, and I do believe that social democracy is the best system,' she says. 'In this book I'm using Marxist tools to analyse social organisation: looking at who profits, whose incomes would be jeopardised by change. But that doesn't mean I'm a Marxist, because I'm not.'

She certainly isn't – there was a media frenzy 18 months ago when Time magazine revealed that Wolf had been paid $15,000 a month to advise the Democratic presidential candidate Al Gore. The magazine claimed that Wolf was telling Gore he should escape his 'beta-male caste' and adopt a 'reassuring wardrobe palette in order to heighten his attractiveness to women' by wearing 'earth tones', greens and browns. The story was leapt upon by everyone from the talk show comedian Jay Leno to Vanity Fair magazine, which labelled Wolf 'the Lady Macbeth of this drama' (the Clinton/Gore relationship). 'Most of what was reported was an urban myth, complete fabrication,' says Wolf now. So where did it come from? 'The Republican National Committee, of course! I did make one of the remarks, which was taken out of context. I made the point, which was not rocket science, that a presidential candidate has to roll out a vision, whereas a vice-president has to support the president. I used the journalistic shorthand of these two roles as alpha and beta males – it was a kind of joke.' Wolf was, in fact, an adviser to Gore on women's issues.

This was not her first encounter with Democratic politics – Wolf had previously worked for the Clinton strategist Dick Morris, who was caught with a prostitute in the 1996 campaign and had to resign. 'We don't need to go after people for their personal lives, just for their ideas,' she says. 'People have weaknesses, people have failings. I don't think it's anybody's business.' For Clinton, too? 'No. Absolutely not. I'm proud to say that I was one of the first feminists to take a line against 'our guy' – because it was a work-place issue. Meritocracy is so important, and if you're rewarding your staff on the basis of sexual favouritism, that is corrupting.' It was quite a turnaround for the woman who, in 1993, had declared, 'I am a Clintonite feminist.' 'The Clinton administration was exciting at the beginning,' she says now. 'Finally, some of the things we cared about were being addressed.'

So, then, why did Gore lose? 'You mean, why did he win so narrowly that he lost?' she laughs. 'I think he had a very tough job running in an environment that was about being mediagenic – and he's a guy who's full of stature, full of great ideas, who's not particularly mediagenic. He was running after the most medi-agenic president since Kennedy, and against someone who is as shallow and callow and devoid of ideas and depth as you can imagine, but who actually plays well on television, and plays to American sentimentality.'

But Gore was, Wolf says, good on women. (No wonder – she advised him.) 'I believe his agenda for women was a really historic agenda. I was honoured to bring the concerns of women to Gore's table, I'm sorry that he didn't win and the controversy was worth it for me.' Much of the controversy focused on those earnings. 'I make no apologies for my salary,' she says. 'I am absolutely enti-tled to it as a professional. The reporters should have done some work to find out what men at my level in that campaign were paid. Because, guess what? Hello! They were paid more!'

Why, then, was Wolf the only one, among all Gore's advisers, who was picked on? 'Oh, that's too easy,' she says. 'Any woman who is a visible feminist gets criticised. Gloria Steinem faced 10 times worse than I did. I take responsibility for the fact that I take strong positions and go after vested interests, so fair enough.'

This tendency to take responsibility for what she provokes in others is an unusual trait and a powerful one, which has the effect of stalling her attackers. For example, the writer Camille Paglia once called Wolf 'the Dan Quayle of feminism – a pretty airhead who has gotten any profile whatsoever because of her hair', she called her 'a Seventeen magazine level of thinker' and a killjoy 'Little Miss Pravda'. And yet Wolf's answer to these bitchy attacks is mature and responsible. 'Yes, she was very personal with her attacks on me, but I was very personal with my attacks on her.' (Indeed she was. A scorching article she wrote in the New Republic labelled Paglia 'the nipple-pierced person's Phyllis Schlafly [a rightwing activist]' who 'poses as a sexual renegade but is in fact the most dutiful of patriarchal daughters', full of 'howling intellectual dishonesty'.)

The exchange with Paglia was, says Wolf, a 'turning point' for her. 'I did some serious soul-searching about what kind of life I wanted to lead; I asked myself if it was my task as a writer to level scathing personal attacks. I had a crisis because I thought, if I don't do that, then I won't have a career as a journalist, I won't go to any parties, no one will think I'm interesting. But I'm very glad I did it. It's about learning how to rebut an idea with respect for the other person. That's all.' Around this time, Wolf made a 'substantial personal commitment financially' to help set up the Woodhull retreat, where we meet – a non-profit institute that teaches young women 'the compassionate use of power'.

She can be terribly earnest – she says things like, 'I feel blessed with my subject matter' and 'I encountered an ethical challenge', and rather than ask if I'm Jewish, she wonders, 'Do we share an ethnic heritage?' But Wolf can also be sparky and funny; when asked if the penis was the enemy, she quipped, 'Hey, lots of women go home at night after a hard day's work thinking of the penis as their friend.'

In fact, she encompasses several contradictions. On the one hand, she is an outspoken, visible feminist and sophisticated political operator. On the other, she often says things that cause problems for feminists and glee for anti-feminists: such as when she writes that she felt it was 'dangerous' to be a feminist when her baby was young, because all that mattered was not to 'rock the fragile, all-important little boat of the new family' or discusses her white wedding dress or says that 'male sexual attention is the sun in which I bloom . . . the male body is ground and shelter to me, my lifelong destination' or says she has trouble with the idea of abortion, as she wrote in Our Bodies, Our Souls. When I ask if she would have written such an article now, with Bush threatening abortion rights, she says, 'Yes, I would, because I believe it is true, and I believe you have to tell the truth as you see it without bowing to situational ethics. A feminism that is not based on women speaking their truth simply won't accomplish its goals – or if it tailors the truth to meet even the most laudable goals, it will not be worth getting there in the end.' (She adds that she would put a strong frame around the essay, addressing Bush's threat to abortion rights and ending with a detailed strategy and call to arms.) In other words, she believes in honesty – even if that honesty can be used by your opponents. It is a risky tactic.

And take a look at her life: it looks un-radical, encompassing all the tradition and convention of a white wedding, two children, a high-earning media husband, house in the country. Why does she write how important it is that women have certain rights, while maintaining a personal distance from those rights herself? 'The reason for this difference has to do with the very definition of feminism in my mind,' is her response. 'To me, feminism is not a rigid set of given positions, an agenda, an ideology. It is far more radical than that: it is a premise of freedom. When the premise of freedom takes hold for women in the world, then every woman will have the right to make her own choices according to her own wisdom and conscience, and those choices will not be monolithic.'

Which all sounds very well, but how long do we have to wait? 'Well, before, I wanted the world to change in, say, 30 years' time,' she says, pushing back the hair from her face. 'Since I had my daughter, I want the world to change before she is 21. Before she is 10. Tomorrow. Yesterday.'

25 MAY 2002

Abortion: still a dirty word?

JULIE BURCHILL

Last week, my boyfriend and I saw our friend's baby for the second time. The minute I saw the baby, I fell, in every way possible, fell down on the floor and babbled at him for an hour and a half, finally to be rewarded by that singular finger-gripped-by-tiny-fist routine and that priceless gummy smile. Then I went home with my boyfriend and watched EastEnders, from which I learned that having an abortion renders a woman 'cold and empty' for ever more (Dot) and that even giving up a baby for adoption wreaks havoc with one's mental health (Sonia). I just knew that there was something in my back pages that I was supposed to be remembering now, probably 'wistfully' and preferably tearfully, and just a little cerebral prodding shook it loose. My abortions! All five of them.

Exposure to Polly's breastfeeding, followed by Dot and Sonia's breast-beating, should by rights have launched me into a right royal depression, or at least a bit of 'bittersweet' brooding over my barren terrain. But – and I examined my psyche closely for signs of self-delusion here – all I felt was happy to be home, alone, with my boyf.

But I didn't want to seem like a smug cow, so I said tentatively, 'Isn't Louie gorgeous?'

'Bloody lovely – and he certainly liked you.'

'I love babies,' I said, surprised at the simplicity of my statement. And then immediately, perfectly naturally, 'I'm so glad I had all those abortions.'

Now, I know this is an unusual statement to make. Even East-Enders, which is ceaselessly condemned by the Daily Mail as being irretrievably 'PC', has an amazingly censorious attitude to abortion. Think of key scenes featuring Carol, Bianca, Natalie, not to mention Dot's life sentence of sorrow. Yet I remember, as a child in the early 1970s, hearing Diane, the waitress heroine of the decidedly reactionary soap Crossroads, saying matter-of-factly to a miserably pregnant woman, 'Abortion's not a dirty word, you know!'

Where did the recent creeping foetus fetishism come from? And how do we – excuse the phrase – get rid of it? Some of it must be blamed on Tony Blair's bowing of the knee to Rome. Cherie Blair can call herself a feminist all she likes, but any feminist worth her salt would have made a point of having a termination – on the NHS, naturally – when she got knocked up the last time. Wantonly giving birth to a fourth child on a planet buckling under the strain of over-population certainly isn't any sort of example to set for gymslip mums, who can at least plead ignorance and rampant fertility.

Me-Ism – psychiatry, psychoanalysis, any sort of navel-gazing – has to take part of the blame for the demonisation of abortion. The idea that everything we do or have done to us stays with us for ever is a reactionary and self-defeating reading of modern life. No doubt if you're the sort of lumbering, self-obsessed poltroon who believes that seeing Mommy kissing Santa Claus 30 years ago irrevocably marked your life, you wouldn't get over an abortion, as you wouldn't get over stubbing your toe without professional help. But you choose to be that way, because you are weak and vain, and you think your pain is important. Whereas the rest of us know not only that our pain is not important, but that it probably isn't even pain – just too much time on our hands.

The Good Birth lobby has to take some of the blame, too. Whenever a pop star has a caesarean, there's always some milch cow who calls herself a feminist popping up to tut-tut to the Mail that anyone who has the nerve to reject the blood, sweat and tears of natural childbirth (not to mention the honour of ending up with a vagina the size of the Channel Tunnel) is some sort of dysfunctional Barbie doll-wannabe, concerned only with the symmetry of her sex organs. Of course caesareans are 'unnatural' but so is anaesthetic – would we seriously say relieving pain during any other life-threatening medical procedure robs the patient of a valuable experience? What a load of old eyewash!

The ever-growing emphasis on the inherent integrity of the 'natural', no matter how well-meant, adds to the demonisation of modern abortion, which is nothing if not highly technical medical intervention. (When it's any good.) To be consistent, the anti-caesarean 'womanist' should also be against the legal medical termination of unwanted pregnancies, favouring a return to the old days when 'wise women' fed terrified girls dodgy roots and left them to get on with it.

In a recent Mori poll for the British Pregnancy Advisory Service, only 7% of those asked about abortion declared themselves totally opposed to it, yet it remains the last taboo. Famous women would rather admit to having been sexually abused as children than to having had a termination – Cybill Shepherd and Barbara Windsor are the only ones I can think of who refer to theirs with good-humoured straightforwardness. 'No woman takes abortion lightly,' even the valiant pro-choice spokeswomen have taken to saying, not realising that they are adding to the illusion that abortion is a serious, murderous, life-changing act. It isn't – unless your life is so sadly lacking in incident and interest that you make it so.

Myself, I'd as soon weep over my taken tonsils or my absent appendix as snivel over those abortions. I had a choice, and I chose life – mine.

1 JULY 2003

What women want

Equal pay for equal work is a noble demand, so why does feminism seem so embarrassing these days?

ZOE WILLIAMS

The Equal Opportunities Commission publishes a new report tomorrow. It has rather a broad reach, but its main points are that women earn less than men and, furthermore, undertake the lioness's share of domestic chores – not because we are forced to, but because we choose to. It's only natural; having cash in our pockets ruins the line of most quality garments and, besides, why do you think we have smaller feet? So we can get closer to the sink (oh, the old ones are always the best – I'll tell you why dogs are better than girlfriends in a minute*).

If this doesn't sound terribly equal, nor, for that matter, loaded with exciting opportunity, don't blame the commission. All it did was assign the survey, which was undertaken by the Future Foundation, and contains a wonderfully mysterious quote from a Young Southern Woman: 'Every time I think of feminism, I just get this really awful feeling.' And that's all there is to explain the absurd claim that women 'choose' lower pay for the same work – to complain about it would be feminism, which is kind of icky.

Now, the word 'survey' is misleading, given that the sample was only 35. This is rather like Research As Conducted By Columnist ('I went to a dinner party, asked all my chums, and this is the way life is'). Its author, Sue Tubules, deals with this by calling it 'indicative' rather than 'representative'. Furthermore, its findings are shored up by similar surveys. Only last week, the Office for National Statistics found that six out of seven mothers would rather be at home, looking after the kids, than working.

Before we take all this to indicate the terminal decline of feminism, we should consider the possibility that it's an indictment of work. Domestic work and childcare have always had a low status compared with the fabled 'career' option, and feminism, rightly, undertook to redress this by storming the workplace. But truthfully, every job, however high-powered, is principally made up of talking to people who aren't really listening, and moving bits of paper.

Quite how this differs from tending children is unclear, except that you get paid for the first, and not the second. Since most pay packets (even before the 19% pay cut you get for having breasts) are cause for resentment rather than rejoicing, it's hardly surprising that thinking people are re-evaluating the nature of worthwhile toil.

But this isn't biological or natural, it has nothing to do with hormones or body clocks. It is, if anything, a neo-Marxist rejection of wasting one's finest years on employers to whom we are all completely interchangeable. I bet men feel exactly the same, only people rarely ask them whether they'd be happier doing childcare, and even if they were asked, they couldn't say yes, since it pleases the modern world to think of all men who like children as irredeemable perverts.

And yet, we're still left with feminism and the 'really awful feeling'. There is no doubt that people are, if not renouncing, certainly distancing themselves from this movement. Young women, according to the EOC 'survey', see it as dated and ball-breaking. The men involved see it as an excuse to marginalise the elderly (by which, one assumes, they mean elderly men) in the workplace. Speaking more generally (from a sample of my dinner party friends – this is indicative, not representative), young women no longer describe themselves as feminists, preferring 'post-feminist', which boils down to a trenchant demand for parity, while at the same time reserving one's right to wear push-up bras.

The women's movement has been castigated for more than its underwear choices: it is also the malign force behind boys doing badly in exams, behind the wider crisis in male identity, behind the pain of accidental childlessness (this theory is most rabidly advanced by Americans. If you're ever having a flat day and want to re-energise yourself with some heart-stopping misogyny, I refer you to Baby Hunger, by Sylvia Ann Hewlett, and The Miseducation of Women by James Tooley). Feminism has been reduced to one of two crude stereotypes: the humourless, lentil-eating battleaxe who won't swallow and the power-dressing, self-seeking career bitch who uses the movement to justify and advance her relentless amassing of cash.

Maybe there's a grain of truth in these, but they are irrelevant sideshows to the point of the movement, which was equality – not grinding down men, not edging them out of work, not missing our fertility window and whining about it, not making any kind of sartorial statement at all, and certainly not possessive individualism.

It was about rooting out an unfairness that was poisoning relationships at both a private and public level. It was about the power and (yes!) beauty of collective action. It was as noble and important as any other civil rights movement, and yet we seem to take no pride in it. We are crazy to disown it like some kind of embarrassing old aunt. If the workplace is a disappointment, that's not a failure of feminism, it's a failure of capitalism.

*Because the later you come home, the more pleased they are to see you.

6 NOVEMBER 2003

Brutal legacy of war in Congo

Harrowing evidence of systematic sexual violence against girls and women surfaces as fighting recedes

EMILY WAX

She walks slowly in padded slippers inside a hospital ward. Bohoro Nyagakon is a woman with gentle eyes and a frail five-foot frame, with a friendly five-year-old daughter playing nearby. She is waiting in this cramped room – with dozens of others – to undergo a harrowing procedure: reconstruction of her vagina.

Gang rape has been so violent, so systematic, so common in eastern Congo during the country's five years of war that thousands of women are suffering from vaginal fistula, leaving them unable to control bodily functions and enduring ostracism and the threat of debilitating lifelong health problems.

Around the world, cases of ruptured vaginal tissue are usually caused by early childbirth and seen in such African countries as Ethiopia, Nigeria and Mali, where brides as young as 12 are too small to give birth. What makes the fistula cases in Congo so jarring to medical professionals here is the large number of them caused by rape.

In the past few months, as a peace agreement has taken hold and fighting has slowed, the extent of the brutality has become evident, physicians say. There are so many cases that the destruction of the vagina is considered a war injury and recorded by doctors as a crime of combat.

'There are thousands of violated ladies showing up. It's like nothing we have ever seen anywhere in the world,' said Jo Lusi, head of a Congolese-run hospital in the eastern city of Goma that is working with the US-based aid group Doctors on Call for Service.

'We are here repairing an organ that is so important to women and to our country and to our dignity,' Lusi said. The UN Children's Fund is building a special ward at the hospital for women suffering from fistula and other effects of rape.

Village health posts are reporting far more cases than those arriving at hospitals, because journeys from the country's interior are long and difficult, according to healthcare workers at the British aid agency Merlin.

'I think we are addressing the tip of the iceberg because access to health care is so limited,' said David Tu, a doctor at the Bukavu branch of Doctors Without Borders-Holland. 'For every one case there could be 30 more in the rural areas that we aren't hearing about.'

Still, doctors say hundreds of women have arrived in recent months in Goma, Bukavu, Shabunda and several other cities in eastern Congo to wait for an operation that will deliver them from life as a village recluse – unable to work, or to have children or sexual relations. Many local women's groups have joined to help the women make the journey by foot through miles of jungle to city hospitals. Some patients go through three or even four painful operations – each requiring 21 days of bed rest. Each operation costs about $300 but is paid for through international donations.

In Congo, it is often said that women have paid the highest price in the war that began in 1998, pitting government forces against rebels backed by Uganda and Rwanda. Young soldiers from the dozens of factions that roam eastern Congo – wired on cocaine, drunk from palm wine – have turned rape into a primary weapon of war, as common as looting or setting light to a hut. Rape has even been encouraged by commanders as a way to gain control of such scarce resources as food, water and firewood, intimidating the women on a continent where women do nearly all the labour in the fields.

An estimated 3.5 million people in Congo have died in the past five years, mostly from disease and starvation. Rape has become so prevalent that some aid groups estimate that one in every three women is a victim. With Congo lacking a functioning court system, no one has been punished.

But there has been a remarkable response by women around eastern Congo, who at times have launched spectacular protests to bring attention to the issue.

In March, for instance, hundreds of women stripped naked in the center of Goma and challenged thousands of dumbfounded onlookers, mostly men.

'If you are going to rape us, rape us now, because this must stop today,' Mama Jeanne Banyere, head of the Federation of Protestant Women in Goma, recalled telling the crowd.

The women chanted that they would no longer accept rape. They demanded healthcare for women suffering from fistula, who were being abandoned by husbands and ostracised by the community.

'So many women have it and so many were raped. Some were even raped by men sticking branches and guns up their vaginas,' said Banyere. 'We couldn't just cry . . . We had to fight back.'

After the protest, the healthcare workers at Doctors on Call for Service moved quickly to find Congolese physicians who could perform the operations for fistula patients. They predicted in April that 50 such surgeries would be needed. Instead, they have performed more than 150 of the operations.

Inside a ranch-style complex of wards, 55 women are housed under white tents in what used to be the hospital's garden. Girls as young as eight and women as old as 73 sat on small wire cots wrapped in gray blankets donated by Unicef. All had been raped and were undergoing counselling for trauma. Some said they considered killing themselves after surviving multiple rapes. Some had puddles of urine under their seats because of their condition.

A vast majority of the women in the tents were waiting for operations, sometimes a second or third procedure. About 10 more women arrive each week, doctors said.

Nyagakon, 30, was waiting for her third procedure at the Panzi hospital in Bukavu, capital of South Kivu Province. The story of how she arrived here began on May 12, 2002, when rebel fighters demanded that she disrobe in her home. It was 8pm. She was eight months pregnant and had finished a long day of cooking and washing.

'Five of them came at me. I closed my eyes. They told my husband to get in another room and they held him down. They were shouting that they would kill him,' she said, looking down. 'Then they each had sex with me, five of them.'

After the rebels left, her husband carried her through the banana trees under the cover of darkness and onto a boat for the five-hour ride from her town of Niabembe to Kabare, a bigger town with a hospital.

In the middle of the night, the doctors had to cut her abdomen open and remove the dead foetus.

'Afterwards my mind was really gone,' she said, her eyes tearing. 'I was thinking how would I survive like this.'

Her husband, who teaches the Bible at a local church, took her home and was kind to her, she said. For that she felt lucky, because many husbands have left their wives after they were raped and suffered from vaginal fistula.

He could not help her, though. She stayed in bed for 10 months trying to survive the humiliation of a condition that often leaves women foul-smelling because of a tear in the bladder or the rectum. In some villages, women with fistula are told to sleep with animals. Finally, a friend of her husband from a women's group at his church told him of a place in Bukavu where she could have an operation. They left right away on the two-day journey.

Her first operation was unsuccessful – doctors said it was because she had suffered such severe ruptures to her bladder wall. The second, three months later, went far better. She can now control most bodily functions.

Nyagakon said she was encouraging other women to talk about what they went through. One woman in the hospital had been shot in her vagina with a gun. Some of the women are pregnant, others are HIV-positive. The hospital has had 897 rape cases since March.

24 November 2003

Buy your son a Barbie for Christmas

The desire to make little boys more masculine is becoming worse and worse. This can only spell bad news for women

Natasha Walter

I'm in Hamleys, walking through a dream of glitter and fluff and shine. Everywhere I look there is pink: Think Pink accessories, Disney Princess dolls in pink net skirts, Baby Chou Chou with her pink potty and, of course, the distinctive sugary tint of Barbie. After a while I go up to the next floor and it's as though a blue filter has been put over a camera lens. Everything pink has turned into the navy and green of Action Man and Crush'n'Smash Hulks. There are shiny things here but it's not a silky, soft shine – rather it is the hard-edged gleam of trains and cars and Armoured Deluxe Mega Battle Power Rangers.

I have a daughter, so there is no doubt which floor I am meant to be shopping on. It is so obvious that it hardly seems worth remarking on; there are toys for her and there are toys for boys. Yet when I was a child my mother took a classic feminist approach to girls' and boys' toys. She subscribed to Simone de Beauvoir's belief that 'One is not born a woman, one becomes one.' So my sister and I weren't allowed to have Barbies and we were expected to play with trains and Lego as much as our dolls. Sure, we were a bit unusual among our peers, but when I had a child of my own I expected that children's behaviour would have moved on from the 1970s, and that, say, encouraging boys to push a doll in a pram would be par for the course. But I quickly learnt that when it comes to where you shop for children's toys – the pink or the blue floor – the world can seem as divided as ever.

Tridias, a family-owned business that sells good-quality toys, produces a catalogue that shows little boys and girls playing with their wares. Flick through it and you will see photographs of girls playing with dolls' houses, dolls' beds, a microscope, a karaoke machine and dolls' prams. You see boys playing with bows and arrows, a car, a garage, a train set, a work bench and drums.

Sophie Coleman, the director of Tridias, is well aware that the catalogue promotes a traditional divide – and one that she herself is not very keen on. 'We have become more gender specific in recent years. Because it does make a difference with sales. You need to get a fast response from the reader to the picture, and you get that response if you show a girl with a girl-biased product. Personally I don't think that girls and boys do necessarily play differently. But I can see that parents want to make those choices for them.'

So we are all caught in this loop – parents respond to traditional marketing, and the traditional marketing gets more intense. Big brands such as Disney and Mattel are particularly astute in bolstering traditional values, even when they sound as if they are being progressive. When, last year, Mattel launched Ello – the pastel-coloured, curvy building range for girls – its resident psychologist, Dr Michael Shore, said, 'While "building" is generally associated with boys' play patterns, there are several ways that girls "build". Girls also "build" stories and characters with their traditional doll play . . . The Ello creation system . . . stimulates role play and storytelling in a way that is relevant to girls.'

In other words girls build with feelings, not with bricks. Indeed the new popularity of evolutionary psychology – the theory that men and women evolved different brain structures because of the conditions in which prehistoric humans lived – has made it harder to question the idea that boys and girls must play differently. One recent study, by Gerianne Alexander from Texas University, purported to show that vervet monkeys played with different toys – a ball or a doll – according to their gender, and this was then taken to be relevant to human children. 'There are certain aspects of objects that appeal to the specific sexes and these aspects may relate to traditional male and female functions dating back to the dawn of the species,' says Alexander.

But the problem with the theory that girls and boys must play differently is that it ignores the way that human brains are so plastic, especially in the early years, and that connections in the brain develop according to exterior influences as well as hormones. Vervet monkeys are of limited relevance to our children, because humans can both influence their environment and adapt to changes in ways that monkeys cannot begin to imagine.

Yet rigid theories of gender differences in our brains threaten to pathologise children who do not fit the boxes. Some specialists in transsexuality have suggested that over-identification with the other sex's playthings can be evidence of disordered gender identity. Dr Lyndsey Myskow, a sex therapist at the Royal Infirmary, Edinburgh, was recently quoted as saying that transsexuality could be picked up by the age of three. 'If girls are playing primarily with trucks and footballs, and boys with dolls and prams, then there is very likely a problem.'

However gentle the approach, such insistence on innate differences reinforces a lazy fatalism about how our children should behave. There may indeed be differences in the ways that girls and boys like to play. In any playgroup you can see boys building train sets or girls talking to dolls. But at the moment there is no way of telling how natural those differences are, as children's choices are put under such pressure by so many influences – including their parents. I asked a mother of two boys aged three and five, 'Do you choose particular toys just because they are boys?'

(Their playroom was the usual mass of trains, buses and garages, with a few brightly coloured animals thrown in.) 'Oh, no,' she said. 'Have you ever bought them a doll?' I asked. 'No, no . . . But they don't like them. Whenever girls bring dolls over here they don't know how to play with them. I remember David carrying one about by dragging it with one arm, and the little girl picked it up and cradled it.'

But then, when first presented with a doll, my own daughter seemed uninterested, and certainly started off by dragging it around by one arm. But her first sparks of interest in dolls were encouraged, while those of her male friends were being snuffed out. Because a boy's interest in girls' toys is constantly thwarted, even when it is quite clear that the interest is there. When my daughter takes her dolls' pram to the park, I can bet that a little boy will try to play with it. Whenever boys come to play with her toys, they seem inexorably drawn to the dolls' house.

The last time this happened, I was talking to the boy's mother about how bored one could get playing children's games. 'There is a limit to how much time one can spend dressing dolls,' I laughed. 'Oh, I'd love to spend hours changing dolls' clothes,' she said. 'Why don't you?' I said. 'I have a boy.' And that was that, though at that moment her boy was carefully putting my daughter's dolls to bed. But what are we doing when we encourage little boys to believe that playing with pretend babies is not for them – suggesting that caring is necessarily female? What are we doing if we dissuade them from acting out domestic scenarios, if not ensuring that they will always play second fiddle when it comes to housework?

Girls are currently less limited in the ways they are expected to behave, especially before they go to school. Although they may go through early life in a froth of pink, they aren't expected to turn away from mechanical toys and active play. Feminism has caused a huge shift in what we feel is acceptable feminine behaviour. Boys are far less free. The careful policing of the limits of masculinity seems to arise from a fear of effeminacy and homo-sexuality – even though there is no reason to assume that a boy who dresses in pink and loves his dolls will end up gay. 'There is generally an absolute terror of enabling boys to express a feminine side,' says Jenni Murray, author of That's My Boy!.

Of course that pressure does not necessarily come from parents. Many families who are relaxed about crossing these boundaries tell tales of how their boys chose dolls, pink things, frills and ballet – until they went to nursery or school. Anne Longfield, chief executive of the Kids Club Network, remembers how her son once adored playing out complicated games with Barbie dolls. 'But that stopped once he was at school. There is a lot of peer pressure, even if it is often implicit rather than explicit.'

The desire to preserve masculinity against incursions of girlishness from an early age seems to have become more rather than less entrenched over time. In the 18th century, little boys were allowed to be as girlish as they liked – if you look at Joshua Reynolds' portrait of the two-year-old Francis George Hare it is hard to believe that you are looking at a little boy, with his soft curls, silky dress and gentle gaze. It brings home how at such an early age boys are pushed into being little men, complete with grey-and-navy sportswear and shorn heads.

Perhaps we encourage our children to be so traditional because we live in a changing world, and we find it reassuring if we see that our children are not being too buffeted by those changes.

'The pressures on little boys and girls to behave traditionally are stronger than they are for teenagers and adults,' says Dr Becky Francis, author of Power Plays, and the mother of two young boys. 'Although when we grow up there is more acceptance of crossing over boundaries, little children are expected to slot into traditional roles. It is very important for them and for us that they take up a stable gender identity.'

Of course, many parents and teachers and children are eager to behave in ways that outrun these rigid boundaries. But as long as the pink and blue boxes are there, most children are being encouraged to fit into them, rather than choosing what suits them best at what should be the freest time of their lives.

It may sound absurdly old-fashioned to talk about equal opportunities in children's toys, but this is not some experiment that was once tried and failed, it is a change that is still waiting to happen. We could all start this Christmas: why not put a Barbie in your son's stocking – what are you afraid of?

22 MAY 2004

The sexual sadism of our culture, in peace and in war

The Abu Ghraib images have all the hallmarks of contemporary porn

KATHARINE VINER

I received some horrific photographs by email yesterday. Purporting to be from Iraq, they depicted the sexual abuse of women by US servicemen. On some, chadors were hitched up over the women's heads. On others, the women were naked while they were raped by groups of men. It is impossible to tell whether the photographs are real – those images we know have been seen by American senators – or faked. They make you sick to your stomach. And they look strangely familiar – like the XXX films in hotel rooms, like those 'live rape!' emails sent to internet users, like porn.

If the photographs are genuine, they are the visual evidence of the sexual abuse of Iraqi women – abuse which we already know is common, with or without these grotesque images. We know that such images exist, because a US government report confirmed it. And we know that Iraqi women are being raped throughout the country, because both Amal Kadham Swadi, the Iraqi lawyer, and the US's own internal inquiry say that abuse is systemic and widespread. We also know this because all wars feature the abuse of women as a byproduct, or as a weapon. The ancient Greeks considered rape socially acceptable; the Crusaders raped their way to Constantinople; the English invaders raped Scottish women on Culloden Moor. The first world war, the second world war, Bosnia, Bangladesh, Vietnam – where the gang rape and murder of a peasant woman by US soldiers was photographed in stages by one if its participants.

But even if the pictures are mocked up, it makes you wonder where the images came from. Some woman, somewhere, had to be raped, or make it look like she was being raped. The poses, the large numbers of men to one woman, the violence – they have all the hallmarks of contemporary porn. Indeed, there is suspicion that the photos are part of a gruesome new trend – the manufacture of films showing the rape of women dressed as Iraqis by men dressed as US servicemen.

There's a difference, of course, between the making of pornography for money and the photographing of pornographic poses as war trophies: the consent of the woman involved. But to the consumer of these images, there's no way of knowing if there's been consent or not. They look the same.

Modern porn has become increasingly savage. 'You're seeing more of these videos of women getting dragged on their faces, and spit on, and having their heads dunked in the toilet,' says even the pro-porn campaigner Nina Hartley. At the same time, the multibillion-dollar porn film industry, bigger than Hollywood, is widely seen as acceptable – just this week, the EastEnders actor

Nigel Harman told Heat magazine: 'I have always wanted to make porn, I think the industry is very underrated.' It is aggressively mainstream.

Nevertheless, right now the American pornography industry is in shock. Not only has the military stolen its thunder, with ritual sexual humiliations of its own performed for the camera, but also three performers have tested positively for HIV, which means that no porn films will be made for 60 days, until all actors are tested. So, in an intriguing quirk of timing, while the making of porn itself is halted, pornography is still being generated – by US soldiers recreating the images many will have seen at home.

Lara Roxx is 18, and arrived in California's San Fernando Valley, the capital of the US porn industry, only days before she contracted HIV. She had moved down from Canada with the aim of making quick money. She was infected while being penetrated anally by two men, simultaneously, neither of whom was wearing a condom. This act is the vogue in pornography today: condoms are rarely used, and the double penetration of a single orifice, whatever the physical consequences or limitations, is seen as hot.

Porn directors are devastated by the news of Roxx's infection. David Brett, chief executive of Passion Pictures, told the industry's website, AVN: 'I would be mortified if anyone got sick in connection with one of my projects. I have to sleep at night . . . I would never earn my living at the expense of some other human being's health and safety.' So now there is some discussion of compulsory condoms. But there is no discussion of how 'healthy' and 'safe' it is to brutalise teenagers in the name of entertainment.

Roxx's interview with AVN itself shows the fluidity of 'consent' in these matters. 'I told [my manager] I wasn't interested in anal at all, and I was a little freaky about the no-condom thing too,' she said. On arriving at the film shoot, she was pressured into performing the 'double anal' scene by the director, Marc Anthony. She says: 'So I get there and Marc Anthony tells me it's a DA, which stands for double anal. And I'm like, "What? I've never done a double anal". And he was like, "Well, that's what we need. It's either that or nothing". And that's how they do it . . . I think that sucks, because he knew double anal was dangerous.' Later, she says, she was in pain and could not sit down.

It is hard not to see links between the culturally unacceptable behaviour of the soldiers in Abu Ghraib and the culturally accepted actions of what happens in porn. Of course there is a gulf between them, and it is insulting to suggest that all porn actors are in the same situation as Iraqis, confined and brutalised in terrifying conditions. And yet, the images in both are the same. The pornographic culture has clearly influenced the soldiers at the very least, in their exhibitionism, their enthusiasm to photograph their handiwork. And the victims in both don't have feelings: to the abusers, they didn't in Abu Ghraib, to the punter, they don't in pornography. Both point to just how degraded sex has become in western culture. Porn hasn't even pretended to show loving sex for decades – in films and TV most sex is violent, joyless. The Abu Ghraib torturers are merely acting out their culture: the sexual humiliation of the weak. So Charles Graner and his colleagues can humiliate Iraqi prisoners because the prisoners are dirt, they can humiliate women, forcing them to bare their bodies and raping them, because that way they can show their power.

The annihilation of Lynndie England, while her superior Graner, clearly in control and already with a history of violence against women, was left alone, fits this story too. They are both repulsive, torturers – but she has been vilified for her involvement, while his is passed off with a shrug. Some women in the military – if they are not themselves being raped by male soldiers (in February, US soldiers were accused of raping more than 112 colleagues in Iraq and Afghanistan) – seem to have to prove that they are one of the guys by sexually humiliating the only people less important than they are: Iraqi prisoners, of whatever sex. It's a chilling lesson, that women can be sexual sadists just as well as men. Just give them the right conditions – and someone weaker to kick. It's proof that sexual aggression is not really about sex or gender, but about power: the powerful humiliating the powerless.

The real images of sexual abuse of Iraqi women, if they are ever released, will at once appear on pornographic websites. They will be used for sexual gratification. People are already joking that England (though not Graner) can have a nice little future career for herself in porn. Of course we are horrified by these images. But we should be horrified too by their familiarity, and how much they tell us about our own societies.

13 DECEMBER 2004

Two to the power of 2 million

We black women face a double whammy when it comes to political representation

HANNAH POOL

The debate about Labour's all-women shortlists makes for depressing reading if you are a black woman. As the Labour party decides how to fill seats left vacant by retiring MPs such as Tony Banks, one minute it's 'we need more female MPs', the next it's 'but not at the expense of having more ethnic minorities', the assumption being that all-women shortlists prevent others – namely black or Asian men – from being given a chance. But hang on a minute, what about me?

The debate goes eerily quiet, everyone looking to the floor with embarrassment, when the subject of black women, the least represented group of all, comes up.

There are just two black female MPs, both Labour (Diane Abbott and Oona King), of 13 black MPs, 119 women and 659 MPs in total. That's right, two. Given that there are well over 2 million ethnic-minority women in this country, that's an awful lot of representation left to Abbott and King.

The argument around shortlists has polarised two camps used to squaring up to each other: Labour women are, rightly in my book, arguing for more all-women shortlists. Meanwhile, black male commentators and groups such as Operation Black Vote (OBV) are arguing for open shortlists in areas where there is a high proportion of ethnic minorities, their thinking being that a black or Asian man might succeed against a white woman. But aren't both groups missing the point? Why are black women so appallingly under-represented? Surely, instead of trying to steal each other's seats and wasting their energies arguing across each other, they should come together and argue the case for more black women candidates? As it stands, pro-shortlist Labour supporters are falling over themselves to represent me as a woman, and OBV is standing up for my rights as an ethnic minority, but both shirk the responsibility of giving me what I really want: to see myself represented in the corridors of power in terms of gender and race. The choice, it seems, is that you can be represented by your gender, or by your colour, but it is simply too much to ask for both.

It feels like I'm being asked: which would I rather lose, my sight or my hearing? And for black women it's an all too common feeling. We are constantly either completely ignored or asked to pledge our allegiance – which matters to you most, your race or your gender? – before anyone will listen. If the debate is about women's equality, we are expected to agree with white women because they are women – if the debate is about race, we are expected to agree with black men. What I resent most about the current debate is that, once again, someone is making decisions on my behalf: Labour women are assuming I'd rather be represented by a woman, OBV is assuming I'd rather be represented by a black man.

Sure, both groups make the right noises about wanting to represent black women, but I have yet to see any evidence. 'In principle, there's absolutely no reason why an all-women shortlist shouldn't be used to promote black women candidates as there are lots of strong black women around,' Katherine Rake of the feminist Fawcett Society told BBC news this month. 'What this [lack of candidates] points to is the broader problem the Labour party, indeed all political parties, have in promoting black candidates. But it's not all-women shortlists per se which are discriminatory.'

All very laudable, but it would be much more believable were it not for the fact that since 1997 (and 50 selections using all-women shortlists) not a single black woman has been selected.

Meanwhile, some in the black community have started to complain that all-women shortlists are at the expense of other minorities – it seems that the idea of campaigning for more black women in parliament hasn't even occurred to them, or if it has, they'd rather sort the men out with some seats first. 'In a constituency which has more than 50% black and ethnic minority communities they really ought to also think about addressing the even-bigger deficit, which is the lack of black and ethnic minority MPs,' said Simon Woolley of OBV earlier this month. An even bigger deficit than two MPs out of 659? I don't think so.

How refreshing it would be if someone suggested that getting more black women MPs was a matter of urgency. What a difference it would make if just once the duality of black women's identity was seen as an electoral bonus, not as an irritation. No minority should be arguing against women-only shortlists: instead they should be arguing for themselves to appear on them. And, by the same token, the Labour party should look long and hard at its selection process and wonder why no black women get through. Or perhaps they should call it what it is: an all-white-women-only shortlist.

2 MARCH 2005

Life after birth

Breeding women may play havoc with the rota. But isn't it worth a bit of bother to keep a few of them in the workplace?

EMILY WILSON

When I got knocked up, I was told that thanks to crazy new European rules I was eligible for a year's leave. A year's holiday! Hah! I was staggered by my good fortune. Who cared if I'd only be getting paid for half of it – somehow I'd manage. After all, it wasn't just a holiday – it was also about spending a year with my baby-to-be. Or like, whatever. A year off!

A childless male colleague found the news of my year off hard to swallow. Why should I get a year off, half of it paid for, while he, if he chose never to breed, would never be given similar perks? Why was that fair? He was quite logical about it, and – dizzy as I was with my year-off plans – it didn't seem like an argument worth having.

Actually, you will be amazed to learn, my year off didn't have quite the gap-year vibe that I'd looked forward to. I spent the first three months of it in hospital. After that, I spent three months so entirely shattered from sleep deprivation that when visitors came round, I was sometimes too tired to lift my head from the sofa to greet them. Then a month after that I went back to work, five months earlier than planned, because it turned out that the first months of a baby's life aren't a great time to save money, and the money that was meant to last a whole year had been spent.

I wasn't ready, not by a long chalk, for the boy to be handed over to a stranger. And I wasn't ready to stop breastfeeding. But luckily, very luckily, my employers let me work from home part-time and, very luckily again, the baby's father was on hand to care for him while I worked. Which made it all extremely bearable, and a billion times better than the deal most British women get.

If my employers hadn't been so flexible (all praise to the Guardian), I would have quit my job, and the baby's father would have had to pick up the breadwinning baton. No big deal to the world at large, quite the reverse – another thirtysomething woman takes an off-ramp. But it would have been a big deal to me – I would quite likely never have got another staff job in newspapers. And of course there are an awful lot of women of breeding age taking off-ramps, which is why women are still getting paid so much less than men, and why there are so few senior women in the workplace.

The government's plans to increase paid maternity leave from six months to nine months sounds so eminently sensible that I'm rather astonished by them. Another three months of pay would have made a difference even to relatively-rich old me, never mind that it would only have been at the rate of £100 a week (rather than the 90% of pay that you get at the start of your maternity leave). The fact that, in the future, women may be able to hand over six months of this leave to their male partners sounds even more astonishingly sensible. Great for the fathers, of course, and for the babies, but also, if you're concerned about women being squeezed out of the workplace, really great for mothers – after all, the next best thing to being at home with baby, is baby being at home with daddy. Lots of women may even prefer it that way.

Would my childless male colleague approve of the government's plans? Probably not. Offices are all about fair deals for the individual, not about the greater good. But I realise now that it is an argument worth having. The bald fact is that if you object to the swing towards better maternity rights, you are basically saying: women can't have everything, so stuff them. And you are placing yourself in some rather unpleasant company.

Just last month 'female boss' Sylvia Tidy-Harris was bleating on in the Daily Mail about how she would never employ a woman under the age of 45 for fear of her getting pregnant – or even a woman with young children, for that matter, as she'd be far too distracted to do her job properly. ('I don't have the same qualms about fathers,' Tidy-Harris added. 'But I would check at an interview that any man isn't in sole charge of his children.') Yesterday Tidy-Harris was back at it in the Telegraph, describing the government's plans to extend paid leave as 'ludicrous'.

Tidy-Harris hangs her hat on the old damage-to-small-businesses chestnut, but basically she's no different than a man I know who works in the Foreign Office who says that he never employs women (other than as secretaries) because 'they're more trouble than they're worth' and play havoc with his rotas. People – there's still a fight to fight, and it's a good fight, and let's not forget it.

10 DECEMBER 2005

A year of killing

All the people featured on the following pages met their death in one
year at the hands of partners or ex-partners. The overwhelming majority
are women

KATHARINE VINER

Every woman on the cover of today's magazine was killed by her
partner or ex in one year – and yet how many of their stories do
we know? Few are reported in the national press, and we wanted
to discover who these people are, and what happened to them.
The list makes shocking reading.

Initially, there is the number. Up to 120 women are killed by
their partners each year. For December 2003 to December 2004,
the period of our research, we found 68 cases that had resulted
in convictions for murder or manslaughter, or in which the perpetrator had committed suicide (many cases are still ongoing, or have
yet to come to court). All those women, young and old, but mostly
young, smiling for the camera, their lives unlived, yet to be killed
by the men they may have loved.

Next there is the level of abuse most of the women endured
before death: years of violence, physical and verbal assaults, harassment, intimidation and bullying. Some of the men who killed
them were subject to restraining orders or facing charges of assault,
but the authorities didn't do enough to protect those at risk. There
are the ordinary situations that might explain upset, but not
murder: an affair, the suspicion of an affair, a misplaced phone

call, the woman's desire to separate. There are the murderers who kill their children too.

But perhaps the most shocking thing is the sentencing. Time and again, men who kill their wives get short sentences because courts believe a woman's infidelity, or even her 'nagging', is bound to provoke a husband to commit murder. A recently reported example is Paul Dalton's killing of his wife, Tae Hui. Dalton punched her, she died, then he cut up her body with an electric saw, and stored the pieces in a freezer. He was cleared of murder on the grounds of provocation; the judge said that he had suffered 'no little taunting on her [his wife's] part'. Dalton received just two years in jail for her manslaughter, but got three years for what many might consider the lesser crime of preventing a burial. He is appealing against the sentence.

Last month, new guidelines were drafted by the lord chief justice, Lord Phillips, which promised tougher sentences and said that nagging, or a man's discovery that his wife was unfaithful, did not justify a lighter sentence. But from the evidence we found here, the overwhelmingly male judiciary has a long way to go if it is to stop appearing to consider it understandable, or even reasonable, for men to kill their partners.

Here we list 68 women killed by men, two women killed by their female partners, and 10 men killed by women. The reasons men and women kill those close to them are very different. Women most often kill their husbands because they are themselves the victims of domestic abuse and can no longer cope – as in the famous case of the late Emma Humphreys, who killed her violent husband and was released on appeal. Or, more rarely, it's for money – the 'black widow' syndrome – or when a woman has a history of domestic violence towards her partner.

The much more common story is of men who kill their wives, girlfriends, lovers and exes, and many have tried to work out why. Men commit almost all violent crime in the UK – 90% – but why do so many kill their intimate partners? Defence lawyers and judges often claim that wife-killers are just ordinary men who snap in a moment of extreme provocation. But this is quite unusual: there is only a small number of men who murder their partners without having previously used violence against them.

Far more common in murder cases is a history of violence by the offender against the victim. This may not have resulted in a criminal record, as often domestic violence is not reported to the police or courts or even friends. On average, according to Canadian research, a woman is beaten 35 times before her first call to the police. Our list represents the tip of the iceberg: not all domestic violence ends in murder, and for every woman killed there are thousands more who suffer years of abuse – one in nine women in the UK are severely beaten by male partners each year.

In a new study, Professors Rebecca and Russell Dobash of Manchester University found that male murderers who used violence against their female partners tended to have more 'conventional' backgrounds than, say, men who murder other men – they tended not to come from difficult homes, or to have fathers who used violence against their wives. However, they were likely to have used violence against previous or current partners – they 'specialised' in violence against women.

Often, as is made plain from our evidence here, the state of the relationship is a catalyst for the killing. In many of the cases in our list, either the woman was in the process of leaving the relationship or it had already ended. This is considered particularly dangerous if the woman initiated the break-up and the man contests it. The months around separation from a violent partner are crucial.

'The thread that runs through this,' say Dobash and Dobash, 'is the man's sense of ownership of the woman, and his control over the continuation or cessation of the relationship.'

Indeed, men's power over women is at the heart of this

depressing story. Very often women are killed when they challenge that power, by trying to separate from their partners, or seeing someone else, or doing something that their partner doesn't want them to do. Perhaps we should not be surprised by the fact that two men a week kill their partners, when courts say that women can consent to sex while almost unconscious, when rape itself has a conviction rate of 5.3%, when twice as many men now visit prostitutes than a decade ago. Britain is not getting any safer for women, however many get to be chief executives.

Violence against women is mainstream – the British Crime Survey from 2004 shows that an astonishing 50% of all adult women have experienced domestic violence, sexual assault or stalking. (It was only in 1991 that it was made illegal for a man to rape his wife.) And we use euphemisms about domestic violence against women such as 'a row that got out of hand' and 'a volatile relationship', which make abusive relationships sound equal, just a bit of sparring. Press reports say, 'Police are treating it as a domestic incident', as if that makes it a lesser crime.

As long as there is a perception that violence between people who know each other is none of our business, and in fact is publicly acceptable, nothing will change. The actor Sean Connery said, 'Sometimes there are women who take it to the wire. That's what they are looking for – the ultimate confrontation. They want a smack.' (He claimed the quote was taken out of context.) Mike Tyson, the former boxer and convicted rapist who last month enjoyed a lecture tour around Britain, hit his ex-wife Robin Givens in the face and described it as 'one of the best punches I ever threw'. And the late George Best, lamented as a flawed hero in reams of tear-stained articles last month, said in support of fellow woman-beating footballer Paul Gascoigne, 'I think we all give the wife a smack once in a while.' He certainly did so himself.

So how much is our society colluding with this? When we lionise abusers, feel sorry for those who kill women who nag, and sentence men who've killed their lovers to paltry terms in jail, you have to ask: are so many women killed by their partners because society lets men get away with it?

Audra Bancroft, December 8 2003: Bancroft, 36, was murdered by her boyfriend, Gary Walker, a policeman, in their flat in Burton-upon-Trent. She was four months pregnant, and sustained more than 50 injuries. Walker, 40, was sentenced to life imprisonment in October 2004.

Geraldine Paxford, December 9 2003: Paxford, 53, a mother of two, sustained more than 100 injuries over two days of violence from her partner, William Barcock, 45, in Cowley, Oxfordshire. Barcock admitted hitting Paxford with a mug, pulling out her hair and breaking her ribs. He was ordered to serve a minimum of 13 years for her murder. Judge Hall told him, 'It wasn't the first time you attacked her. You had broken her ribs on a previous occasion. People had tried to keep her away from you but she succumbed, went back to you and you killed her.'

Gemma Horstead, December 16 2003: Horstead, 20, was found dead in the Manchester bedsit she shared with her boyfriend, Richard Butcher, 40. Butcher had hanged himself. Their bodies were too decomposed for pathologists to determine the cause of Horstead's death, but the coroner believed she had been put in the position in which she was found (her hands neatly folded across her chest). He concluded, 'I find it hard to think it was a suicide pact. All I can do is talk about possibilities – and it's possible her life was ended by Butcher.'

Lisa Higgins, Christmas Eve 2003: Higgins, 25, and her two young daughters were stabbed to death at home in Wolverhampton. Higgins' partner, Spencer Smith, 30, hanged himself while on remand for their murders in Blakenhurst prison. Higgins' mother said she had begged her daughter to leave Smith: 'He made Lisa's life hell for six years.'

Clare Mace, Christmas Eve 2003: Mace, 23, a police officer, was stabbed to death by her estranged husband, Richard, 26, at home in Clayton-le-Moors, Lancashire. He was found dead with his wrists cut in the bathroom.

Catherine Campbell, Christmas Day 2003: Campbell, 43, from south Wales, was found dead in a hotel in Goa the day after beginning a holiday with her partner, Adrian Duggan, 37. She had been stabbed in the neck and chest. In August 2005, a court in Goa found Duggan guilty of murder and sentenced him to life imprisonment. Duggan, who maintains his innocence, is planning an appeal.

Louise Beech, December 29 2003: Beech, 24, was beaten and strangled by her estranged husband at their home in Gosport, Hampshire. He then stripped and had sex with her body, before attempting suicide. Shaun Beech, a 41-year-old navy reservist, denied murder but admitted attacking his wife. In November 2004 he was found guilty of manslaughter on the grounds of diminished responsibility, and sentenced to seven years' imprisonment. The jury accepted that he had been severely depressed at the time of the killing.

Christine Longworth, January 1 2004: Longworth, a 36-year-old mother of five, was killed by her 16-year-old boyfriend, Joseph Parr, on New Year's Day. She was stabbed and died of internal bleeding at her home in Gateshead. Her body was not found until January 27. Parr was jailed for life in October 2004.

Nicola Edge, January 2 2004: Edge, 31, was stabbed in the neck with a kitchen knife by her girlfriend, Tracie Grundy, 39, in Birkenhead, Merseyside. Grundy was convicted of her murder in July 2004 and sentenced to life. She was ordered to serve a minimum of 13 years.

Constance Fish, January 2 2004: Fish, 70, died in the bath at her home in Croydon. Her husband of 53 years, Ernest, 74, hit her over the back of the head with a baseball bat and then took an overdose. He survived, and in August 2005 was sentenced to three years for manslaughter.

Susan Peters, January 9 2004: Peters' body was found at her home in New Brighton, Merseyside, by police. She and her three-year-old daughter had been stabbed several times. Her husband, Ian Peters, a navy chef, was sentenced to life for their murders in November 2004, and ordered to serve at least 27 years. Susan was 29.

Julie Borrowdale, January 11 2004: Borrowdale, 36, died when her estranged husband, William, 41, stabbed her 30 times in front of their 15-year-old son. He attacked his wife as she sat in the driver's seat of her car, outside her home in Sawston, Cambridgeshire. He was jailed for life in December 2004. The court heard how he had previously attacked his wife with a bottle in a pub.

Emily Bates, January 24 2004: Bates, 21, was stabbed 23 times by her partner, Kieron Carpenter, 30, at their flat in Wisbech, Cambridgeshire. He then attempted suicide. At Northampton crown court, Judge Charles Wide said, 'You ended a young, happy, promising life. She was just emerging from the relationship with you in which you accept you were possessive and dominant.' In March 2005 Carpenter was sentenced to life, to serve at least 13 years.

Azmat Bismal, January 25 2004: Bismal, a 35-year-old mother of six, suffered years of violent abuse before her husband, Mohammed, 34, strangled her at their home in Luton. In 2002 she had gone to a women's refuge; in 2003 her children had been placed on an at-risk register. Mohammed was sentenced to life in February 2005, to serve a minimum of 14 years and 74 days.

Anupama Damera, February 1 2004: Damera, a 36-year-old radiologist, was found stabbed to death in a car in Ipswich. Her husband, Jayaprakash Chiti, 41, a surgeon, jumped into the River Orwell holding their two-year-old son. Both died. They were survived by their 11-year-old son. In July 2004 a coroner recorded two verdicts of unlawful killing and one of suicide.

Anne Jalland, February 6 2004: When Jalland, 40, a care worker, apparently disappeared from her home in Harlesden, north-west London, leaving her 13-month-old daughter behind, her estranged husband, Raymond, 58, repeatedly appealed for her return. In April he was charged with her murder. In June 2005 he was sentenced to life. He is appealing. Her body has not been found.

Irena Pearson, February 13 2004: Pearson, a 50-year-old mother of two, was beaten to death at home in Poole, Dorset, by her husband, Maurice, 56, who later led appeals for help in finding her killer. He was found guilty of her murder and sentenced to life in September 2004.

Debbie Hodgkiss, February 14 2004: Hodgkiss's body was found in a flat in Nottingham beside the body of her friend, Daniel Staniforth. The pair, both 36, had been murdered by Hodgkiss's ex-partner, Brian Tedds, 46. Tedds, who had previous convictions for violence, was jailed for life in June 2004 and told he must serve at least 20 years.

Chantelle Lynch, February 17 2004: Sixteen-year-old Lynch was stabbed to death by her girlfriend, Shantelle Campbell, 18, at Campbell's home in Coventry. Lynch died from a single stab wound to the chest. Campbell, who has never denied the killing, was convicted of murder and sentenced to 12 years in September 2004, reduced on appeal in March 2005 to nine years because of her history of overdosing and deliberate self-harm.

Melanie Horridge, February 27 2004: Horridge, 25, a mother of three, was attacked as she pushed her baby in his pram in Chorley, Lancashire. She was repeatedly stabbed in the neck and bled to death. Her ex-partner, Bevon Williams, 27, a professional cricketer, was charged with her murder and jailed for life in July 2004.

Karin Brookshaw, March 10 2004: Brookshaw, 47, was murdered 'in a jealous rage' by her partner, George Wilson, at their home in Shrewsbury. Wilson, 53, who admitted to unlawful killing by strangulation, claimed he had not meant to harm Brookshaw. He was convicted of murder in November 2004 and told he would serve a minimum of 14 years.

Odell Rowlands, March 18 2004: Rowlands, 45, was stabbed by her partner, Peter Middleton, 59, who cleaned her wound and then fell asleep next to her body at their flat in Skegness, Lincolnshire. Middleton was found guilty of murder in December 2004 and jailed for life, to serve a minimum of six years.

Sally Rose, April 9 2004: Rose, 26, was killed by her partner, Andrew Tinley, 35, at their home in Paignton, Devon. Exeter crown court heard that Rose had poured a pan of boiling water over Tinley's lap as he slept on the sofa, and that Tinley had then hit her over the head with an unopened champagne bottle. Tinley, who has three children, admitted manslaughter and was sentenced to five years in December 2004.

James Donoghue, April 23 2004: Donoghue, 35, was shot as he watched TV at home in Stevenage, Hertfordshire, by Christopher Reed, 53, who was having an affair with Donoghue's wife, Elizabeth, 40. They were both convicted of his murder: the court heard how Elizabeth had directed Reed to her husband by a mobile phone call, and earlier persuaded her husband to take out a £144,000 life insurance policy. Both were sentenced to life and told they would each serve 30 years. She is appealing.

Bharana Krishna Namoonty, April 30 2004: Namoonty's body was found in a Coventry hotel. The 29-year-old PhD student had been strangled by her boyfriend, Emachi Eneje, 24, who was arrested after crashing his mother's car as he left the hotel. Eneje had twice been hospitalised for mental health problems, and pleaded guilty to manslaughter on the grounds of diminished responsibility. He was detained indefinitely in a secure hospital.

Bronwen Jones, May 14 2004: Jones, 55, was hit in the head and strangled by her husband, John, 69, at their home in Rhyl, north Wales. She had been her husband's registered carer. He then went to Benidorm on holiday, and was arrested a week later on his return. He pleaded guilty to manslaughter on the grounds of provocation, claiming he was angry that his wife had been too drunk to go on holiday. He was sentenced to six and a half years in October 2004.

Sarah Jane Dudley, May 16 2004: Dudley, 33, a mother of two, was burned to death when her ex-boyfriend, Anthony Frost, pushed a lit carrier bag through the letterbox of her home in Bargate, Derbyshire. Frost, 47, told Nottingham crown court he had called Dudley but dialled incorrectly and flew into a rage when a man answered. He denied murder, but admitted manslaughter and reckless arson. He was jailed for 10 years in December 2004.

Hayley Davenport, May 19 2004: Davenport, 23, was shot by her lover, 32-year-old drug dealer Jarvis Mayfield Johnson, at her home in Wolverhampton when she tried to end their relationship. She was found the next day by her two small children. Johnson was jailed for life in September 2005 and ordered to serve at least 25 years.

Nicola Finch, May 21 2004: Finch, 38, died at the home she shared with her husband, Adrian, 47, and their two children in Crediton, Devon. After months of verbal abuse, she had been stabbed to death using three different knives. In August 2004, Finch was found hanged in his cell in Exeter prison while awaiting trial for murder.

Kevan Oram, May 26 2004: Oram, 41, was stabbed by his wife, Julie Telford, 39, in their caravan near St Austell, Cornwall. Oram had suffered brain damage following a road accident, and had the mental age of a teenager. In January 2004, he had been cautioned by police for common assault after attacking and threatening to kill Telford. Police had been called after further incidents in February and April. Telford admitted manslaughter on the grounds of provocation and was jailed for four and a half years in April 2005.

Roger Osliffe, June 6 2004: Osliffe, 35, was stabbed by his wife,

Catherine, a week after their honeymoon, at home near Clitheroe, Lancashire. Preston crown court heard that the couple had a 'stormy and volatile relationship'. She was found guilty of manslaughter in February 2005 and sentenced to five years.

Tae Hui Dalton, June 7 2004: Dalton, 38, was found by her husband's parents in a series of packages in a freezer at the couple's home in London. Paul Dalton had punched his wife, then cut up her body with an electric saw. He told the Old Bailey he had suffered years of provocation from his wife and did not mean to kill her. Mr Justice Gross said, 'You lashed out at your wife in the course of an argument and in my judgment after no little taunting on her part.' He was cleared of murder, but convicted of manslaughter and preventing a burial, and sentenced to two and three years respectively. He is appealing.

Nyarai Nyamatanga, June 16 2004: Nyamatanga, 22, was found dead in a car in Leigh, Wigan. She'd been killed with a stab wound to the neck. Her partner, Leon Katina, 30, who had moved from Zimbabwe with her, was found hanging in the couple's flat. A coroner's inquest concluded in June 2004 that there was no third party involved.

Hazel Dix, June 19 2004: Dix, 54, was stabbed and dismembered in her kitchen in Redditch, Worcestershire, by her husband, Glyn, 50. He had already served a life sentence for the murder of Pia Overbury, a mother of two, in 1980. Dix, who admits stabbing his wife, is receiving treatment for schizophrenia. He is due to be sentenced next week.

Gareth Evans, June 24 2004: Evans, 18, was stabbed with a kitchen knife by his girlfriend, Hayley Wallbank, 18. Cardiff crown court heard that he had told her he had sex with her friend while she was downstairs in their flat in Crosskeys, south Wales. She was convicted of manslaughter in March 2005, and will serve six years in youth custody with two years on licence. The court heard that she had a history of self-harm.

Anna Duncan, July 3 2004: Duncan, 30, was killed by her former boyfriend, Craig Donaldson, 29, at his flat in Aberdeen following an argument over the custody of their two children, who partially witnessed the attack. Duncan suffered more than 35 stab wounds. Donaldson pleaded guilty and was jailed for life in March 2005. He was ordered to serve at least 14 years. An inquiry into police handling of the case is ongoing, following concerns raised by Duncan's family.

Jacqueline Johnson, July 18 2004: Johnson, 43, was stabbed in the leg and left to bleed to death in her flat in Windsor. Her partner, Stephen Bird, 53, later admitted manslaughter and was sentenced to six and a half years.

Janet Courtney, July 19 2004: Courtney, 47, was found dead at her home in St Anne's, Lancashire, by her daughter. A wheelchair user, she had been strangled. Her husband, Brendan, 49, pleaded guilty to manslaughter on the grounds of diminished responsibility and in February 2005 was detained indefinitely under the Mental Health Act.

Charles Shaw, July 30 2004: Shaw, 33, was stabbed in the throat by his girlfriend, Jenny McAdam, 29, at their Liverpool flat. She had a history of mental illness and in August 2005 was found guilty of manslaughter on the grounds of diminished responsibility. She has been detained indefinitely at a secure unit in Cardiff.

Natalie Jenkins, July 31 2004: Jenkins, 24, was killed by her former partner, Mark Redwood, 31, during a 'ferocious' attack at his home in Risca, south Wales, after they argued over their four-year-old daughter. Redwood, Chester crown court heard, had once cut off his finger and sent it to an ex-fiancee. He was jailed for life in February 2005.

Abigail Rowan, August 1 2004: Rowan, a 32-year-old mother of one, was stabbed more than 20 times by her boyfriend, Michael Taylor, 45, at their home in Eversley Cross, Hampshire. Her body was discovered on a neighbour's doorstep. Taylor admitted manslaughter on the grounds of diminished responsibility, claiming he could remember nothing of the murder, but was convicted of murder and jailed for life in June 2005. Witnesses said that Rowan was often seen with bruises and had become withdrawn.

Stuart McKibbin, August 9 2004: McKibbin, 40, was killed in a house fire started by his girlfriend, Amanda Hewitt, 32, in Burry Port, west Wales. Hewitt was jailed for seven and a half years in August 2005 for manslaughter. She is appealing.

Nusrat Ali, August 16 2004: Ali, 25, was stabbed to death with a kitchen knife outside her house in Middlesbrough by her husband, Amir Shazad, 30. They had had an arranged marriage in Pakistan in 1999, but had little contact until he moved to the UK in 2003. He pleaded guilty to murder at Teesside crown court and in February 2005 was sentenced to life, to serve a minimum of 10 and a half years.

Gregory Robertson, August 16 2004: Robertson was stabbed with a knife by his girlfriend after a barbecue in Hitchin, Hertfordshire. Wendy Mathias, 30, stabbed Robertson through the lung and heart, and was found guilty of murder in June 2005. She was jailed for life and told she must serve at least nine years.

Adele Corpe, August 21 2004: Corpe, a 33-year-old mother of two, was stabbed to death by her boyfriend, Edward Kearney, 46, at their home in Riddings, Derbyshire. He pleaded guilty to murder at Nottingham crown court in November 2004 and was jailed for life. He had convictions for violence and assault dating back to the age of 14.

Barbara Dhillon, September 4 2004: Dhillon, 49, was bludgeoned to death by her husband, Sat, 49, at their home in Crewe, Cheshire. Her body was discovered after he committed suicide on a nearby railway line. An inquest jury recorded a verdict of suicide and unlawful killing.

Vincent Keningale, September 13 2004: Keningale, 61, was stabbed by his wife Doris, 43, after they argued in the kitchen of their home in Newport, south Wales, over her plans to launch a jewellery business. She said that she had not intended to kill him, but he 'was so aggressive I could not cope any more.' Cardiff crown court heard how she had suffered years of verbal abuse. She admitted manslaughter and was given a three-year community rehabilitation order.

Lorraine Macdonald, September 14 2004: Macdonald, 43, was stabbed 12 times and strangled by her husband at their home in Bognor Regis. Shaun Macdonald, 38, admitted manslaughter on the grounds of diminished responsibility, after telling Lewes crown court that he was haunted by his service in the armed forces. He was jailed for four and a half years in July 2005.

Ann Edwards, September 21 2004: The body of Edwards, 44, was discovered by police at her home in Northwood, Kirkby. She had sustained more than 50 injuries to her head and neck, caused by forceful impact with the floor or wall. Her partner, Robert Gallagher, admitted her murder and was sentenced to serve a minimum term of 11 years in March 2005. Her daughter Joanne told local reporters she had begged her mother to leave: 'She was too scared and she stayed.'

Christine MacCowan, September 22 2004: MacCowan, 54, was attacked at home in Balmedie, Aberdeenshire, by her husband, Hamish, 55. He hit her with a sledgehammer before strangling her with a tie. His defence told the court that he had been suffering from a depressive illness. He was found guilty of culpable homicide and detained at a medium secure facility at the Royal Edinburgh Hospital.

Margaret Gardiner, October 4 2004: Gardiner, 55, apparently disappeared from her home in Helensburgh, Scotland. Her body was never found, but after a forensics team searched her house, her husband, John, 58, told police she'd fallen on concrete steps, causing a fatal head injury. He said he'd then disposed of her body in the River Leven. He was jailed for six years for culpable homicide, plus six years for perverting the course of justice. He is appealing.

Natalie Cox, October 4 2004: Cox, 75, was assaulted by her husband in their home in Ammanford, south Wales, and died nine days later in hospital. The prosecution decided not to press charges of murder or manslaughter, but Charles Cox, 78, a wheelchair user, admitted grievous bodily harm with intent in May 2005. Last month he was made the subject of a guardianship order under the care of Carmarthenshire council.

Pauline Jones, October 8 2004: Jones, 53, from Cwmbran, south Wales, was killed with a claw hammer by her former boyfriend, Melvin Stewart, 45, after she refused to resume their relationship. In September 2005, he was found guilty of murder and jailed for life.

Nicola Johnstone, October 10 2004: Johnstone, 23, and her partner, Kevin Braid, 41, were killed by her ex-husband at Braid's home in Leslie, Fife. Former soldier Shaun Alexander, 32, stabbed Johnstone eight times, and stabbed and hit Braid with a crowbar. The high court in Edinburgh heard that Alexander had constantly followed his ex-wife after they separated. She had applied for a restraining order, which had not been granted by the time of her death. In June 2005, Alexander was jailed for 20 years, increased from 17 years after the Crown appealed against the leniency of the initial sentence.

Vicky Reay, October 17 2004: Reay, 19, was strangled by her boyfriend, Andrew Maguire, 34, at her home in Hexham, Northumberland. He told police his cousin had told him to do it because she 'knew too much' about his criminal activity. Maguire, who confessed to her murder, hanged himself days later in Durham prison.

Julie Harris, October 19 2004: Harris, 41, was stabbed to death by her former partner, Andrew Millard, 42, after he broke into her home in Cheltenham. Hours before, she'd asked Gloucestershire police to arrest Millard, who was the subject of a harassment order. She was told they had 'other commitments'. He was sentenced to life. In 2000, he had been jailed for three years for stabbing his then girlfriend in the face, and in 1994 to five years for stabbing his wife's friend. An inquiry into police handling of the case is ongoing.

Linda MacDonald, October 20 2004: MacDonald's body was found at her home in Buckfastleigh, Devon. She'd been beaten with an iron bar. Her husband, Hibiekoun Hien, 54, who'd recently emigrated from Burkina-Faso, pleaded guilty to manslaughter. He was jailed for five years. The court heard that he'd become depressed and disoriented, believing that MacDonald, 53, was going to kill or sell him.

Ela Maisuria, October 22 2004: Maisuria, 46, was stabbed to death in Southall, Middlesex, by her husband, Prabodh, 52. Her body lay undiscovered for several days, during which time Prabodh begged for help in finding her killer. He pleaded guilty to manslaughter on the grounds of provocation, but in June 2005 was sentenced to life for murder. He was ordered to serve at least 13 and a half years.

Paula Owens, October 22 2004: Owens, 41, was strangled and stabbed in the chest by her partner, Anthony McCormack, 54, in their home in the Wirral. She was six months pregnant. He was convicted of murder and destruction of the child she was carrying, and sentenced to not less than 20 years. In 1998 he had served five years after cutting an ex-girlfriend's throat. He had faced a charge of stabbing Owens in 2003, but was cleared due to insufficient evidence.

Amanda Lewis, October 24 2004: Lewis, 42, died from a single stab wound at her home in Suffolk. Her husband, Gareth, 43, who said he could not remember killing her, pleaded guilty to manslaughter due to diminished responsibility. Ipswich crown court heard that he had a history of depression. In June 2005 he was sentenced to three years and four months.

Mary Crilly, October 31 2004: The bodies of Crilly, 40, and her partner, Brian Smith, 47, were found at their home in east Belfast. Smith, a former prison officer, had shot his wife dead before killing himself. Crilly's 15-year-old daughter was treated for gunshot wounds. Her 21-year-old son, also in the house at the time, escaped injury.

Jenni Gordon, November 15 2004: Gordon, 15, was strangled and left to die in sub-zero conditions in a lane near Dunfermline, Fife, by her boyfriend, Kenneth Fraser, 16. He said in court she had told him she had contracted chlamydia. He was sentenced to life in June 2005, to serve a minimum of 20 years. He is appealing.

Simon Neglia, November 18 2004: Neglia, 29, was stabbed five times by his girlfriend, Anna Gray, 35, at their flat in Hatfield, Hertfordshire. She told Luton crown court that the attack was in self-defence after Neglia tried to drown and strangle her. In July 2005, she was jailed for six years for manslaughter by reason of provocation.

Mandy Skedd, November 22 2004: Skedd, 30, a childminder, was looking after two children at her home in Nottingham when she was stabbed by her ex-partner, Mark Odeyemi, 47. He left a note on her body saying, 'Tell Eddie thank you', a reference to her new partner. He pleaded guilty to murder and was sentenced to life, to serve at least 21 years and five months. Paul Mann QC, prosecuting, said, 'It is the crown's case that the defendant could not come to terms with the break-up. He became possessive.'

Research by Isabel Eden, Kristin Aune, Kearan Ramful and Guardian research department

17 FEBRUARY 2006

This bawdy world of boobs and gams shows how far we've left to go

In the new raunch culture, the freedom for women to be sexually provocative has usurped genuine liberation

ARIEL LEVY

A few years ago I noticed something strange was happening in my native US. I would turn on the television and find strippers in nipple-tassels explaining how best to lap-dance a man to orgasm. I would flip the channel and see babes in tight, tiny uniforms bouncing up and down on trampolines. Britney Spears was becoming increasingly popular and increasingly unclothed, and her undulating body ultimately became so familiar to me that I felt like we used to go out.

In my own industry – magazines – a porny new genre called lad mags were hitting stands and becoming a huge success by delivering what Playboy had only occasionally managed to capture in the past: greased celebrities in little scraps of fabric humping the floor.

Some odd things were happening in my social life too. People I knew (female people) liked going to strip clubs (female strippers). It was sexy and fun, they explained, it was liberating and rebellious. My best friend from college, who used to go to Take Back the Night marches on campus, had become captivated by porn stars. Only 30 years (roughly my lifetime) ago, our mothers were supposedly burning their bras and picketing Playboy, and suddenly we were getting implants and wearing the bunny logo as symbols of our liberation. How had the culture shifted so drastically in such a short period of time?

What was even more surprising than the change itself were the responses I got when I started interviewing the men and – often – the women who edit magazines such as Maxim and produce reality television series about strippers. This new raunch culture didn't mark the death of feminism – it was evidence that the feminist project had already been achieved. We'd 'earned' the right to look at Playboy – we were 'empowered' enough to get Brazilian bikini waxes. Women had come so far, I learned, that we no longer needed to worry about objectification or misogyny. Instead, it was time for us to join the frat party of pop culture where men had been enjoying themselves all along. If male chauvinist pigs were men who regarded women as pieces of meat, we would beat them at their own game and be female chauvinist pigs: women who make sex objects of other women and of ourselves.

I tried to get with the programme, but I could never make the argument add up in my head. How is resurrecting every stereotype of female sexuality that feminism endeavoured to banish good for women? Why is labouring to look like Paris Hilton empowering? And how is imitating a stripper or a porn star – a woman whose job is to imitate arousal in the first place – going to render us sexually liberated?

This new raunch culture is being replicated in the UK too. As Natasha Walter noted after the publication of Naomi Wolf's new book last month, there's 'a general feeling that feminism had become tolerant of cultural sexism'. And that cultural sexism is linked to underlying political and economic inequalities that make it not so ironic or funny.

There is a widespread assumption that, simply because my

generation of women has the good fortune to live in a world touched by the feminist movement, that means everything we do is magically imbued with its agenda. But it doesn't work that way. 'Raunchy' and 'liberated' are not synonyms. It is worth asking ourselves if this bawdy world of boobs and gams we have resurrected reflects how far we've come, or how far we have left to go.

Many women today, whether they are 14 or 40, seem to have forgotten that sexual power is only one, very specific, kind of power. And what's more, looking like a stripper or a Playboy bunny is only one, very specific, kind of sexual expression. Is it the one that turns us – or men – on the most? We would have to stop endlessly re-enacting this one raunchy script to find out.

We have to ask ourselves why we are so focused on silent girly girls in G-strings faking lust. This is not a sign of progress, it's a testament to what's still missing from our understanding of human sexuality with all of its complexity and power. We are still so uneasy with the vicissitudes of sex that we need to surround ourselves with caricatures of female hotness to safely conjure up the concept of 'sexy'. It's kind of pathetic.

Sex is one of the most interesting things we as humans have to play with, and we've reduced it to polyester underpants and implants. We are selling ourselves unbelievably short.

Without a doubt there are some women who feel their most sexual with their vaginas waxed, their labia trimmed, their breasts enlarged, and their garments flossy and scant. I am happy for them. I wish them many blissful and lubricious loops around the pole. But there are many other women (and, yes, men) who feel constrained in this environment, who would be happier and feel hotter – more empowered, more sexually liberated, and all the rest of it – if they explored other avenues of expression and entertainment.

This is not about the sex industry – it's about what we have decided the sex industry means . . . how we have held it up, cleaned it off and distorted it. How we depend on it to mark us as an erotic and uninhibited culture at a moment when fear and repression are rampant. In 2004, George Bush, the leader of the free world, proposed an amendment to the United States constitution to for ever ban gay marriage – which was already illegal. In opinion polls, about 50% of respondents said they thought Bush had the right idea. If half my country feels so threatened by two people of the same gender being in love and having sex (and, incidentally, enjoying equal protection under the law) that they turn their attention – during wartime – to blocking rights already denied to homosexuals, then all the cardio-striptease classes in the world aren't going to render us sexually liberated.

Women's liberation and empowerment are terms feminists started using to talk about casting off the limitations imposed upon women and demanding equality. We have perverted these words. The freedom to be sexually provocative or promiscuous is not enough freedom – it is not the only 'women's issue' worth paying attention to. And we are not even free in the sexual arena. We have simply adopted a new norm, a new role to play: lusty, busty exhibitionist. There are other choices. If we are really going to be sexually liberated, we need to make room for a range of options as wide as the variety of human desire. We need to allow ourselves the freedom to figure out what we internally want from sex, instead of mimicking whatever popular culture holds up to us as sexy. That would be sexual liberation.

If we believed that we were sexy and funny and competent and smart, we would not need to be like strippers or like men or like anyone other than our own specific, individual selves. That won't be easy, but the rewards would be the very things Female Chauvinist Pigs want so badly, the things women deserve: freedom and power.

18 FEBRUARY 2006

Embarrassment of riches

When female health workers won a colossal £300m equal pay claim last year, few cared to share in their celebrations. Why?

BEATRIX CAMPBELL

Last year, 1,600 women, all of them health workers at two Cumbrian hospitals, won the biggest ever equal pay deal: a total of £300m. At a time when the pay gap between men and women is actually growing, the settlement should have sparked a clamour for equality. Instead, there has since been an eerie silence. The story of how the women, underpaid for years, spurned an offer of £1.5m compensation and achieved £300m, all from one health authority, has been mysteriously buried, as if it were an embarrassment. They sense a fear of 'mutually assured destruction' wafting around the headquarters of their union, Unison, which represents more than a million public service workers: a feeling that the settlement was too huge, and the ramifications of it just too enormous – what would happen if it triggered equal pay claims across the whole of the public sector?

The front of the Unison building on Euston Road, central London, is adorned with a fetching tabard portraying the modern face of public service trade unionism – a woman. The Cumbrian women expected head office to rejoice at their victory and be proud that the union had lived up to its image. In fact, says one of them, 'You'd have thought someone had died.'

'Nobody called us, or asked how we'd done it, how we could

help other people do it,' says Christine Wharrier, one of the local Unison negotiators, 'and nobody came up from the union to celebrate with us.'

The reaction from others who spend their lives working for equality and fair pay was also strangely muted. 'Off the record, it's brilliant,' said an Equal Opportunities Commission insider. 'It's brilliant – and potentially devastating,' said a senior union official who won't be using the case as a template for the rest of the public sector. 'It could destroy the union' and, worse, the government could use it to 'destroy the public sector', he added.

The Cumbrian settlement was agreed a year ago. Wharrier recalls: 'Nobody wanted to know: it's been like a radioactive leak. It's because we [the union] have been affiliated to Labour for so long. People ask, "Where will the government get the money?" It's awful. I think to myself, we're the third richest country in the world, we are not a third world country.'

The claims were initiated by Peter Doyle, Unison's full-time organiser in Cumbria. To make the case, he and his associates had to find 'comparators', men who did equivalent work to the female health workers for higher pay. The evidence collected was so compelling that, in the end, Doyle, Wharrier and her colleagues won their settlement before the case even went into an employment tribunal – a sign that everyone, by now, understood the strength of the women's claim. The health authority realised it couldn't win.

Who are these women, and why do they feel like untouchables? Wharrier is a hospital worker and a Unison convener – this was her first big confrontation. She joined the health service 28 years ago, first as a domestic, then as an auxiliary nurse. 'I was known as a woman who stood up for everybody,' she says – and, after getting a divorce in her 40s, she had to start standing up for herself. 'I couldn't afford a pension. I had a mortgage to pay and two teenagers to take care of. I'd never thought equal pay was relevant to me . . . What this deal means to me personally is that I've been able to do something I've never been able to do: open a savings account. People on low incomes have to do everything very expensively, because they've got to get a loan to pay for everything.'

Her friend Marlene Airlie has worked as a nurse for 38 years, many of them on night shift. The deal upgraded her status and her salary by £9,000 and, like the others, she received a lump sum, backdated – at most to 1991 – for the extra amount she would have been paid if she'd been a man in a similar job (not the same job: male and female nurses are paid at the same rate, as are doctors and others in professional grades). 'Do I feel guilty?' Airlie asks. 'I'm sorry, no. This is for the 38 years I've given.' The case, she says, exposed 'how undervalued we are. My comparator was an engineer. He was upset about the result – not because we'd won, but because all those years he hadn't been aware of what we were earning.'

Sheila Lyle became a cleaner 22 years ago, with no qualifications and three children to care for. 'It is the nature of the job and the environment we work in that we give a lot of goodwill; it's unlimited. And now we've been recognised for it.' Her job took her from the mortuary to the operating theatre, vacuuming, washing and buffing the floors – until privatisation, to her disdain, reduced cleaning to one task: washing. 'I've always liked my job – cleaning is important.' But it was not until this campaign that everyone else recognised its value.

Elsie Murdoch started as a cleaner at 26. She works nights and during the day cares for a disabled child. 'You're aware of the importance of cleanliness to recuperating patients – and I like talking to the patients.' She was always a union woman and, like her colleagues, applauds Doyle for taking on the battle. 'It's lovely to see a man recognising the value of our work and doing something about it.'

Kathleen Wallace's story is also the chronicle of privatisation. She is a seamstress approaching retirement who has worked for 26 years in the health service. Her department worked on staff uniforms, hospital curtains, bed linen and patients' linen. Everything eventually went out to tender, and when they moved to the new infirmary there was no laundry, so her department 'dwindled to one person, part time – me'. Her comparator is a wall-washer. 'I wouldn't say I'm skilled, or a proper dressmaker. I can wash a wall, but I don't think a wall-washer could do my job.' Now she faces retirement with an unexpected bonus: 'I know I won't have to worry.'

Vanessa Brown is a theatre nurse coordinator at Carlisle's Cumberland Infirmary, the first private finance initiative (PFI) hospital to be built in Britain, where she organises the comings and goings of patients, clinicians, information and equipment, prior to operations. 'When our levels of responsibility and accountability were compared with a foreman electrician, the men were found to be on £9,000 a year more. That's almost a wage to some of our women.' When the women won, 'We wanted to shout it from the rooftops, we wanted it on the front pages.'

Instead, it was downplayed. After the deal was announced, the union initially insisted that it was a local negotiation, with no national implications, it said it would be 'irresponsible' to use it to launch other claims. Now it is inviting members to contemplate cases – after being warned that it might be sued for encouraging women to settle for less than they might otherwise achieve.

The sense of crisis around the case is 'because the figures are so scary', says one sex discrimination lawyer. The deputy prime minister, John Prescott, did nothing to allay fears about the consequences of such claims when he met the unions and public service employers in 2004 and insisted that the public sector would get no extra money to fund equal pay.

The Cumbrian story starts in 1995. Peter Doyle had been looking for a way to raise women's pay. 'I aimed everything at our low-paid staff,' he says. 'The assumption was that if you took equal pay claims for women at the top, it would trickle down. But it didn't. So I devised the trickle up.' A big man with big glasses, a big laugh and the bad health that goes with big stress, he has doubled the county's Unison membership during the life of this case.

His proposed equal pay claim was dropped that year, because Unison feared that such a challenge would encourage an already hostile Conservative government to abolish national pay structures in the NHS. But, emboldened when Labour was elected in May 1997, Doyle resurrected it. He canvassed female members at two North Cumbria Trust hospitals. One, a raggy slab of a building, looms over the Solway Firth at Whitehaven, once one of Britain's slave-trade ports, now a modestly handsome township where men depend on Sellafield for work and women on the public services; the other is the Cumberland Infirmary. At the time it was a Victorian shambles.

The unions were now faced with another challenge: the PFI. The Cumberland Infirmary was to be rebuilt with private finance. Equal pay would be regarded as a burden on investors. Doyle suggested converting the burden into a weapon: 'The union was opposed to PFI. I argued the equal pay claim would bugger up PFI. I said we should lodge the claim before the private company signed a contract.' They did, and momentarily it stopped the negotiations. 'But then they came back. The government had indemnified them for 15 years!' So, the private sector wouldn't lose a penny, whatever the cost of the claim. 'It was a tactical mistake,' says Doyle. 'If we'd lodged it after they signed, it might have collapsed the deal.' The comparison between the cost of settlement and the cost of Carlisle's PFI hospital, built in 2000, is not lost on the Cumbrian women: their deal is worth £300m, whereas the new infirmary cost £87m to build, but PFI means the NHS will have to pay to use it – at a cost of an estimated £1bn over 30 years.

The claim was possible because of 'equal value', a concept contained in a European directive announced during a late sitting in the Commons 20 years ago by a reluctant, and drunk, employment minister, Alan Clark. It allows different jobs to be compared for skill, complexity and responsibility; it focuses on the work, not the job. In detail, the claim translated the gothic arithmetic and arcane patois of industrial relations into the everyday life of men and women: everything, from bonus, to pension, to the length of the working week, to a working life. 'It took a while to convince some of them that what they did was not only of equal value to a man, but more important,' says Doyle.

A job evaluation expert, Sue Hastings, assessed the Cumbria dossier and reported that the cases were a golden equal pay opportunity for 'exactly the people who ought to get it' – nurses who had been undergraded for decades, cleaners, telephonists and sterile services staff, who prepare instruments for surgery and who had been stuck on the same grade as washers-up since the health service was founded. Doyle had found men willing to stand as comparators: a wall-washer earning £3,000 a year more – and working 104 fewer hours a year – than a seamstress and sterile services staff; a plumber earning more than a nurse; a specialised nurse on a cancer ward, at the top of her scale, earning £8,000 a year less than a plant maintenance man; a nurse on £9,000 less than an engineer. The report did not provoke enthusiasm. The union was frightened of the scale of the claim and its implications for public services all over the country. If these women won, the government – their government – could react by privatising public services.

But the cases had been lodged, expert opinion had been enlisted, the claim was on its long, slow march through the tribunal system, the employer had to respond. Independent experts showed that the women's jobs were focused on 'responsibility for the health of people, whilst the men's jobs tended to be responsible for things.' Their radical critique showed that 'looking after equipment was more highly rated than looking after people.' Clerical responsibility for the management of information – a matter of life and death – was undervalued. So, too, was the 'emotional labour' invested in patient care.

'Often, people aren't aware of what exactly they do, and it is part of our job to make them aware of it,' explains Kay Gilbert, an independent expert.

The trust first offered £1.5m to be shared between the 1,600 claimants. The women said no, and they kept saying no. By the time the trust offered £5.6m, the union head office wanted to settle. Doyle and Wharrier conceded that, yes, it was big, 'but it was 100 times less than [what they would get] if we fought it out'.

The women received their own legal advice: if the union accepted a deal that was less than they could expect to get at a tribunal, then the women could sue their union. They rejected the offer. 'Doyle was right,' says an equal pay specialist, 'though he had serious battles with the union. He is inspirational – the number of women he can get to an evening meeting in a dusty old hall is staggering.'

Finally, the trust agreed to talk bigger in direct negotiations with Doyle and Wharrier. 'It was real short sword stuff, in close,' says Doyle.

'The management kept saying it would bankrupt the trust, that it would come out of patient care. But that was just a threat,' says Wharrier. After days of tough talk, they emerged with the £300m deal.

It was back pay that made it so mighty. Economic sexism was endemic and historic. Doyle argued that the women should attract the same kind of redress as, for example, industrial injury. If the government was prepared to bankroll massive funds to compensate workers for physical injury, why not economic injury? Why not deal with what they were due in the past as well as the present and future? That is what pushed some settlements into six-figure sums. They were beneficiaries of European law that allowed the deal to date from six years before it was lodged, in this case 1997. The £300m included compensation for lower hourly rates paid to women, lesser pension contributions, and the non-payment of bonuses and attendance allowances that had been paid to men – all of it backdated a total of 14 years, all with compound interest. In addition, Doyle cleverly insisted that the higher union dues the women would have paid had their earnings been higher should also be part of the settlement. Hence, the union's case paid for itself.

Union hierarchies may be reluctant to follow the example, but not the veteran employment lawyer Stefan Cross, who was involved in the early stages of the Cumbrian claim. Formerly a Labour councillor in Newcastle upon Tyne, he describes himself as an inveterate Blairite. That hasn't saved him from becoming a hate figure in Labour circles: for encouraging women to challenge deals that don't offer back pay, for setting up his own firm specialising in equal pay claims, and for offering to take no-win-no-fee cases for women who feel they've been failed by their unions. 'I scratched my head trying to work out why unions were taking such a bizarre and intransigent position: they were lining up with the employers against women.' Cross calculated that payouts averaging under £2,000 to manual workers were much lower than they'd get if their case went to a tribunal. 'It was outrageous.' Cross is taking 7,500 equal pay cases, and 700 claims against trade unions alleging that women were encouraged to sign away their entitlements. Mention of Cross's name makes union officials incandescent. Unison in Scotland issued a press release in August last year after his firm set up a Scottish office, describing him as a 'Johnny come lately' and urging employers to co-operate with the union or leave themselves vulnerable to this purported 'cherry-picker'.

Some observers, recognising the dilemma faced by local

authorities that have consistently underpaid female employees and are now having to make up the shortfall, believe there is only one way to proceed: co-operation between unions and employers.

Partnership is the imprimatur of Agenda for Change, a new pay structure for the health service negotiated on the eve of the Cumbria settlement and, many believe, inspired by it. It is not phasing out unequal pay so much as phasing in equal pay – sceptics also see it as a way of blocking equal pay litigation. Men's privileged pay will be protected until 2011.

However, there is no equivalent of Agenda for Change in local government, which foots the bill for many public services. 'It is being made explicit that the pursuit of equal pay will be at the expense of jobs and services, and that is unfair,' says Nicola Dandridge, head of equality at Thompsons Solicitors, the law firm that does most trade union work.

It remains to be seen how fiercely the public service unions will take up the battle. Unison HQ rebuts any criticism of its conduct of the Cumbrian claim. The Cumbrian members, it says, were mistaken in feeling that head office did little to help them: 'The union gave all its support to the case. And we think the payout was the best possible outcome.'

The four main NHS unions (GMB, Amicus and T&G, as well as Unison) have invited members to come forward if they think they've got an equal pay claim. There are already 8,000 cases being processed by Thompsons. Dandridge reckons many thousands more women may have a case. 'This is a national, collective problem, but the problem is that the law only addresses it through individuals.' This kind of claim, she says, flags up the need for class actions, which the unions have campaigned for.

When Doyle and Wharrier knew they'd got a deal, they convened a confidential gathering of the women to give them details of the offer. A cleaner was sitting quietly doing her own sums. One of her companions gasped, 'Oh my God . . . she's away.' She slumped to the floor, people rushed to her with offers of water, then the gasps became laughter. The woman had fainted when she'd read her own arithmetic and realised what she had won. She recovered, read out her sums and asked, 'Is this right?'

'Yes, you are right,' Doyle replied, 'but you've made a little mistake. You've missed something, you've missed the future.' When the woman calculated her new salary, she burst into tears.

As Doyle tells this story, his voice breaks, his eyes fill. 'Phew,' he murmurs when he finds his breath. 'Aren't we privileged to be able to do work like this? It's the best buzz in the world.'

6 APRIL 2007

How the web became a sexists' paradise

Everyone receives abuse online but the sheer hatred thrown at women bloggers has left some in fear for their lives

JESSICA VALENTI

Last week, Kathy Sierra, a well-known software programmer and Java expert, announced that she had cancelled her speaking engagements and was 'afraid to leave my yard' after being threatened with suffocation, rape and hanging. The threats didn't come from a stalker or a jilted lover and they weren't responses to a controversial book or speech. Sierra's harassers were largely anonymous, and all the threats had been made online.

Sierra had been receiving increasingly abusive comments on her website, Creating Passionate Users, over the previous year, but had not expected them to turn so violent – her attackers not only verbally assaulting her ('fuck off you boring slut . . . I hope someone slits your throat') but also posting photomontages of her on other sites: one with a noose next to her head and another depicting her screaming with a thong covering her face. Since she wrote about the abuse on her website, the harassment has increased. 'People are posting all my private data online everywhere – social-security number, and home address – a retaliation for speaking out.'

While no one could deny that men experience abuse online, the sheer vitriol directed at women has become impossible to ignore. Extreme instances of stalking, death threats and hate speech are now prevalent, as well as all the everyday harassment that women have traditionally faced in the outside world – catcalls, for instance, or being 'rated' on our looks. It's all very far from the utopian ideals that greeted the dawn of the web – the idea of it as a new, egalitarian public space, where men and women from all races, and of all sexualities, could mix without prejudice.

On some online forums anonymity combined with misogyny can make for an almost gang-rape like mentality. One recent blog thread, attacking two women bloggers, contained comments like, 'I would fuck them both in the ass,' 'Without us you would be raped, beaten and killed for nothing,' and 'Don't worry, you or your friends are too ugly to be put on the black market.'

Jill Filipovic, a 23-year-old law student who also writes on the popular blog Feministe, recently had some photographs of her uploaded and subjected to abusive comments on an online forum for students in New York. 'The people who were posting comments about me were speculating as to how many abortions I've had, and they talked about 'hate-fucking' me,' says Filipovic. 'I don't think a man would get that the harassment of women is far more sexualised – men may be told that they're idiots, but they aren't called "whores".'

Most disturbing is how accepted this is. When women are harassed on the street, it is considered inappropriate. Online, though, sexual harassment is not only tolerated – it's often lauded. Blog threads or forums where women are attacked attract hundreds of comments, and their traffic rates rocket.

Is this what people are really like? Sexist and violent? Misogynist and racist? Alice Marwick, a postgraduate student in New York studying culture and communication, says: 'There's the disturbing possibility that people are creating online environments purely to express the type of racist, homophobic, or sexist speech that is no longer acceptable in public society, at work, or even at home.'

Last year I had my own run-in with online sexism when I was invited to a lunch meeting with Bill Clinton, along with a handful of other bloggers (I edit the site feministing.com). After the meeting, a group photo of the attendees with Clinton was posted on several websites, and it wasn't long before comments about my appearance started popping up. ('Who's the intern?' 'I do like Gray Shirt's three-quarter pose.')

One website, run by the law professor and occasional New York Times columnist Ann Althouse, devoted an entire article to how I was 'posing' so as to 'make [my] breasts as obvious as possible'. The post, titled 'Let's take a closer look at those breasts,' ended up with over 500 comments. Most were about my body, my perceived whorishness, and how I couldn't possibly be a good feminist because I had the gall to show up to a meeting with my breasts in tow. One commenter even created a limerick about me giving oral sex. Althouse herself said that I should have 'worn a beret . . . a blue dress would have been good too'. All this on the basis of a photograph of me in a crew-neck sweater from Gap.

I won't even get into the hundreds of other blogs and websites that linked to the 'controversy.' It was, without doubt, the most humiliating experience of my life – all because I dared be photographed with a political figure.

But a picture does seem to be considered enough reason to go on a harassment rampage. Some argue that the increased visibility afforded people by the internet – who doesn't have a blog, MySpace page, or Flickr account these days? – means that harassment should be expected, even acceptable. When feminist and liberal bloggers slammed Althouse for her attack on me, she argued that having been in a photo where I was 'posing' made me fair game. When Filipovic complained about her harassment, the site responded: 'For a woman who has made 4,000 pictures of herself publicly available on Flickr, and who is a self-proclaimed feminist author of a widely disseminated blog, she has gotten pretty shy about overexposure.'

Ah, the 'she was asking for it' defence. 'I think there's a tendency to put the blame on the victims of stalking, harassment or even sexual violence when the victim is a woman – and especially when she's a woman who has made herself public,' says Filipovic. 'Public space has traditionally been reserved for men, and women are supposed to be quiet.'

Sierra thinks that online threats, even if they are coming from a small group of people, have tremendous potential to scare women from fully participating online. 'How many rape/fantasy threats does it take to make women want to lay low? Not many,' she says.

But even women who don't put their pictures or real names online are subject to virtual harassment. A recent study showed that when the gender of an online username appears female, they are 25 times more likely to experience harassment. The study, conducted by the University of Maryland, found that female usernames averaged 163 threatening and/or sexually explicit messages a day.

'The promise of the early internet,' says Marwick, 'was that it would liberate us from our bodies, and all the oppressions associated with prejudice. We'd communicate soul-to-soul, and get to know each other as people, rather than judging each other based on gender or race.' In reality, what ended up happening was that, online, the default identity became male and white – unless told otherwise, you would assume you were talking to a white man. 'So people who brought up their ethnicity, or people who complained about sexism in online communications, were seen as "playing the race/gender card" or trying to stir up trouble,' says Marwick.

And while online harassment doesn't necessarily create the same immediate safety concerns as street harassment, the consequences are arguably more severe. If someone calls you a 'slut' on the street, it stings – but you can move on. If someone calls you a 'slut' online, there's a public record as long as the site exists.

Let me tell you, it's not easy to build a career as a feminist writer when you have people coming up to you in pubs asking if you're the 'Clinton boob girl' or if one of the first items that comes up in a Google search of your name is 'boobgate'. And for young women applying for jobs, the reality is terrifying. Imagine a potential employer searching for information and coming across a thread about what a 'whore' you are.

Thankfully, women are fighting back. Sparked by the violent harassment of Sierra, one blogger started a 'stop cyberbullying' campaign. This was picked up by hundreds of other bloggers and an international women's technology organisation, Take Back the Tech, a global network of women who encourage people to 'take back online spaces' by writing, video blogging, or podcasting about online harassment.

It won't mean the end of misogyny on the web, but it is a start. Such campaigns show that women are ready to demand freedom from harassment and fear in our new public spaces. In the same way that we should be able to walk down the street without fear of being raped, women shouldn't have to stay quiet online – or pretend to be men – to be free of threats and harassment. It is time to take back the sites.

8 June 2007

What would Beth Ditto do?

Today's dilemma: How should I respond to catcalls in the street?

Beth Ditto

I have been 130lb as well as 215lb. I have had blond, strawberry blond, green, pink and purple hair, and none of that has ever exempted me from having lewd comments flung at me in the street. This happens to all women, and it can be really upsetting, but we shouldn't feel hopeless about it – I really believe that if men and women start communicating about this, it's something that we can tackle together.

First things first . . . we have to stop referring to this as a 'catcall'. Women aren't cats, we aren't pets, we are just people trying to cross the freaking street to get an ice-cream cone. (Well, in my case, anyway.)

I struggled with this question, asking, 'Beth, what would you do?', and then I remembered all the times I've shouted back: 'Show us your cock! That's right – let everyone here see how huge it is! Oh wait! What's that? I didn't hear you! You're walking away?!' Using my voice is always my first instinct. In good conscience, though, I know that this kind of harassment happens in varying degrees and that shouting back isn't always appropriate. Harassment can also stir up strong feelings, which can ruin your day. So, taking all that into consideration, I've written a handy list of scenarios and sketched out exactly how to respond!

No 1: If you find yourself on the receiving end of some crude dude's remarks, it is up to you to decide how much energy to give the jerk. It's understandable to feel too tired, or afraid, or even embarrassed to confront a stranger who hasn't the sense to respect you as a human being. If you feel up to it, though, go right ahead! Just be careful and know how to protect yourself.

No 2: If you find yourself feeling powerless after someone has shouted at you, you need to remember that this is the masterplan of sexism. The guys in question may not know it, but every time they 'catcall' a girl they are reminding her of her vulnerability in a system designed to do just that. As women, we need to remember the power that lies within.

No 3: If a friend or partner tells you that catcalls are a fact of life and to 'just get used to it', it's worth recognising that they are fuelling the harasser's fire and extinguishing yours. It can be particularly annoying when a boyfriend does this – it's not fair for someone who has the privilege of taking a risk-free stroll in the park, day or night, to dismiss your reaction. The next time he says something like that then you should arrange to get some of the most annoying, frightening women, young and old, ugly and beautiful, thin and fat, to stare at him for a week, pointing and remarking on his body. He'll just have to get used to it! Seriously, though, I suggest that you nip any comments like that in the bud. You can't be yourself with a partner who writes off your feelings.

No 4: This advice is for the boys . . . If you want to give a woman a compliment, there is nothing wrong with just saying, 'You look beautiful.' But the over-the-top stallion attitude is intimidating and, let's face it, doesn't really work for anyone. I mean, seriously? When was the last time it actually got you a date?!

28 July 2007

The really bad girls

Those who collude in the public degradation of gifted young women are beneath contempt

Bidisha

Who doesn't love to speculate about good girls gone bad? Well, people who like and respect women don't. Nor do people who recognise that the rules prescribing what constitutes a 'good' female are bigoted and hypocritical. A good girl is charming and comely, and never does anything to upset the status quo. A good girl does not dare to challenge the position society has put her in. A good girl is the ideal helpmeet for a man, with neither a hair nor a thought out of place.

So it's a nasty shock for reactionaries to see Lindsay Lohan's latest police mugshot, in which she sends a fabulous look of 'Yeah, I've been arrested. So what?' straight through the camera into the miasma of prurient dreck that is pop culture. So Lohan likes a drink. What's the problem? Women get drunk, fall over and hit the double standard face first. Further proof that womankind is pushing things a step too far is the news that Britney Spears acted brattishly at a recent photoshoot, wiping her hands on one dress and letting her pooch defecate on another.

Again, so what? Male power players have been abusing subordinates ever since they created the first hierarchies. Nobody points out that male violence is destroying the world. A drunk young rich guy is a crazed creative genius and cultural messiah who lives on the edge – his female counterpart is a sad strumpet. Or, in Britney's case, it's all put down to her ongoing 'meltdown'.

That is not to say that I want to even things up by watching talented women sabotage themselves with as much dedication as men. There is no glory in substance abuse or depression. They are debilitating conditions, deeply saddening for any friend, family or fan who must watch, wondering how they might help. But the avid readers of What Lindsay/Britney Did Next are not wondering that. The people who like to see a good girl go bad do so not because it provides young women with a vicarious means of joyful rebellion, but because they like watching a gifted woman get destroyed.

The strategy is the same whether we're talking pop princesses or actual ones. First, the target is goaded, speculated about. She is said to be too fat, too thin, unstable, unprofessional, a bad mother. Then, understandably, she begins to freak out and unwittingly vindicates the gossip. Then she is hounded some more until something – an arrest, an accident, a scandal, an eating disorder, a suicide – degrades her so much that the public finally sits back, satisfied that another promising female has been taken out of action.

The media that deal in pop freakouts don't report these stories so much as create them. If Britney Spears has had any kind of meltdown, who can blame her? She is followed wherever she goes by stalker-violators: some have cameras and call themselves paparazzi; some have notebooks and call themselves journalists; some have vaginas and call themselves concerned women of the world. All relish the harassment that they perpetrate. It is women (writers and readers) who are enjoying and encouraging the exposure of Lohan's drink and drugs hell or Spears's identity crisis, while saving space for a snide comment about their outfits. It is women who are getting off on other women's difficulties, while men in power carouse, abuse (and self-abuse) with impunity.

Who are the real 'bad girls'? Not Lohan or Spears. The gossip magazines may be as punchy as a dose of Splenda, but they offer evidence that women have obediently taken on the values of a woman-hating world. We must recognise the part women play in the degradation of women: the ultimate betrayal.

11 DECEMBER 2007

'You're consenting to being raped for money'

Appalled at the sanitised picture The Secret Diary of a Call Girl paints, a woman who charges for sex describes her life

EMINE SANER

A flat in a block in a suburb of London: Karen (not her real name) thinks her neighbours probably realise she sells sex for a living. Of all the myths and stereotypes surrounding prostitution, the reality is more likely to be found in banal places like this. It is as far away from a cliched sleazy Soho walk-up as it is from a room in a luxury hotel. The bed is made, the bathroom clean. There is a pair of black plastic strappy shoes with a transparent high heel on one side of her computer desk, tucked down the other side is a pair of fluffy, white slippers.

The ITV drama The Secret Diary of a Call Girl, which has been commissioned for a second series despite terrible reviews, brought prostitution into the mainstream – and with it a lot of controversy. The makers of the programme, which was adapted from the book and blog by 'Belle de Jour', the pseudonym of a supposedly high-charging escort, were accused of glamorising prostitution and portraying an unrealistic image of the sex industry. 'It is highlighting in a big way a very tiny segment of the industry,' says Karen, who wanted to talk to the Guardian about her experiences in light of the hype surrounding the programme. 'The majority of what this industry is about is a lot of pain, misery and distress. It annoys me that the media like to highlight only the prostitutes who say how empowering this is. There might be a few out there who think that at this moment in time, but that is not true for the vast majority. What pisses me off about [Belle de Jour] is that you're very rarely going to have a client that you like having sex with. You have to learn to disassociate your body from your mind which is dangerous for your psyche. For the vast majority of prostitutes, it isn't glamorous – it is damaging and dangerous – yet it seems to be promoted as some kind of career option.'

It is hard to understand why a woman who isn't a drug addict would become a prostitute, but then there are a huge number of reasons why someone finds themselves in this situation, says Karen. In her 20s, she was the victim of a horrific attack and sexual assault, which left her with an anxiety about men. She thinks she has tried to counteract it by putting herself in what she sees as a position of power over them. 'I'm the one in control, they're paying me. I'm not stupid – [the assault] probably does have something to do with proving to myself that I can be the one in control, that I can have something at the end of it. I can say when he walks out the door.'

She came to prostitution late – she is in her early 50s but looks much younger – having left her full-time job as an administrator six years ago after being bullied. It left her depressed and unconfident. She has a history of alcohol abuse and also had ME, which left her unable to get another full-time job. 'Just driving to work and back every day would exhaust me,' she says. 'I have to factor in a lot of rest in my life. I know my limitations and I keep within them as much as possible.'

A few years earlier, Karen had left an unhappy marriage and began using internet chatrooms to meet men. 'I started going on blind dates and it slowly started to evolve into having sex with strangers'. It wasn't such a huge leap, she says, into charging for what she was giving anyway. 'I had a bad month, financially, as I invariably would, and it started as a trickle. I had always been curious about doing it – I think I was trying to prove to myself that actually prostitution was OK. But now I realise that it isn't.' She put an ad offering massage in a newsagent's window and found that sex work would fit in around the hours of rest she needed to control her chronic fatigue. 'To keep myself going and pay my bills and save for my pension, I probably need to see five a week,' she says. 'I can almost control my workload. The most I've ever seen in one day was three. I don't have a stream of men coming.' She charges £130 an hour – it used to be £170 but the influx of eastern European prostitutes, charging low prices, has pushed prices down.

For a while, Karen worked for an escort agency in London. 'You got the best-paid jobs through the agency, but the woman who ran it would take 30%,' she says. 'One guy one night wanted me at 11 o'clock and I left at two in the morning. He ended up giving me £1,500. But these are the exceptions. Another guy paid me an extra £700 for unprotected sex – I walked out of there with £1,200. It was a godsend because I wasn't working much at the time.' She never agrees to unprotected sex now. 'I don't provide anything that's unsafe and it is probably pretty basic compared to some women out there. The more desperate you are, the more you're going to put yourself in danger.'

She left the agency because she was angry at how much money the proprietor took. She tried working in flats used as brothels, but these jobs never lasted long. 'One Christmas I was getting really desperate so I asked for work at a flat. It was dirty, they took out money for maid service, commission and cleaning, so I only got about half the money I earned. I'd rather work away from home, but you don't get the money and you're in somebody else's control. If I really can't face it I just won't answer the door. I'm lucky I can control that.'

An estimated two-thirds of prostitutes have experienced violence from clients. Has she? 'Nearly. When I first started, I got trapped on a building site with a client. He locked me in a building with him. He made it clear that all the security guards had gone home because it was a Sunday evening. I hadn't realised that he was very drunk. He started talking about wanting a threesome and I said I'd ring my friend and ask her to come over. I rang this made-up number on my phone and pretended to speak to her, then I told him I had to go out and meet her. He let me out.' Once she was out of sight, she ran and ended up having to climb over two 8ft fences. 'Another time, I had one guy who kept insisting that I have anal sex but I wouldn't. He became extremely violent – he kept grabbing my hair and pulling it back. And you have to act like you're enjoying it. How that cannot damage somebody is . . . you don't know what they're going to do if you say stop.'

Then there are the scammers and time wasters, the ones who ring her up and ask what she is wearing so they don't have to ring a premium-rate phone line. 'I had one man who came round and said he would only pay if he could see what he was getting. I undressed in front of him and he said, "You've got a great body for your age, but I could go into London and pay the same money for a girl that looked like a model and was 25." I said, "Fine, off you go then." I made him leave but it was so demeaning.'

'You're going to get creepy men. That's a fact. I've had clients who have made my life hell. One guy came in and foolishly I didn't ask him for the money first.' Afterwards, he claimed to have forgotten his wallet and Karen kept phoning him about the money. He turned nasty and threatened to burn her house down, then he started harassing her and would come by at two in the morning or would ring from different numbers pretending to be someone else. 'You have to be careful not to piss someone off,' she says. 'Most of the time I would say the men I meet, when I have sex with them I feel neutral about them. I don't fancy them but they don't repulse me either – they're just middle of the road. Some men have actually turned my stomach – I could hardly bear for them to touch me and those are generally the ones who find it hard to find someone who will see them again, so they start to pester you.'

What sort of men visit her? A lot are older, 'Either their wives have gone off having sex with them or they want to prove to themselves that they can still turn a woman on. They seem to block out the fact that having to pay a woman to do this kind of cancels that out. Some men are quite upset that you don't enjoy it, but those are the few. Some people say that prostitution is actually a man paying to rape a woman.' Does she believe that? 'I think that is true in a lot of cases. Although it is a business arrangement, he is getting off on the fact that the woman doesn't want it. Basically you've consented to being raped for money.'

Even in the past couple of years, Karen says she has noticed changes in the men who come to see her and what they expect. 'I've noticed that the paedophile scenario has started creeping in. Recently, I had a man who said, "I'd like to try a 14-year-old. Can you find me one?" I've been asked to include another woman – that's quite a new thing. Two years ago, I remember men who would be upset at the idea that a prostitute they were using had been trafficked. Now I don't think it bothers them. The desensitisation process doubles up on itself every year. They want to tally up what's going on in their heads with your body. Sometimes they're not even looking at you.' How does that make her feel? 'Sometimes I think, it's just a performance. But it's not, it's more than that and it's very harmful.'

How does she think it has harmed her? 'That word disassociation comes back. I know the difference between sex for money and sex with someone you love, but if I was younger it might have damaged me more. You become hyper-vigilant. You worry about who is going to walk through the door or if the client is going to turn nasty. There is the constant worry about money.'

Karen would like to be able to stop working, but doesn't know what else to do (she is waiting to hear whether or not she will be able to claim disability benefit). Would she ever be able to have a 'normal' relationship with a man? 'Even if I found a man I could tell what I've done, at the back of his mind he will not trust me. It puts you in quite literally a no-man's land. I will never trust a man again. In fact, I'm almost glad that I have done this because I know what men get up to. Their wives don't know. The likelihood, if you've got a boyfriend or husband, of him cheating on you is probably quite high.' When I tell her I don't really believe this, she looks at me as though I'm stupid.

She calls herself a feminist, but how does she square that with being a part of the sex industry, perpetuating it? 'When I first started, I thought I was getting my own back. Men were meeting me and expecting sex for nothing so I thought, why not make them pay? It does bother me that I am perpetuating it but I don't know what else to do. I try whenever possible to counteract that with clients, in subtle ways. For instance, when a man asks me to be with another girl I say, "Well, would you go with another man?" I try to make them stop and think.'

She describes what she calls the 'surround sound' of pornography – on television, in advertising, on the internet, in pop videos. 'Younger women are being coerced into valuing themselves by what they look like and men's definition of how a woman should be valued. It's like being at the top of a hill and looking down and I can see all the little cultural landmarks, like the launch of Playboy, the internet, music videos celebrating a "pimp and ho" culture, lads' magazines, burlesque. Women are being told that their bodies should be accessible at all times to men. I believe there is a conspiracy to turn women into readily accessible semen receptacles. Men are twisting this now to make women think it's a level playing field and it's equal and liberating. No, it suits men, it's convenient for men. That's what is so insidious.'

22 DECEMBER 2007

Porn is screwing up young men's expectations of sex

The revelations about Manchester United's party reflect the parlous state of our supposed sexual liberation

MARINA HYDE

Truly, nothing says Christmas like a footballer-party rape allegation. It's getting so Pavlovian that the first story suggesting one guest might have enjoyed herself rather less than the others at some club's festive bash has become as evocative as the smell of mulled wine or wilfully spun reports suggesting the Muslims are stealing our Christmas.

Facetious? Most of the responses to the fact that a 19-year-old Manchester United player has been accused of raping a 26-year-old woman at the club's Christmas party early on Tuesday have been about as nuanced. They have run the gamut from 'footballers are lawless scum' to 'the girls are no better: they all deserve each other'. There were some 'she probably made it ups' in there, too, and maybe the odd 'women are just meat to these beasts'.

Yesterday further revelations about the party surfaced. One 'very drunk' woman was 'roasted' by five or six men, according to another guest, who told a newspaper that 'I asked her if she was OK and she said, "Yeah, why wouldn't I be? They said I was a great shag."'

There will be people – some would even count themselves as third-wave feminists – who can read that statement and accuse anyone who feels the vaguest sense of unease about it of being straitlaced, or repressive of this woman's natural sexuality. These people like to think of themselves as sexual cognoscenti – a bedroom version of those television chefs who tell you they always get their truffles from a family supplier in Puglia and assume you'll do the same. For their bondage tips, they go to the Marquis de Sade in the original French.

If they're that smart, though, they should appreciate that not everyone indulges in these things with quite the same degree of consequence-free delight and rationalised abandon as they do – and it's inverse snobbery to pretend that it is so.

And so to a vexing riddle of our times. Namely, if six footballers can have six girls each, why do they only want one between them? The answer is actually incredibly simple (and has nothing to do with repressed homosexuality). It might be partly that they enjoy team activities and it's a kind of extended goal celebration, but it is primarily because that is what they see in porn. And porn is screwing up sex. Not sex in relationships, but the kind of casual sex in which it would be nice to think people could indulge in a mutually enjoyable, non-exploitative fashion. In this context, footballers are not qualitatively different from plenty of other young men, it's just that being regarded as demigods makes it easier to act in this way.

Several years ago Naomi Wolf pointed out that the proliferation of porn, particularly on the internet, was the way most young men and women were now, in effect, taught about sex – 'what sex is, how it looks, what its etiquette and expectations are'. It had a significant impact on the way they interacted. She wondered whether all the sexual imagery around represented the true liberation of sex, or whether 'the relationship between the multibillion-dollar porn industry, compulsiveness, and sexual appetite has become like the relationship between agribusiness, processed foods, supersize portions, and obesity'.

No matter where you stand on it, porn has undoubtedly skewed many young men's expectations of sex, and many young women's sense of sexual obligation. The marvellous website jezebel.com touched on this theme recently, having identified an experiential trend among the staff's acquaintances. Several of these women had been on a first date, ended up sleeping with the guys, and the men had ejaculated on their face without asking. The reader responses were revealing. It transpired that lots of people had had this surprise experience, and while there was debate about whether the act referred to was rank misogyny or something you could truly love, there was unanimous concurrence that it should be on the 'have to ask first list' – and that the presumption even in a few people that it wasn't signified a shift in popular male imagination. Several younger readers wrote in saying that they found men their age were so conditioned by porn that 'they don't think sex is "good" unless it's somehow fetishy'.

Now, either these guys were just borderline rapists, or – way more likely and way more scarily – they simply didn't know any better.

It would be nice to think we could reclaim the right to say people don't know any better without being accused of snobbery, because the longer we allow the argument to be short-circuited in that fatuous way, the longer the debate remains buried. And there are plenty of questions, wherever you stand. Is this the only sexual liberation we're going to have, or are we due another rethink? Are both genders having better sex than they did 10 or 20 years ago?

Could it be that women who queue up outside a hotel just itching to be told they are 'a great shag' by an assortment of footballers have bad sex most of the time? If we placed more emphasis on addressing these issues, would there be fewer of what we might, with immense charity, call 'misunderstandings'?

15 FEBRUARY 2008

Banda sisters

In one of India's poorest regions, hundreds of pink-clad female vigilantes are challenging male violence and corruption

RAEKHA PRASAD

Under a scorching summer sun, a swarm of 400 furious women engulfed the scruffy electricity office of Banda district in north India. They were all dressed identically in fluorescent pink saris. For more than a fortnight they and their families had had no electricity, plunged into darkness at dusk and stewed in sweat at dawn. But they had all been sent bills demanding payment for power they had never received.

It was at noon one day last May that the group, brandishing sticks, first surrounded and then charged into the office, punching the air and shouting slogans of solidarity. They wanted to confront the officer in charge but met instead his cowering juniors, at whom they bawled to telephone the boss. When the man refused to come to the office, the women became incensed. They snatched the office key, roughed up the terrified staff and, after herding them outside, locked the door and ran away, vowing to return the key only when they had electricity again.

There are few places on earth where life is as short and brutal as in Bundelkhand, the desolate region straddling the southern tip of Uttar Pradesh where Banda lies. Farming is the principal livelihood; wages are as little as 60p a day for men and half that for women. Bonded and child labour are rife. Corruption is routine. Its reputation in India is that of a place where people still die of hunger.

But what has made Bundelkhand infamous is banditry. Scores born out of feudalism and caste violence are settled by bullets. It was here that Phoolan Devi, the Bandit Queen of India, used to lead her gang of robbers in vicious acts of retribution on rich, upper-caste villagers. Products of this cruel environment, the hundreds of pink-clad women knew that their electricity supply had been disconnected by corrupt officials to extract bribes from them to get the power switched back on. With no functioning law to fall back on, they knew also that the only way to get a power supply was to take matters into their own hands. Within an hour of their absconding with the key, the electricity was restored.

It is just one victory in a list of successes achieved by the Gulabi Gang since it formed two years ago. Gulabi means pink, and refers to the electric shade of the uniform worn by the 500-plus members, who hail from Banda's arid villages. The women have become folk heroes, winning public support for a series of Robin Hood-style operations. Their most daring exploit was to hijack trucks laden with food meant for the poor that was being taken to be sold for profit at the market by corrupt officials.

The targets of the Gulabi Gang's vigilantism are corrupt officials and violent husbands. The gang has stopped child marriages, forced police officers to register cases of domestic violence – by slapping them – and got roads built by dragging the official responsible from his desk on to the dust track in question.

The gang is led, and was created by, 46-year-old Sampat Devi Pal. When I meet her, she is demonstrating self-defence moves with a stick. 'We always carry them but only for protection,' she explains, twisting the weapon high over her head and thwacking it hard against her opponent's.

The daughter of a shepherd, Pal was put to work on the family's land while her brothers went to school. Married at 12 to a 20-year-old man from a neighbouring village whom she had never met, she was pregnant by 15. She wanted to be sterilised after having two daughters but her mother-in-law wouldn't allow it until she had produced a son. Another four children followed.

As is common among Hindu families in rural north India, her in-laws wanted Pal to veil her face and remain silent in the presence of male family members, as a sign of respect for authority. 'I never did either,' she giggles throatily.

Pal is difficult company. Those not showing her the utmost respect get crude abuse. Yet in a place where expectation of female restraint is so faithfully observed, only someone as irascible as Pal could defy it. I meet her husband in the couple's home, which is built in a ditch with plastic sheeting for a roof. He is mute and utterly obedient to her every order. Later, an astonishing role reversal takes place as half a dozen loyal and obedient male hangers-on are sent running at the snap of her fingers to fetch us tea and guavas.

To them Pal is someone who can defend the weak, which, in the badlands of Bundelkhand, is rare indeed. Although 80% of the gang's actions are on behalf of women, they are increasingly called upon by men. When 7,000 Banda farmers decided to take to the streets to demand compensation for failed crops earlier this month, they asked the Gulabi Gang to be there.

The gang's challenge to the throttling grip of male authority has brought new confidence – and dangers – to its members. I meet Radha, 40, the leader of the ambush on the electricity office, walking with a friend in the market. 'Before I joined the gang I was in purdah and never went out of the house,' she says. 'Now I've tackled ministers and officials and I've done away with my shyness – and the veil.' Others have been less fortunate. A few days before I arrive in Banda, one of the gang's youngest members, a 14-year-old girl, had been attacked with a sickle as she went for her morning ablutions in the fields. She had put up a fight when a 16-year-old neighbour tried to rape her.

Meanwhile, Pal herself is in danger of being criminalised. Following a complaint by the police, she is waiting to hear if she will be formally charged with 11 offences, including unlawful assembly, rioting, attacking a government employee and obstructing an officer in the discharge of duty. 'To face down men in this part of the world, you have to use force,' Pal says. 'I didn't do anything wrong. I have faith that justice will prevail.'

It took Pal over a decade to muster the foot soldiers for the gang she now calls her 'army'. Travelling from village to village, she amassed hundreds of female fans by belting out her repertoire of protest songs. 'I wanted to lift them out of the black hole they'd been pushed into,' Pal says, like a true orator. Only 20% of women in Bundelkhand's villages can write their name and most are child brides. 'I realised that without education, women are steeped in superstitious beliefs.'

Eventually, hundreds of women were turning out to hear Pal. They also brought their problems: land grabbing by powerful thugs that left whole families homeless; their violent husbands' alcoholism and drug abuse; how officials demanded bribes even for payment of a widow's pension.

'I realised that if I could have this kind of control over women then I could get them out of the clutches of their husbands,' Pal says, narrowing her eyes. There is not the faintest hint of a smile on her lips.

22 FEBRUARY 2008

Mothers need not apply

Maternal profiling is illegal in the UK – but it is flourishing

VIV GROSKOP

The unlikely new face of radical women's activism in the US? Meet Kiki Peppard, a 53-year-old switchboard operator and grandmother from Pennsylvania who claims she is one of millions of victims of 'maternal profiling'. Defined as 'employment discrimination against a woman who has, or will have, children', feminist groups say that maternal profiling has reached epidemic proportions – and is getting worse. In essence, it involves employers building up information on a woman's age, marital status and family commitments to determine whether to hire her, how much to pay her and how much responsibility to give her. Is she likely to have children and need maternity pay? Will she want to work shorter hours?

All these factors push women up against a 'maternal wall' – which has been described as the new glass ceiling – potentially stopping them from landing a job for which they are specifically, even uniquely, well qualified.

Peppard has spent the past 14 years campaigning unsuccessfully for a law to ban the practice in Pennsylvania. She experienced maternal profiling first-hand in 1994 when her husband left her and she moved from Long Island, New York, to Effort, Pennsylvania ('The name is appropriate,' she sighs over the phone). She was rejected from 19 job interviews in a row because she was a single mother to James, then 14, and Carissa, then 11.

'The first question was always, "Are you married?" The second was, "Do you have children?" After that, they stopped the interview.' After a year on welfare she finally got a job as a secretary at a high school where they asked no questions about her child-care responsibilities.

Unbelievably, then as now, it was perfectly legal in 28 states, including Pennsylvania, for interviewers to ask questions about a job applicant's marital status, family plans and caring responsibilities. At the end of 2007, the New York Times called 'maternal profiling' one of the political buzzwords of the coming year. Moms Rising, the increasingly high-profile US campaigning group which promotes mothers' rights and has doubled its membership to 140,000 in the past year has championed Peppard's case. And maternal profiling is edging its way on to the election agenda: Hillary Clinton pledged her interest when campaigning in New Hampshire in October last year.

In the UK, asking questions in a job interview about a woman's maternal status would leave an employer open to a sex discrimination case, yet there is a great deal of evidence that such profiling goes on unspoken. And it is a practice that affects not just mothers, but all women of childbearing age. Whether or not you intend to have children, the possibility that you might could well be enough to put off a potential employer.

Last year, a survey by the new Equality and Human Rights Commission, headed by Trevor Phillips, found that 70% of recruitment agencies had been asked to avoid hiring women who were pregnant or likely to get pregnant. The commission also found that mothers face more discrimination in the workplace than any other group. Those with children under 11 were 45% less likely to be employed than men, with that figure rising to 49% among single mothers.

A YouGov poll of 1,000 UK directors, also conducted in 2007, revealed that 21% knew of instances where their company had avoided hiring women of child-bearing age – 19% admitted to making this decision themselves. In the same poll, more than two-thirds of senior executives said that the bureaucracy surrounding parental leave posed a 'serious threat' to their companies. And in 2004 an extraordinary survey by the HR information provider Cromer found that eight in 10 human resources managers would 'think twice' before hiring a newly married woman in her 20s. (They had fewer reservations about hiring mothers with older children, they said, as they would be 'less likely to take maternity leave'.)

All of which reflects the fact that women of child-bearing age increasingly seem to be seen as 'difficult' employees. So much so, that earlier this month Alan Sugar commented that the laws preventing employers asking women about their family plans and childcare arrangements have resulted in him throwing some candidates' CVs in the bin. 'Everything has gone too far,' said Sugar. 'We have maternity laws where people are entitled to too much. If someone comes into an interview and you think to yourself "there is a possibility that this woman might have a child and therefore take time off", it is a bit of a psychological negative thought.

'If they are applying for a position which is very important,' he continued, 'then I should imagine that some employers might think "this is a bit risky". They would like to ask the question: "Are you planning to get married and to have any children?"'

(In the last series of The Apprentice, of course, Sugar caused heated debate by quizzing candidate Katie Hopkins on her childcare arrangements during the final interview process.)

In the weeks since Sugar made these extraordinary comments, cyberspace has been full of (mostly anonymous) owners of small businesses cheering him on. One blogger writes: 'It is high time someone of high profile said what every employer is scared to say: "I would not employ women." [. . .] The reason I do not employ women is that I run a small business and there is no way that I could fund maternity benefits.' Another replied: 'I know where you are coming from as we too are the same . . . if we do look for a female staff member, we would want somebody in her late 40s or early 50s.'

And this last comment reflects an observation made by Moms Rising, which estimates that women are only safe from maternal profiling after the age of 44, when they are considered to be past child-bearing age. As one of the group's activists writes on a 'maternal profiling' blog: 'My life and career path have not made it possible for me to settle down and have children. However this does not keep people from discriminating against me by "assuming" that I either have children or plan to have them soon. As if they can hear my biological clock ticking.'

This discriminatory behaviour has always taken place, of course, but it is hoped that by giving it an emotive name – with its connotations of racial profiling, and offender profiling – the problem might gain new recognition and an organised campaign of opposition. As Kristin Rowe-Finkbeiner, president of Moms Rising, points out: 'Sexual harassment is a phrase that helped to spark major legislative and cultural changes. Widespread use of the phrase "maternal profiling" can similarly help to spark major changes.' She describes the incidence of discrimination as 'jaw-dropping,' quoting a recent US study that showed that mothers are 79% less likely to be hired than non-mothers with equal employment experience. 'If you're a mother in America maternal profiling is likely to have happened to you.'

For her part, Peppard says she has never forgotten the humili-ation of having to present her food stamps at the supermarket all those years ago when she was being turned down for job after job. Her most recent attempt to pass the law stalled before it reached the state senate in November 2007. 'Initially I kept up the momentum in the hope that I would get this law passed before my daughter was ready to enter the workforce,' she says. 'Now I'm doing it for my granddaughter.'

The Miami-based lawyer Michael Casey, who specialises in employment law, says that 'so-called "family responsibility discrimination" claims are probably going to constitute the next wave of major litigation directed at employers in the US.' Some US companies are already voluntarily showing support to parents, regardless of their state laws, because they fear future litigation. But there is a knock-on effect even to these pre-emptive moves. 'Giving preferential treatment to people who have familial responsibilities has created a backlash involving employees who lack such responsibilities,' says Casey, and, in future, these childless employees could bring 'reverse discrimination' suits over the injustice of always being the ones asked to work late and at weekends. 'Lawyers will be happy with that result, at least,' he adds wryly.

Meanwhile, in Pennsylvania, Peppard is happy to fight on as long as it takes. 'I have written to Oprah Winfrey twice a year for the past 14 years and I contacted her again last week. I think if she knew about this personally, she'd call me.' Peppard is dismissive of the (mostly male) legislature who won't pass her bill. 'I wonder if their own mothers know about what they're doing to punish women,' she says. 'Maybe they think mothers don't vote and don't matter. But we do.' Perhaps she might do us all a favour, and write to Alan Sugar next.

21 MARCH 2008

I was only telling the truth

When Rachel Cusk wrote A Life's Work, she was shocked by the vicious reaction it provoked from other women. The experience forced her to question herself as a writer and a parent

RACHEL CUSK

In 2001 we were living in the sticks. It was a beautiful place in the Brendon Hills in Somerset, the rattling ghost of a grand estate, where a miniature ornamental lake still languished in the overgrown pleasure gardens, and the trees in the neglected orchard shed rare red, heart-shaped apples like the apples in a medieval tapestry. It lay remotely, far from town, in a lush green crease of hills that rose steadily up to meet the moor. There was me, my husband, my husband's eight-year-old daughter, and our own two children: a baby who cried passionately each time I moved out of her line of vision, and her sister, older by 15 months, whose abundant hair exactly matched the electrifying palette of autumn in the pleasure gardens that year.

We were renting a house in the grounds of the estate, abandoned by its lineage in the 1940s. It had the portrait of a lady at the top of the stairs with particularly penetrating eyes. I was a little frightened of the house at first: those eyes followed me doggedly, and at night, when the darkness was fathomless, the house embarked on long interior monologues, the water groaning in its old pipes, the floorboards clicking and creaking, the damp walls sometimes emitting a profound shudder or sigh, while outside the wind roared in the oak trees and over the black shapes of hills. There were other houses on the estate besides ours: a cottage, and a flat in the tumble-down stable block opposite our house, and a recherche dwelling called the Elephant House. The people who lived in these places were mostly artisans and artists. They were welcoming and warm, for in this community people came and went frequently. It was easy for us to fit in.

All through a drizzling Exmoor winter I had been writing a book, in a tiny rented place up on the moor where we stayed while we looked for somewhere to live. My husband walked the baby around the lanes in her pram so that I could concentrate. It rained and blew a gale. It would have been more pleasant for them inside: the imposition was so direct that I wrote as quickly as I could. I had written other parts of the book in some uncomfortable places: the cold cobwebbed vestry of my parents-in-law's local church, to which my mother-in-law had the key; the attic of another, earlier house whose stairs were so narrow for my increasingly pregnant body that it seemed possible I might one day get permanently stuck up there. By the time we moved to the house beside the pleasure gardens, which had a study, I was nearly finished.

Adversity was the hallmark of this book, though I didn't notice it at the time. It was a book – called A Life's Work: On Becoming a Mother, and published in 2001 – that set out to describe the psychical events of childbirth and early motherhood, and though I very much wanted to write it, it was difficult to do when in the thrall of the events themselves. But that was how it had to be, for I was using myself as the template. I had to live it and to analyse it, both at the same time. I was four or five months pregnant with my second child when I began, and when I reached the end, that child existed, an ardent 10-month-old baby whose power of love has ever since been fused in my mind with the risks and rewards of self-exposure. By the time the book came out, she was one and a half, her sister three: that summer I peacefully harvested the gooseberry bushes at the back of the house, swam in the orna-mental lake, shooed out the bats that sometimes flew around the rafters of our room on summer evenings. It was my sincere belief that nobody would read it or care about it, and in all honesty I didn't blame them. I didn't particularly want anyone to read it. It had been important for me to make a record, that was all, of emotional and physical states I was unlikely to experience again.

First of all there was a letter, from a writer friend I had sent a copy to. Be prepared, she said: your book is going to make people very angry.

I read this sitting in the foot-high summer grass that grew through the terrace, above a wild sea of rhododendron bushes. I didn't know what to make of it. Which people? Why would they be angry? What did it have to do with them? A day or two later my sister called. Don't listen to anything they say, she said. It's a very good book. Just ignore them.

These signs and portents soon crystallised into something tangible. I went into town and bought a newspaper, and turning the pages came across the first review of A Life's Work.

'If everyone were to read this book,' it said, 'the propagation of the human race would virtually cease, which would be a shame.' The reviewer was a woman. I had met her, in fact, at some literary festival or other years before. She had seemed harmless enough: I would not have suspected her of such drastic reach, such anni-hilating middle-class smugness ('which would be a shame'). She went on to accuse me of 'confining [my daughter] to the kitchen like an animal'. Perhaps strangely, it was the second remark that troubled me more than the possibility that humanity would be extinguished by my hand. How did this person presume to know what I did with my daughter, and where? Where had she come upon such bizarre information? Had someone told her I treated my child like an animal? It took me a long time to realise that her accusation came from the book itself, from a falsification of its personal material. She had searched it, I saw, for 'evidence' of my conduct as a mother, and as such she could permit herself to misrepresent me, for she was not judging the book as a book. She was judging it as a social situation.

I returned to the house. When I laid eyes on my children I was instantly overcome by powerful feelings of guilt and shame. There is always shame in the creation of an object for the public gaze. This time, however, I felt it not as a writer but as a mother. I felt that I had committed a violent act. I felt that I had been abusive and negligent. I felt these things not because of anything I had physically or actually done to them ('she confines her daughter to the kitchen like an animal'), but because I had written a book that had malfunctioned, and had allowed our relationship to be publicly impugned. I see now that it was the reviewer who was violent, with her careless, self-congratulatory brutality ('Believe it or not, quite a few people enjoy motherhood,' she went on, 'but in order to do so, it is important to grow up first'), the reviewer who, while claiming saintly qualities of motherhood, proved with these lines her utter lack of respect and care for children.

Another review, in a different paper: this one long and articulate where the first was brief and blunt.

'What is really startling about A Life's Work is that it is genuinely post-feminist, not in the sense that we do not need feminism any more, but in the sense that it implicitly points to the holes in the familiar feminist discourse. If we do away with the notion that the personal is political, as feminism-lite is wont to do, who gets left holding the baby? This is the contemporary crisis of feminism. An equality founded on what Cusk might call public significance has produced an emphasis on work as the only measure of parity. Motherhood, as it is lived, is still individual, personal, private, and therefore deeply undervalued, sometimes even by those of us (and nowadays that is most of us) who move between the 'real' world of work and the shadow world of family life. Between these worlds,

Cusk has crafted a work of beauty and wisdom. And belly laughs. A lovely thing.'

The sun shines again: the shame goes away. After all, it seems that I have done something good, not bad. I even feel a certain pride, as a mother, that is. My writer-self feels nothing at all. It can't afford to.

'Frankly, you are a self-obsessed bore: the embodiment of the Me! Me! Me! attitude which you so resent in small children. And everything those children say or do is – in your mind – really about you. Sooner or later, you end up in family therapy, because it has never occurred to you that it might be an idea to simply bring children up to be happy, or to consider happiness as an option for yourself . . . Talk about navel-gazing.'

'Cusk anatomises motherhood as Montaigne anatomised friendship or Robert Burton anatomised melancholy . . . Some alchemy of her prose renders this most fascinating and boring of all subjects graceful, eloquent, modest and true.'

'I have about as much interest in babies as I have in cavity-wall insulation. You might feel moved to describe the moments of desperation that follow nine hours of incessant wailing. It might not occur to you that, just because it's a horrific experience doesn't make it interesting. If you had a baby, you did so because you wanted one. If you are suffering sleep deprivation so severe you're hallucinating, that was your choice.'

'I laughed out loud, often, in painful recognition.'

'Pure misery to read. From the way she writes about her first child, God alone only knows how she allowed herself to bear a second.'

On and on it went, back and forth: I was accused of child-hating, of postnatal depression, of shameless greed, of irresponsibility, of pretentiousness, of selfishness, of doom-mongering and, most often, of being too intellectual. One curious article questioned the length of my sentences: how had I, a mother, been able to write such long and complicated sentences? Why was I not busier, more tired? Another reviewer – a writer! – commanded her readers not to let the book fall into the hands of pregnant women. The telephone rang and rang. I was invited on the Today programme to defend myself. I was invited on the Nicky Campbell programme to defend myself. I was cited everywhere as having said the unsayable: that it is possible for a woman to dislike her children, even to regret having brought them into the world.

As writers go, I have a skin of average thickness. I am pleased by a good review, disappointed by a bad. None of it penetrates far enough to influence the thing I write next. This time, it was different. Again and again people judged the book not as readers but as mothers, and it was judgment of a sanctimoniousness whose like I had never experienced. Yet I had experienced it, in a way: it was part of what I had found intolerable in the public culture of motherhood, the childcare manuals and the toddler groups, the discourse of domestic life, even the politics of birth itself. In motherhood the communal was permitted to prevail over the individual, and the result, to my mind, was a great deal of dishonesty. I had identified this dishonesty in A Life's Work: it seemed to me to be intrinsic to the psychical predicament of the new mother, that in having a child she should re-encounter the childhood mechanism of suppression. She would encounter the possibility of suppressing her true feelings in order to be 'good' and to gain approval. My own struggle had been to resist this mechanism. I wanted to – I had to – remain 'myself'.

It was, perhaps, our isolation – idyllic though it was – that sealed these events in a profound melancholy from which I subsequently found myself unable to escape. The world became a bleaker place. I felt angry and defensive and violated. Despite the number of people who had praised and admired it, and the letters I received to that effect from readers, I regretted, constantly, the fact that I had written A Life's Work. I had been asked many times – am still asked – by journalists barely able to contain their excitement lest I say 'yes', whether I regretted having my children. What meaning could such an admission possibly have? My children are living, thinking human beings. It isn't in my power to regret them, for they belong to themselves. It is these kinds of questions that are the true heresy, not my refusal to answer them. But my books are my own, to approve of or regret as I see fit.

These days I have a better understanding of the intolerance to which, for a while, I fell victim. I see that, like all intolerance, it arose from dependence on an ideal. I see that cruelty and rudeness and viciousness are its harbingers, as they have always been. I see that many – most – of my female detractors continue to write routinely in the press about motherhood and issues relating to children. Their interest in these issues has a fixated quality, compared with their worldly male equivalents. I am struck by this distinction, for it is clear that they hunger to express themselves not as women, not as commentators or intellectuals, but as mothers. This hunger evidently goes unsatisfied, and must content itself with scraps from the table of daily news.

I see, too, that there are many women who find motherhood easier than I do, or did. I believe that these things do not lie entirely within our own control. I felt a great need to write, which did not always harmonise with the requirements of my daughters. I was step-parent to a young child with difficulties and vulnerabilities of her own. I have a bad relationship with my own mother and was pitched by motherhood into the recollection of childhood unhappiness and confusion. But this, too, is a common enough reality: why should it be mocked or censured? Penelope Leach gives, I think, an accurate definition of postnatal depression: she says that in postnatal depression the mother believes that there is something faulty or abnormally difficult about her child. This was not my position. My great love for my children and step-child slowly liberated me from much of what I felt about the past. I freed myself – or them – by trying to be honest, by being willing to apologise.

Nevertheless, I remain uneasy in the public places of motherhood – the school gate, the coffee circuit – where the skies can unexpectedly open and judgment rain down on one's head. I find that I like women less than I did, and wonder whether other feminists have been in the same uncomfortable position. It used to be incomprehensible to me that women of the time attacked early feminists so violently, that they loudly objected to their own sex being given the vote. It isn't any more.

Every morning I cycle with my daughters to school: it is a good 10-minute ride, uphill most of the way. We used to go on the pavement, but people protested so now we go on the road. Every single day, some woman with her child strapped into the front seat of her car shakes her head at us. Today, a woman in a Range Rover pulled up at a junction where we had stopped, and rolled down her window. 'You're making me very nervous,' she said to me loudly. I looked at her, at the child sitting beside her. Did she not care that my daughters could hear what she said? Did they not exist for her, panting and proud of their cycling, stridently moral about pollution? Could she not see that it was she, in her car, that represented the very danger she congratulated herself for pointing out? She was so certain that she was protecting her child better than I was protecting mine. I will never defeat that certainty. All I can do is endeavour not to be crushed by it. I smiled politely, and we rode on.

17 DECEMBER 2008

'We are the future'

So many men were killed during the Rwandan genocide that women have increasingly found themselves in positions of power. How is that changing the country?

CHRIS MCGREAL

Judith Kanakuze pauses at the mention of her family. 'God saved me,' she says. 'He did not save them.' Fourteen years ago, 11,000 Tutsis were murdered in Kanakuze's home province of Kibuye, in the west of Rwanda, in the town's Roman Catholic church. Almost everyone in her extended family had fled to the chapel for sanctuary. The next day another 10,000 people were murdered in the town stadium in a pogrom led by Kibuye's governor.

Kanakuze does not want to say much more. The survivors of the genocide often speak of the pain of being 'condemned to live'. But she admits to an unexpected optimism as a member of the first parliament in the world to have a majority of female MPs. 'This is a different time,' she says. 'We are transforming our society, and women are part of the solution.'

In September, Rwanda's parliamentary election saw women win 45 of the 80 seats. Nearly half were elected in women-only seats, with the rest triumphing in open ballots.

The women MPs include former rebels and genocide survivors, war widows and peasant farmers, and although the election was a landmark, the women's success was not unexpected. Under the requirements of a new constitution, women already held a third of cabinet posts – including the foreign, education and information portfolios. The heads of the supreme court and the police are also women, as are a majority of the country's prison governors.

Before 1994, women held only around one in five parliamentary seats. The genocide changed everything. When the killing ended there were twice as many women as men in Rwanda, and while the gap has since narrowed, more than a third of households are still headed by women. Women also make up 55% of the workforce and own about 40% of businesses.

Aloisea Inyumba is a Tutsi former rebel fighter, who has been part of the Rwandan Patriotic Front-led (RPF) government since it overthrew the extremist Hutu regime in 1994 – serving first as minister for women and the family, before moving to the gender and social affairs brief. She is now a senator in the upper house of parliament, and says that women began to exert political muscle partly as a means of survival. When the killing ended, widows were sometimes left destitute because the existing law didn't permit women to inherit land or property.

That prompted Inyumba to press for change. 'After the genocide there were property disputes,' she says, 'so we worked on a strong family bill. For the first time the women of this country were given rights to inherit. Traditionally, if a woman married a man, the property belonged to him. If your husband died, the property would go to the in-laws. This bill has become a legal protection for families. Women can now inherit, women can own property. A girl child and a boy child have equal entitlement to inheritance.'

Another issue that women forced the government to address is rape. Sexual attacks were an integral part of the genocide, with local political leaders running what amounted to rape camps in some villages.

The international tribunal for Rwanda – which tried some of the organisers and perpetrators of the killings – defined rape as an act of genocide under international law, if part of a systematic move to wipe out an ethnic group. Yet when it came to Rwanda's own law to punish genocide, rape was almost relegated to a relatively minor offence. The draft genocide law split offences into four categories, with sentences of death or life imprisonment for murder. But rape was placed in the lowest category, alongside offences such as looting, with the draft law requiring only a light prison sentence or community service.

Groups such as the Widows of the Genocide and Ibuka, the survivors' association, were outraged. Many Tutsi women who had been raped had been infected with HIV, while others bore the children of their attackers. 'The women were not happy with that draft law,' says Inyumba, and so 'we advocated for a change. We regarded the genocide law as very important in ensuring that the issue of sexual abuse was taken seriously. There was a proposal and an agreement that all the issues dealing with sexual violence would be included as category one. That was a great victory for women.'

As the politicians moved beyond the immediate legacy of genocide, Kanakuze joined the committee that was drafting a constitution, as a 'gender expert'. She pressed for the 2003 constitution to require that at least 30% of seats in parliament and the cabinet be held by women. 'Before we were listened to on social issues and gender equality and about violence against women,' she says. 'But now women will be a majority on the committees that were controlled by men – security, finance.'

This transformation seems all the more unlikely given that it was engineered by what had been a male-dominated rebel group. But Inyumba says a focus on gender equality infused the RPF from the start because the party was focused on a broader rejection of discrimination of all kinds – beginning with the official persecution of Tutsis by successive Rwandan Hutu administrations. 'The important generation is the next generation,' she says hopefully.

'My children are 20 and 18. They do not speak this language of ethnicity.'

But many Rwandans still do and the government's critics say that discrimination is only being papered over. Public recognition of ethnicity is officially discouraged but that cannot hide the fact that a new Tutsi political elite – mostly made up of former exiles – has emerged dominant and privileged. Only 15% of the Rwandan population are Tutsi, and it has not gone unnoticed that a sizeable number of the new women MPs are of this ethnicity, leading some to question how well they can represent the mass of Hutu women who live in poverty.

The MP Euthalie Nyirabega declines to discuss her ethnicity, but says that although she went on to become a sociology professor at the national university, her background is close to the grassroots poor. She served in local government and in a number of women's organisations before being elected to parliament. 'I'm from a rural area,' she says. 'It's important that people in this building understand what women in rural areas are thinking. Not everyone here has that background.'

Men have, on the whole, remained silent on the new laws. But Evarist Kalish MP, a member of the Liberal party and the chair of parliament's human rights committee, says that many men recognise that women may provide the best leadership.

'More than men, women are the victims of the war,' says Kalish. 'They have different priorities to those of men. They have more concern about issues related to violence in general, and gender-based violence in particular. Women have faced discrimination so they want to put a stop to discrimination. All of this will contribute to preventing another genocide.'

30 JANUARY 2009

My sexual revolution

Thirty years ago, a group of radical women began arguing that all feminists should be lesbians

JULIE BINDEL

In the late 70s a group of lesbians in Leeds, known as revolutionary feminists (RFs), made a controversial move that resonated loudly for me and many other women. They began calling for all feminists to embrace lesbianism. Appealing to their heterosexual sisters to get rid of men 'from your beds and your heads', they started a debate, which reached its height in 1981 with the publication of an infamous booklet, Love Your Enemy? The Debate Between Heterosexual Feminism and Political Lesbianism (LYE). In this, the RFs wrote that, 'all feminists can and should be lesbians. Our definition of a political lesbian is a woman-identified woman who does not fuck men. It does not mean compulsory sexual activity with women.'

The message of LYE immediately provoked a strong and often negative reaction. While some radical feminists agreed with the group's arguments, many went wild at being told they were 'counter-revolutionaries', undermining the fight for women's liberation by sleeping with men. The main author of LYE, Sheila Jeffreys, says that the backlash to the booklet 'even among lesbians, was quite shocking. Quite a few were angry with the group for writing it. They felt it exposed them to hostility from outraged heterosexual feminists.'

It's no surprise that the booklet was so controversial. 'We think serious feminists have no choice but to abandon heterosexuality,' it reads. 'Only in the system of oppression that is male supremacy does the oppressor actually invade and colonise the interior of the body of the oppressed.' It also asserted that penetration 'is more than a symbol, its function and effect is the punishment and control of women.'

Tina Crockett was one of the RFs who gathered in a holiday cottage in the Yorkshire Dales to write LYE. She says that while the booklet's insistence that lesbianism could be a choice was controversial, debate was equally heated around the suggestion that men were the enemy. 'We were trying to challenge the excuses used by some heterosexual feminists as to why they lived with Nigel or John,' she says. 'They said, "Oh, but my man is OK," as a way of refusing to look at the fact that some men really do hate women.'

Alison Garthwaite was another of the authors, and she stands by the original argument. 'Sexuality is not determined by a gene which we are born with,' she says. 'It can change over time, and is determined by both your circumstances and the choices you make.' Garthwaite is keen to reassure heterosexual feminists, however, that their role in feminism is not redundant or unwanted. 'Perhaps the original paper implied that heterosexual feminists were of no use, and that they need not bother. I don't think that.'

Both Crockett and Garthwaite can see why LYE upset people. 'The arguments in LYE were a stick of dynamite up a very cosy feminist convention,' says Crockett, 'that heterosexual feminists must never be criticised for choosing men over women.'

The publication of LYE was one of the first times that the notion of sexuality as a choice had been publicly raised in the UK women's movement. Many feminists considered sexuality purely a matter of personal desire, and the idea that lesbianism could be a political decision was perceived as 'cold-blooded'. 'They believed that one did not choose sexual orientation or feelings, but was over-come by them,' says Jeffreys. 'One could accept them or struggle against them, but not manufacture them.'

The feminist writer Beatrix Campbell was one of LYE's many detractors, arguing that it was far more important to challenge men's behaviour in heterosexual relationships than to insist that women abandon hope altogether. 'The notion of political lesbianism is crazy,' she says. 'It erased desire. It was founded, therefore, not on love of women but fear of men.' Another feminist critic was the academic Lynne Segal, who has written in celebration of hetero-sexuality. 'For me, coming into feminism at the beginning of the 70s, "political lesbianism" was the main position advanced by a tiny band of vanguardist women,' she says. 'Its stance was tragic, because no, all men were not the enemy.' She adds that the media used LYE to 'trash' feminism in general. 'That inevitably added to the bitterness we felt, both then, and ever since.'

For all those who bridled at its message, there were women who took the arguments in LYE to heart. The booklet described lesbianism in glowing terms, which was quite something back in the 70s – after all, out women still face prejudice and exclusion (just yesterday, the Sun used the pejorative 'lesbo' in a headline about Iceland's interim PM). Some women threw out boyfriends and husbands after taking note of claims such as this: 'Being a heterosexual feminist is like being in the resistance in Nazi-occu-pied Europe where in the daytime you blow up a bridge, in the evening you rush to repair it.'

Others, such as myself, found that the arguments in LYE spoke directly to feelings that had already been developing. Opponents of political lesbianism argue that 'genuine' lesbians are motivated purely by lust towards women, rather than a decision to reject men and heterosexuality. For me, however, my lesbianism is intrin-sically bound up with my feminist politics and my campaigning against sexual violence.

When I was growing up on a council estate in Darlington, the expectation was that I would one day marry a local boy, settle down and start producing kids. Frankly, the thought horrified me. I was surrounded by men – my father and two brothers – and at an early age I had picked up on the stories of domestic violence, child abuse and general unhappiness that seemed to emanate from neighbouring households. I was also struck by the drudgery on display. While men were out drinking, embarking on fishing trips and generally enjoying their freedom, women were stuck cooking for them, cleaning for them, and running around after children. For women, heterosexuality seemed a total con.

At 15 then, having only ever had one non-serious boyfriend, I came out as a lesbian. Three years later, I moved to Leeds in search of the scary-sounding feminists I had heard about and, having joined a group that campaigned against pornography, finally met the RFs. They engaged me in discussions about heterosexuality in the pub, and critiquing this mainstream sexual culture made sense to me – after all, the women I had met during my childhood clearly hadn't benefited from it. The RFs told me that, to them, lesbianism was a choice that women could make, and not a 'condition' we are born with. 'All women can be lesbians' was the mantra. I loved the sense that I had chosen my sexuality and rather than being ashamed or apologetic about it, as many women were, I could be proud, and see it as a privilege.

Many of those who embraced political lesbianism in the 70s and 80s still keep the faith today. For Jeffreys, for instance, the arguments in LYE are as relevant now as they were 30 years ago. 'We made the decision to become lesbians because loving and fighting for women was the centre of our lives, and for me it still is. It made little sense to spend our whole time working for women's liberation and to then go home to men.' Crockett also says she stands by the sentiments in the paper, but wishes it had not only focused on the negative aspects of heterosexuality. 'We should have said, "Come on in, the water's lovely," because actually, it is really great fun being a lesbian.'

To me, political lesbianism continues to make intrinsic sense because it reinforces the idea that sexuality is a choice, and we are not destined to a particular fate because of our chromosomes. I also suspect that it is very difficult to spend your daily life fighting against male violence, only to share a bed with a man come the evening. Then there's the fact that working with women towards a common goal means you develop a strong and passionate bond with them – why some feminists then block out the possibility of sexual relationships with their political sisters and instead turn to men for intimacy is beyond me.

I think it's time for feminists to re-open the debate about hetero-sexuality, and to embrace the idea of political lesbianism. We live in a culture in which rape is still an everyday reality, and yet women are blamed for it, as it is viewed as an inevitable feature of heterosexual sex. Domestic violence is still a chronic problem for countless women in relationships with men. Women are told we must love our oppressors, while, as feminists, we fight to end the power afforded them as a birthright. Come on sisters, you know it makes sense. Stop pretending you think lesbianism is an exclusive members' club, and join the ranks. I promise that you will not regret it.

11 MAY 2009

'When I was growing up, one or two girls were beautiful but it wasn't an aspiration. That was what movie stars were for. It wasn't essential for all of us'

Interview with Susie Orbach

DECCA AITKENHEAD

On my way to meet Susie Orbach, it occurs to me that it would be very hard to find a single week when her work isn't relevant to the headlines. It's a depressing sort of tribute, but I certainly haven't managed to find such a week. On the journey to her Hampstead home, I read a report in the day's paper of an Australian beauty pageant featuring a contestant so thin that she would not look out of place in hospital. That same morning I had happened to drop into a chemist and found a queue of women lining up to buy a supply of Alli – the new 'miracle' slimming pill currently thrilling the beauty press, despite a long list of side-effects that include faecal incontinence.

'Oh my God,' Orbach exclaims as soon as I mention Alli. 'So, I'm in Boots yesterday, and there was a queue of women at the pharmacist, each with a pack of it. Not one of the women in front of me conceivably had a BMI of 28 [the minimum body mass index the new drug is supposed to 'treat']. And every one of the women said to the pharmacist, "How much does it cost?" "£50." And these weren't women with money. But they were saying to each other, "I think it's worth it." And the pharmacist was saying, "If you'd lose 2lb normally, then you'll lose three by taking Alli." So I'm like a one-woman campaign I couldn't restrain myself. I said to the pharmacist, "If these women needed this drug, they would be getting it on prescription, and not be needing to pay £50 a month for it." And I said to the women in the queue, "I guess we all walk around feeling fat in the head, but couldn't you dare to feel OK about your body?"'

The psychotherapist gives an incredulous, defeated smile. 'I didn't stand there saying, "Actually, the question isn't losing weight, the question is will you learn how to eat, and feel comfortable with your body?" I didn't do any of the things I might as a propagandist, because I just didn't expect to find this great queue.'

Orbach didn't expect to see most of the mess we've got into with our bodies when she wrote Fat Is a Feminist Issue more than three decades ago. The seminal bestseller was a groundbreaking work, the thesis of which was so simple that no one who read it could dispute its logic. At 31, Orbach had been bingeing and dieting for much of her adult life when she wrote that diets make us fat by distorting our relationship with food, and urged us to restore trust in the natural rhythm of our self-regulating appetite. Yet 31 years later, Orbach acknowledges that we are more disconnected from our bodies than ever before.

Her latest book, Bodies, maps the progress of our alienation, from a time when we took our bodies for granted to one where they are an endlessly perfectible work in progress. 'When I was growing up,' she explains, 'one or two girls were beautiful, but it was not an aspiration, right? We didn't expect to be that sportsman or that beauty queen. That was OK, that was what movie stars were for. That wasn't something that was essential for all of us.' Yet today, movie-star looks are not just an aspiration but an imperative, and ordinary people think nothing of starving or surgically enhancing their bodies in a tireless campaign to make them look as though they belong to somebody else altogether.

Just as Donald Winnicott identified the 'false self', whereby a neglected baby will blame itself for its carer's lack of interest, and create an artificial version of itself in the hope of winning love, so Orbach argues that we are creating false bodies. Assailed by media imagery that celebrates only one type of body and one type of beauty, we assume any discrepancy between our own appearance and this digitally airbrushed 'ideal' must be our fault, and that it's not merely necessary but morally virtuous to do whatever it takes to correct our deficiency. The simultaneous rise of anorexia and obesity is not a paradox, but rather two sides of the same psychological coin – both manifestations of our panic about hunger, in which normal appetite becomes pathologised as the enemy. Crucially, whereas once we might have experienced the pressure to look different as an onerous tyranny, today we tell ourselves that it's empowering.

'We transform the sense of being criticised,' Orbach writes, 'by becoming the moving and enthusiastic actor in our own self-improvement programme. We will eagerly repair what is wrong . . . We see ourselves as agents, not victims. It is the individual woman who feels herself to be at fault for not matching up to the current imagery . . . She applies herself to the job of perfecting that image for herself and so makes it her own, not assaultive or alien.'

Orbach's writing is closer in tone to cultural studies than to the jaunty self-help register of most contemporary books about eating, but in person there is nothing abstractly academic about her. Framed by a mass of curls, she is small, even birdlike, but her sprightly energy conveys a vivid sense of aliveness. Her accent has a faint American inflection, which can sound almost antipodean at times, particularly when her sentences end in a question mark – 'right?'

– and she is surprisingly relaxed, even imprecise, with her words, often letting sentences tail away unfinished. But she is very clear about where we are going wrong.

I've been half looking forward to the meeting, and half dreading it because, although it must be 20 years since I first read what Orbach calls 'Fifi', her work feels uncomfortably relevant to my own current state. She is the sort of woman you find yourself confiding in, and I admit to her that halfway through my first pregnancy, my overriding preoccupation is with weight gain. To my dismay, what I'm really thinking about most of the time is how I'm ever going to lose it. And right there, according to Orbach, is the source of our troubled relationship with food. Mothers transmit their own anxieties to their babies – it all begins in the family.

'The only way to solve the problem is to provide very different help to new mums,' she says briskly. 'Because every mother wants to do right by their kid. It would mean training health visitors and midwives – you'd raise a mother's awareness of her own body. This is an opportunity for both of you to find the rhythm in terms of relation to appetite. I don't think it would be difficult to design. And it would be very cheap. And new mums would really benefit from it. But instead, they are being told to do sit-ups straightaway, and why not even consider having a C-section, so you don't have to get that last month's weight gain? All of that nonsense. It's completely counter to what a baby's mental health requires – and what the mother needs as well, actually.'

What can parents say, I ask, to a 16-year-old girl who is convinced that a regime of dieting and beautification is not self-punishing but empowering? 'Well, it's awfully late at 16. But I'd be saying to the mums: "Watch your own behaviour – how often do you criticise your own body in front of your daughter?" Stop making the body the cause of the problem, or the solution to the problem. The problem isn't how she looks.'

But surely a teenage girl would say that how she looks is precisely the problem? 'But what she'd be picking out aren't imperfections, they're just what makes her her, right?' What if she says she's overweight? 'Well, they all feel overweight. Even when they're tiny, tiny, tiny. But where are they getting that idea? That's why I think the mums are doing something.'

If Orbach were just another voice in the cacophony of finger-pointing that surrounds most discussion about weight, I would be feeling unpleasantly guilty by now. But her analysis of what she calls 'disordered eating' extends beyond mothers and the family, to encompass everything from the diet industry – 'which relies upon a 95% recidivism rate' – to the media, which produces glossy magazines in which 'not a single image is not digitally retouched, up to hundreds of times' – and globalisation, in which a culture of 'aspirational bodies is the mark of entry'.

It is a comprehensive critique, yet one that resists apportioning blame for overeating to individuals, which you would have thought would make her hugely popular, a sort of Claire Rayner of the kitchen. Yet strangely, at 62 she is not the national treasure you might have expected. Before this interview, I'd met Orbach several times, and always found her warm and intensely compassionate. Yet time and again, interviewers report that she is cold, uptight and unforthcoming.

Does she find the characterisation upsetting? 'Yes,' she says simply. 'I do.'

One reason for the public relations problem is probably her reluctance to volunteer much about her private life. Born in 1946 to Jewish parents – her father was a Labour MP, her mother an American teacher – she grew up in north London before moving to New York, where she was married briefly and became involved in the women's movement, before returning to London and training as a psychotherapist. Last year she split from her partner of nearly four decades, a fellow psychotherapist with whom she has a son, 24, and daughter, 20.

'It's just not appropriate, is it?' she says, when I ask why she has always chosen to say little about her personal life. 'I think what's most interesting about me is the work that I do.' In the 90s she found herself besieged by journalists when they discovered she was treating Princess Diana for her eating disorder, and Orbach's refusal to discuss their relationship probably inflamed the media's frustration at knowing so little about Britain's most famous shrink.

'The other thought,' she offers, 'is to do with the role of public intellectuals, and for some reason women don't come off so well in that. So perhaps there is something there about feeling intimidated, and thus narrowing the conversation that occurs, and focusing on personality rather than the ideas one might have.'

I suspect it may also be because the combination of a psychotherapist and a feminist campaigner confuses people. Orbach is not just a therapist and writer, but an activist; she is a consultant to the Dove ad campaign, and runs a website, anybody.org, 'giving women a voice to challenge the limited physical representation of females in contemporary society'. In a media discourse that is endlessly blaming women for being too thin or too fat, for looking hatefully perfect or shamefully flawed, her contribution is too nuanced to quite fit. For example, when I ask if she feels angry with feminists who opt for cosmetic surgery, she says: 'Well, that's where I think being a psychoanalyst puts me in a different category. I'm really not there as a moralist. I've always felt very sympathetic from the first days of writing about women that, whatever the woman, whether she is trying to be a woman in the conventional sense or breaking the boundaries, those struggles are quite difficult.'

So she doesn't think it's helpful to criticise them? 'Well, I don't think it's helpful for me. I think I'm of more use saying, "Right, let's try and work out why we feel this way. What does it mean that women post-pregnancy are being offered reconstructive surgery, as if pregnancy were a disease? Let's think about that." That's where I come in. Rather than say, you shouldn't do this or you should do that. That's irrelevant.'

As a campaigner, Orbach wants to see our visual landscape filled with images of people who look real. 'And gorgeous!' she interrupts. 'I mean, I'm not an anti-stylist, for Christ's sake. I think it is one of the capacities of human beings, to create style. It's the mono-imagery, the one look, that is so disturbing.'

Some feminists take the view that it doesn't matter if models look like Twiggy or Beth Ditto – it's the act of objectification that is so destructive. But Orbach shakes her head. 'I don't buy that, because I think it's unrealistic. Maybe this is too pragmatic but we live in this world, we have got the democratisation of beauty, we have got the notion that we can, should, enter into the representation of ourselves in certain kinds of ways. We're going to do that. So the question is, can we do it and have joy about this, rather than only regarding ourselves critically.'

She is very happy to criticise the diet industry, though, and once tried to sue WeightWatchers. 'I really hoped we could do it, and there was some interest, but you can't do it without a massive amount of money. I think there's still an important discussion point, though. Why haven't they been prosecuted under the Trade Descriptions Act? Why haven't they?' Similarly, when I suggest that the government should take action against the media for irresponsible reporting of a drug such as Alli, just as it would on false advertising, she says at once, 'I think that's an interesting argument, I really do, because the question is: where are the pressure points?

'What could journalists do? It's not enough to blame the media, it's what could they bring to the party. What could they do to change the visual culture? They could write about Alli not in a tongue-in-cheek, maybe-this-time-a-drug-will-work kind of way, but by saying the stats show that 95% of slimming preparations will have a serious failure rate, and you're likely to end up larger than you started. And then you deconstruct what this new drug is about – the marketing of it, the production of it, and all that. So that would be a nice way to do it.'

How can it be that, after all these years, we're still queuing up to buy what we know will probably not work? 'Because of hope,' she says sadly. 'It's about transforming that sense of feeling power-less into feeling powerful. It transforms the image of you as the victim into thinking, "Oh, this is a real opportunity! I could do it this time!"'

24 JULY 2009

Time for a good scrap about what our feminism really is

Bring on 'infighting' if it means rigorous, honest debate about what we believe

LIBBY BROOKS

Oh, it's like ruddy buses. You wait a decade for some Brit-born feminist literature, then four books come along at once. Since Natasha Walter's New Feminism – a work as buoyantly optimistic as the New Labour moment it refracted – came out in 1998, main-stream publishing about gender has been horribly absent in this country.

Sure, there have been the US buy-ins to keep us talking – Susan Faludi's discourse on the consequences of 9/11 for women, Ariel

Levy's roar against raunch culture, Jessica Valenti's Full Frontal Feminism. And undoubtedly there's been a platform shift – the hottest discussions about British feminism now happen online, at sites such as thefword.org.uk, or between clued-in types on Twitter.

So this is really not reflective of my Luddite thrill at having another volume to slot into my bookshelf next to Marilyn French. It's an opportunity to think the hard thoughts and to ballast the resurgence of activism with theory. Over the next 12 months, four very different women, of diverse ages and agendas, offer their slant on contemporary British feminism, hopefully generating a level of debate that we – men as well as women – haven't known for years.

Kat Banyard of the Fawcett Society assesses the 'equality illusion', examining how the language of liberation has become co-opted and arguing that feminism remains the most important motor for social justice of our time. Catherine Redfern, founder of The F-word, surveys the activist trend and uncovers why younger women are engaging like never before. Walter returns to the fray, challenging a cultural sexism she admits she didn't take seriously enough in her last book. All three will be published early next year.

And, lest this read like a roll call of knit-your-own-yoghurt worthiness, Ellie Levenson, a writer with rather less locus than the three aforementioned, has delivered her Noughtie Girl's Guide to Feminism, complete with rape gags and a section on why women bosses are shits. As I write this, she's just tweeted about how she can be a feminist and still have a leg wax. Yawn.

OK, so that last paragraph requires some deconstruction. It's wrong to suggest that Banyard, Redfern and Walter will be received as dull because they're serious. Just as I shouldn't imply Levenson isn't serious because she doesn't have a bachelors in gender studies but does have jokes. It's as well I didn't say that observing feminism won't wind you up in a huge fankle.

But herein lies the particularly scratchy rub. What Levenson suggests, with a spangly cover that renders her book indistinguishable from the latest Marian Keyes novel, is that feminism needs to be rebranded to be made friendlier and more accessible to women born after 1970 who balk at the word, though not necessarily the principles it represents. While agreeing it's a cute marketing ploy to pass off politics as chick lit, I'm already exhausted if we are to have the nomenclature discussion all over again.

Plus, Levenson's invocation of a judgmental cohort of older feminists beating up their daughters for choosing to shag around with shaved legs resurrects another weary canard – that second-wave feminists of the 60s and 70s were po-faced, anti-sex misandrists. And there is a line, not a skip and a jump away from the media's appetite for 'women fight like cats in a bag – again' stories, that suggests all feminists go into lockdown when presented with a thesis that doesn't fit their own prescriptive view.

I just don't buy that. In a blog about initial responses to her book, Levenson says 'infighting' harms feminism. But does it? The women I meet, of every generation, are desperate for debate, especially if it can be conducted under the unflattering lights of the mainstream and take in Katie Price as well as rape conviction rates. And when older women remind younger ones about the history of the movement, it's because many of the answers to our present day questions can be found there.

If infighting means having an unashamedly intellectual, rigorously conducted, unflinchingly honest discussion about what feminism is and what it isn't at the end of the noughties, then count me first in the ring. And I won't be alone. Consider Object, the campaign group that has recently gained traction for its work on lap-dancing club reforms. Its meetings are stuffed to the rafters with twentysomethings – both female and male – who have clocked that their right to choose striptease lessons does not obviate the exploitation inherent in the industry. (And, yes, the presence is predominantly white, middle class and university educated – as are the writers of these books. So let's get infighting about that, too.)

Feminism can never equate with individualism, no matter what the pick-and-mix proselytisers might tell you. That a single woman feels empowered to make a particular choice means nothing if the grassroots organisations and political lobbies don't exist to manifest real social shifts. It is still collective theory and collective action that changes the world. At a moment for British feminism when the theory is fresh and the action is vibrant, all of us should be thinking and doing, and mindful that there's nothing so empowering as a good scrap about what we believe in.

16 APRIL 2010

'I have a rebel gene'

Nawal El Saadawi has braved prison, exile and death threats in her campaign against female oppression. She isn't about to give up now

HOMA KHALEELI

'I am becoming more radical with age,' says Nawal El Saadawi, laughing. 'I have noticed that writers, when they are old, become milder. But for me it is the opposite. Age makes me more angry.'

This is a startling admission. It is hard to imagine how El Saadawi – the Egyptian writer, activist and one of the leading feminists of her generation – could become more radical. Wearing an open denim shirt, with her hair pulled into two plaits, she looks like the rebel she has always been. It is only the pure white hair, and the lines that spread across her face as she smiles, that give away the fact that she is 79. She has, she tells me, 'decided not to die young but to live as much as I can.'

El Saadawi already seems to have lived more than most. She trained as a doctor, then worked as a psychiatrist and university lecturer, and has published almost 50 novels, plays and collections of short stories. Her work, which tackles the problems women face in Egypt and across the world, has always attracted outrage, but she never seems to have balked at this; she has continued to address controversial issues such as prostitution, domestic violence and religious fundamentalism.

This has come at considerable cost. In 1972, her non-fiction book Women and Sex (which included criticism of female genital muti- lation) led to her losing her job as director general of public health for the Egyptian ministry of health. In 1981, her outspoken polit- ical views led to her being charged with crimes against the state and jailed for three months – she used the time to write Memoirs From the Women's Prison on a roll of toilet paper, with an eyebrow pencil smuggled in by a fellow prisoner. In 1993 she fled to the US after death threats were issued against her by religious groups.

Her work continues to be explosive. Her play, God Resigns in the Summit Meeting – in which God is questioned by Jewish, Muslim and Christian prophets and finally quits – proved so contro- versial that, she says, her Arabic publishers destroyed it under police duress. And recently her criticism of religion, primarily on the basis that it oppresses women, has prompted a flurry of court cases, including unsuccessful legal attempts both to strip her of her nationality and to forcibly dissolve her marriage.

As El Saadawi prepares to talk about her life at a Pen literary festival today, she is unrepentant. 'It's all worth it,' she assures me. 'If I went back I would do it all again. That is what I have learned from my experiences, that I was on the right track.' Her energy, she insists, comes from the 10 to 15 letters she receives every day from people who say their lives have been changed by her writing. 'A young man came to me in Cairo with his new bride. He said: "I want to introduce my wife to you and thank you. Your books have made me a better man. Because of them I wanted to marry not a slave, but a free woman."'

El Saadawi is 'a novelist first, a novelist second, a novelist third', she says, but it is feminism that unites her work. 'For me feminism includes everything,' she says. 'It is social justice, political justice, sexual justice . . . It is the link between medicine, literature, politics, economics, psychology and history. Feminism is all that. You cannot understand the oppression of women without this.'

She says she has been a feminist 'since I was a child. I was swimming against the tide all my life.' Her eight brothers and sisters 'were totally different. Some of my sisters are now veiled and they think I am very, very radical. They love me, and we see each other, but we don't visit much.'

In her first autobiography, A Daughter of Isis, she recalls her outrage when she began to realise daughters were not considered equal to sons. When her grandmother told her, 'a boy is worth 15 girls at least . . . Girls are a blight,' she stamped her foot in fury.

In that same book she writes about the horror of female circumcision. 'When I was six, the daya (midwife) came along holding a razor, pulled out my clitoris from between my thighs and cut it off. She said it was the will of God and she had done his will . . . I lay in a pool of blood. After a few days the bleeding stopped . . . But the pain was there like an abscess deep in my flesh . . . I did not know what other parts in my body there were that might need to be cut off in the same way.' Later, while working as a doctor, she saw for herself the terrible physical damage female genital mutilation could cause – she campaigned for 50 years, she says, for it to be banned in Egypt. A ban was finally instituted in 2008, but the practice 'still happens – it is even increasing. Some religious leaders talk against it, but others are for it.'

Circumcision wasn't the only horror El Saadawi faced as a child. Brought up in a middle-class Egyptian household, she was expected to become a child bride, but refused – she blackened her teeth and dropped coffee over one would-be suitor who came to call. 'When I was a child it was normal that girls in my village would marry at 10 or 11,' she says. 'Now, of course, the government is standing against that because it is unhealthy. And it happens much less. But we are having a relapse again, because of poverty and religious fundamentalism.'

El Saadawi's desire to study was so great that her parents were eventually convinced she would benefit from university. She believes that her radical views were formed, at least in part, by training as a doctor. 'When I dissected the body it opened my eyes,' she says. 'Also, I think I have the gene of my grandmother who was a rebel. My sisters and brothers took another gene.'

At medical school she fell in love with a fellow student, Ahmed Helmi, who was engaged in the fight against the British occupation of the Suez. They married and had a daughter – but divorced when he came back from the fighting embittered and turned to drugs. She later married a lawyer, who 'said to me you have to choose between me and your writing. I said my writing.' In her second volume of autobiography, Walking Through Fire, she describes how he refused to grant her a divorce, announcing that, 'It is the man who decides to divorce and not the woman' – in desperation, she threatened him with her scalpel. For the last 45 years she has been married to the novelist, doctor, and former long-term political prisoner, Sherif Hetata, with whom she had her second child, a son.

El Saadawi's daughter, Mona Helmi, has followed in her footsteps, becoming a writer and poet. In 2007, Mona became the target of controversy when 'she wrote a beautiful article on

Mother's Day,' says El Saadawi. 'She asked, "What present can I give to my mother – shall I give her shoes? A dress? The gift I will give is to carry her name."' The article was signed Mona Nawal Helmi. 'They took her to court – they said it was heresy because in the Qur'an women should take the name of the father not the mother.'

Although Mona won the case, El Saadawi says that this, and another court case in 2002 – brought by a lawyer who sought to have El Saadawi forcibly divorced on the basis of apostasy (abandonment of religion) – has left her bruised. 'I feel I am betrayed by my country. I should be awarded the highest prize in Egypt for what I have done regarding injustices against women and children, and for my creative work.' But she says her writing has given her an alternative sense of identity. 'Home to me is the world because my books have been translated into more than 30 languages. People feel they know me and the minute they talk about my life or books I feel at home. Home is where you are appreciated, safe and protected, creative, and where you are loved – not where you are put in prison.'

She still refuses to tone down her work. 'I am very critical of all religions,' she says. 'We, as women, are oppressed by all these religions.' It is religious extremism, she believes, that is the biggest threat to women's liberation today. 'There is a backlash against feminism all over the world today because of the revival of religions,' she says. 'We have had a global and religious fundamentalist movement.' She fears that the rise of religion is holding back progress regarding issues such as female circumcision, especially in Egypt.

In a bid to address this, she has helped to found the Egyptian chapter of the Global Solidarity for Secular Society. She believes religion should be a personal matter, and approves of France's ban on all religious symbols, including the hijab. 'Education should be totally secular. I am not telling people not to believe in God, but it should be a personal matter which should be done at home.'

Despite the fact that her sisters wear the veil, she refuses to accept it as a free choice. 'What do we mean by choice? It is pressure, but it is hidden pressure – she is not aware of it. I was exposed to different pressures from my sisters. We are all the products of our economic, social and political life and our education. Young people today are living in the era of the fundamentalist groups.'

El Saadawi says that she is dismayed by the relaxed attitude of young women who do not realise what previous generations of feminists have fought for. 'Young people are afraid of the price of being free. I tell them, don't be, it is better than being oppressed, than being a slave. It's all worth it. I am free.'

And, she adds, there are more battles for her on the horizon. 'A new university opened in Egypt and I was asked to teach, but the top people said no. They are afraid. So that is the next thing. I will work towards teaching in Egypt.' A fighter to the last.

2 AUGUST 2011

What is the link between the media and eating disorders?

We all know that the way the media judge women's bodies is sick – but how directly this leads to eating disorders is less clear

HADLEY FREEMAN

You know the problem with eating disorders? They're just so photogenic! There are the young women or – even better – girls; the celebrities and fashion magazines that are, of course, the cause of eating disorders; female body shape and, thrillingly, the food that is eaten or, in this case, not eaten to obtain that shape; women who are, you know, a bit tragic and might even die.

With such a catalogue of attributes no wonder the media love a good eating disorder story. In fact, it's hard to think of a single other subject that combines so many pieces of media catnip. It even beats that annual classic, an A-level success story, even ones involving triplets in vest tops getting into Cambridge.

So it's not that surprising that eating disorders made two tabloids' front pages this week. On Monday, both the Sun and the Daily Mail splashed on the story about the number of children being treated for eating disorders according to newly released statistics, focusing in particular on the number of children requiring treatment aged between five and nine.

Pretty much every other newspaper also covered this issue, understandably, as this is indeed a terrible story, although it's hard to imagine a study showing that the same number of children are receiving treatment for, say, schizophrenia getting the same amount of coverage. But then, of course, schizophrenia can't be illustrated with a photo of a little girl lifting up her shirt, as the Sun did.

Both the Sun and the Daily Mail took especial care to blame 'pictures in magazines', as the Sun put it, excusing itself and its fascination with female bodies from the equation. The Daily Mail cited 'ultra-slim celebs' in the headline, 'celebs' who are praised daily by that paper for losing "the baby weight" and other such monumental achievements. And presumably, the headlines writers didn't notice that, just inches away from the anorexia article on the website was another story on its front page debating which female celebrity has 'the best bikini body'.

These stories followed on from news last week that L'Oréal felt compelled to airbrush those old hags Christy Turlington and Julia Roberts in its adverts. This prompted one writer in this paper to claim that 'anorexia and compulsive eating are . . . a response to' this false idealisation of women.

Everyone knows that the way women's bodies are judged in the media is sick – heck, even the papers that do it know this. How directly this leads to severe eating disorders is something I, unlike these newspapers and columnists, feel is less clear cut.

I spent almost three years straight in psychiatric hospitals being treated for severe anorexia nervosa. While I was not five years old, I was very young: young enough to not have even started my GCSEs, young enough to be, always, the youngest patient on the ward.

Unlike some newspaper columnists, I do not feel compelled to talk about my personal experiences with the mental health profession in every article I write, nor turn every story into an opportunity to talk about them. In fact, I try to avoid talking about them altogether, mainly because I hope that I have something more to offer than my history. After working so hard to recover, I'd rather not spend the rest of my life being seen through the prism of my past, permanently labelled 'ex-anorexic'. Talking about oneself in a newspaper is, to my mind, a little like chattering loudly at the cinema: you are not the show the audience came to see.

However, the nonsense that has been spouted of late in the media about eating disorders is too ubiquitous and too stupid, even by the low standards of the media's usual coverage of the illness. And while I would never claim that my personal experience makes me an expert on the subject, maybe it gives me a different perspective than, say, a lazy news reporter churning out cliches under a deadline or a columnist in search of easy outrage and reader traffic.

Like I said, I was very young when I was first hospitalised. Too young for fashion magazines, tabloid newspapers or even 'ultra-slim celebs'. After all, eating disorders have existed for hundreds of years, predating, amazingly, Kate Moss. But this is not to excuse those elements because they did complicate my eventual recovery. And it's certainly not to excuse them the way the fashion industry does, harrumphing that the obesity crisis is a more pressing problem, which is about as stupid as saying we should stop talking about any infertility issues seeing as there's such a problem with teen pregnancies.

The obsession with food and weight in the media mirrored and therefore, to my then sick mind, legitimised my own. Why should I put on weight when there are actresses out there almost as skinny as me and celebrated for it?

Eating disorders do not stem from a desire to be slim: they are an expression of unhappiness through food. The way a woman's body is equated with her human value in the media can, to someone who is subconsciously looking for a way to articulate their unhappiness, feel like the perfect solution. But this doesn't mean that the problem comes from young women looking at too many fashion adverts.

People who claim that the media are the cause of their past or present illnesses are, in fact, undermining themselves. It would be like claiming that a really great Budweiser advertising campaign made them an alcoholic. Your problem, my friend, is bigger than that.

The media is neither the cause of nor irrelevant to eating disorders. Sometimes, unfortunately, life is too complicated to fit in a snappy headline.

12 AUGUST 2011

Layla's story: jailed after reporting a sexual assault

In 2009, Layla Ibrahim told police she had been the victim of a savage sexual assault. So why did she end up in jail?

SIMON HATTENSTONE AND AFUA HIRSCH

Sara Ibrahim says that since the day her little sister Layla was sent to prison, her family has been faced with a simple choice: 'Do we give up and just get on with our lives, or do we clear her name? And we've decided if it takes the rest of our lives, that's what we'll do – we'll clear her name.'

It was a couple of weeks after she reported being attacked in the early hours of a cold January morning in 2009 that Layla Ibrahim, then 21, noticed a change in the attitude of the police. Yes, the police had documented the injuries to the back of her head and breasts, the black eye, the bleeding from her vagina. They had listened closely as she described the two strangers who attacked her, how the main perpetrator had worn a Nike hoodie, how she thought she had temporarily lost consciousness after being knocked to the ground, how she had felt a 'thud' in her vagina but had no clear recollection of what had happened.

The police had seemed sympathetic as she explained how she tried to fend off her attackers with a pair of blunt scissors, and how the second assailant grabbed hold of them and started cutting her hair. Layla told them how eventually she had made her way home, running and bawling, almost feral with fear. The case quickly became high profile, as the local newspaper reported that the police had set up an incident room staffed by 30-40 officers and described it as 'one of the city's biggest manhunts'.

But a couple of weeks later it was as if the police were investigating an entirely different case, one in which the suspect was Layla herself. The police suggested she had acted in a strange manner when they first went to see her – crying one minute, laughing the next; that she had been aggressive. They talked about inconsistencies in her evidence.

At first Layla thought it understandable – of course, the police wanted to clarify what she had told them – but when they kept questioning her story, she became unnerved. She'd told them the batteries were flat on her mobile phone, but they seemed to think it odd that it wasn't working. And they told her the forensics suggested there was no soil on her clothing from the grass where she said she had been attacked.

'That's when I said I didn't want to answer any more questions without a solicitor,' she writes in a letter from prison. 'They asked why I wanted a solicitor and I said, "Because I don't feel like I'm the victim."'

It wasn't Layla who first heard the news her attack was no longer under investigation. Instead, the police contacted her mother at the school in Carlisle where she works as a senior teaching assistant to tell her they suspected Layla of fabricating her story and inflicting the injuries on herself.

'A detective came round and put all these photos of Layla's hair round the floor and said it looked to them as if she'd walked and cut her hair and dropped it,' says Sandra Allen, Layla's mother. The DCI told her she thought the injuries to Layla's knee were suspicious. 'I asked her what she meant, and she said, "Well, it looks as if Layla just took something and slashed herself on the knee." And I said it was winter, she'd fallen, it was iced – why would you think that?'

Layla was told she would be charged with wasting police time if she didn't drop the case. She refused – after all, she said, she'd been violently attacked. Eventually, the charge was upped to the more serious offence of perverting the course of justice. A year later, in June 2010, Layla – then six months pregnant – was convicted and sentenced to three years.

The story of Layla Ibrahim, now 23, is as bizarre as it is alarming. How can a woman end up jailed after reporting an attack on herself? And when there appeared to be powerful evidence of the savagery of the assault?

Layla had been out drinking with friends in Carlisle in early January 2009. They went on a mini pub-crawl, and she was drunk by the end of the evening but, she says, not out of control. She had no money left and says she asked her friend Richard Dent if he could lend her £10 or share a cab. When he refused, she was surprised but decided to walk home through a pathway by the River Eden known as the Cut.

Layla would later describe the two men who sprang out of the darkness as young – not much older than her own teenage brother – and said that the one whose face she saw looked like a drug addict with a 'hollow, sucky-in face'. She struggled home at around 4am, and banged on the door of her oldest sister Samira, who lives round the corner from her mother. Samira called the police, who arrived a couple of hours later.

We are chatting in Sandra's home in Carlisle as Layla's other sister Sara returns to the living room with a tray of drinks and chocolate biscuits. Sandra lived in Libya for many years with her then husband – the Libyan father of her children – and speaks fluent Arabic.

What troubles the family is the evidence they say could have proved her innocence. Male blood was found at the scene, but it was dismissed because it did not belong to one of the suspects and did not match anything on the DNA database. A male blond pubic hair was found on Layla that Rosemary Swain, the doctor who examined her, said would be crucial evidence against her attackers. But the family later learned it had been destroyed in the forensics lab.

The police did not take the cardigan Layla had been wearing for DNA testing. Although it was later handed in by the family, it had been lying around the house and might have been worn by other family members or even washed. Layla's shoes were not tested for DNA, although one shoe was alleged to have been held by an attacker. Her leggings were not tested for DNA, nor was her bra fully checked, although blood was found on it.

Layla's description of one of the attackers closely matched that of a suspect in other attacks in the area. Layla's family and a case worker who represented her believe that one of the many troubling aspects of her conviction is that while Layla is in jail, her attackers are out there, posing a threat to women.

The thing that did most to put Layla behind bars was the pair of scissors. Layla told the police how they were used against her by her attackers. The police claimed she had taken them with her to fake the attack. They pointed to the fact that Layla's DNA was on the scissors, as was fabric from her dress. But Layla says there is a straightforward explanation.

'Of course my DNA was on the scissors – they are my scissors,' she writes. 'I have always carried scissors with me since I was in school. I'm quite big-chested and my bras come undone because the metal bit inside comes out. My mum taught me to always carry scissors, needle and thread.'

Asked about Layla Ibrahim, the director of public prosecutions Keir Starmer – who was briefed on the case after Sara visited him earlier this year but has so far declined to intervene – confirmed the scissors had been a crucial piece of prosecution evidence. 'Much greater store was put on the evidence about the scissors than was put on the inconsistencies [in Layla's account of what happened],' he says.

As so often in such situations, the circumstances are confused. In her first statement, Layla said the second attacker had cut her hair, and it was only later, when running, that she discovered her dress was also torn. Layla later said the boys might have cut her dress, too – she simply couldn't remember. To complicate matters, Layla's mother Sandra had cut the dress under the armpit earlier that evening where it was tight.

The fact that Layla couldn't remember everything was an important part of the case against her, too. She doesn't dispute it; even today her memory of what happened is partial and muggy. 'He [the first attacker] fell on top of me, and I don't really remember a lot after that. I woke up, well, it felt like I was waking up. And it hurt down below,' she writes.

The family are wary of the police. Had they ever had cause to call on them before? Sara and Sandra look at each other, waiting to see who answers first.

The Ibrahims have always felt they stood out in Carlisle. Sara says when she was young there was only a handful of mixed-race families in the town. It wasn't always easy growing up there.

'I was brought up to respect the police,' Sandra says. Her family is from Carlisle, she grew up here, later moving to Libya for work, where she met her husband. She returned to the UK when Layla was nine. But moving back with four mixed-race children brought its own problems. 'My very first dealings with the police were when we came to England and that boy beat you up,' Sandra reminds her daughter.

Sara laughs, quietly. 'I had a few beatings because I was black. I can't remember which one you mean.'

Sandra: 'Sara got seriously beat up and the police didn't want to know. All the neighbours ran out, everyone was screaming and shouting. Sara's head was smashed up. The police came but didn't even look at her. It was just like "these things happen".'

'They arrested *me*,' Sara says, still bewildered all these years later.

'In the scuffle, the boy got a scratch. We were so naive, the police asked us into the police station and me and Mum were like, "Oh, they've just invited us in for a chat" and they arrested me! I was put on bail and we were back and forward to and from the police station.'

Some time later, Sandra's son Taraq, then aged 12, had a series of run-ins with the police. He was arrested time and again by the same officer, but never charged. Sandra went to the Independent Police Complaints Commission. The issue was resolved by Cumbria constabulary, who admitted the officer had 'targeted' Taraq 'to deter him from committingcrime'.

Layla had no history of depression or self-harm before January 2009. A report by an independent psychologist, prepared for the court in advance of Layla's trial, concluded she was suffering from post-traumatic stress as a result of the attack, and found it difficult to explain why she would have fabricated it.

'Motives for false rape allegations have been found to be seeking attention or sympathy from others or revenge against others,' wrote Carolyn John, a consultant clinical psychologist with 21 years' experience and the lead consultant for Newcastle Upon Tyne's acute adult mental health service. 'I could find no motive for deliberate self-harm or for Ms Ibrahim having malingered. I could find nothing in her personality profile that might lead to attention-seeking or a lowered threshold for histrionic or antisocial behaviour that might amount to wasting police time.'

John also pointed to various factors that undermined the evidence used against Layla. In terms of inconsistencies, she cited Layla's dyslexia as a reason for her mislabelling of left/right, and concussion following the blow to her head as a reason for her memory problems. John also raised the conditions in which Layla was interviewed: a lengthy process during which a male officer was present and she was not given anything to eat for hours.

Dr Rosemary Swain, a GP and specialist in sexual assault medical examinations who examined Layla shortly after the incident, reached the same conclusion, forming the view that Layla had indeed been subjected to a sexual assault. Despite working for the police, Swain would later give evidence in Layla's defence at her trial.

But the investigation into Layla continued. In February 2009, a month after the incident, Layla attempted suicide by throwing herself into a river. She was rescued by a passerby and taken to hospital where she seized a used needle and tried to cut her wrists.

Layla was identified as high risk and referred for a psychiatric assessment. The psychiatrist who assessed her did not find any mental health problems but instead enduring trauma resulting from the recent attack. 'This is a 21-year-old woman with evidence of an adjustment disorder in relation to a sexual assault one month earlier,' his report concluded. Sandra says Layla became desperate and despairing, unrecognisable from the daughter she knew.

Layla writes that while it is too late for her to be spared jail, one of the reasons she is determined to draw attention to her case is to help other women in the same position.

'We know of 30 women jailed for so-called false allegations of rape in the past 12 months,' says Lisa Longstaff of Women Against Rape. 'Such prosecutions must be stopped. It is a galling diversion for women to be jailed when the vast majority of rapists are not – 90% of rapes are never reported and only 6.7% of those that are reach conviction on a full charge of rape. The prosecution of women and the disproportionate media coverage they get are putting rape victims off reporting and leaving all of us more vulnerable to attack. Is that what they want?'

Starmer insists that discouraging women from reporting rape is the last thing prosecutors want. Under his leadership, the CPS last monthpublished new guidance stating that individuals who retract rape allegations out of fear will be protected from prosecution. 'Rape and domestic violence victims should be confident in reporting abuse without fear of prosecution if they are later pressured into retracting the allegation,' Starmer said, responding to a controversial court of appeal case in which a woman had her prison sentence overturned after judges found she had been pressured into withdrawing a rape claim by her abusive husband.

Yet this new guidance offers no comfort for the likes of Layla Ibrahim: women who are accused of falsifying rape allegations still face prosecution. The guidance in fact states that prosecution is more likely when the allegation is believed to be made maliciously or over a sustained period of time – in other words, there is now an incentive to withdraw rape allegations if victims feel the police disbelieve them. Starmer has introduced a further check in the system, however, requiring all prosecutions against people accused of falsifying rape claims to be authorised by his office before proceeding. Would this have saved Layla? It's impossible to say, but he acknowledges that there may be women in jail now who would not have been prosecuted under the new regime.

One thing that would have stopped Layla from going to prison is if she had given in to the police's attempts to persuade her to withdraw her account of the attack. But Layla writes that she always felt confident that, as the victim, she would eventually be believed and was concerned that her attackers needed to be caught.

When her case came to court, Layla believes she was a disaster in the witness box. 'I froze. I was like a rabbit stuck in headlights because I was beyond nervous. I didn't really understand what they were asking. I definitely don't think I did a good job.'

There were other reasons Layla ended up being convicted, too. Her ex-boyfriend Nikki White, who had not been with her on the night, gave a statement saying they had argued (about a tomato sandwich). The prosecution argued she had faked the attack as a form of revenge. In his statement, he also said that Richard Dent, who had been out with Layla that night, told him afterwards that when he refused to share a cab home with her, Layla had said, 'If anything happens to me, you will be sorry.' Yet Dent made no mention of this when interviewed at the time, only confirming it was true in a second statement more than a year later.

Layla and her family believed there were criticisms to be made in court of the police investigation. But Jane Mayes, a caseworker at Geoffrey Clapp solicitors in Carlisle who advised Layla, points out that the tone of the trial was set by a horrific crime that had just happened in the area. On 2 June 2010, a local taxi driver Derrick Bird had gone on a shooting spree, killing 12 people. A couple of weeks later, when Layla's trial started, funerals were being held for those killed. A solicitor friend of both barristers and the judge had died in the shootings, and the trial was suspended for one day so they could attend the funeral. The police had been vilified in the national press for not stopping Bird earlier, and Mayes believes there was little appetite in court for further criticisms of the police. 'Lots of little things went wrong at trial,' she says, 'but the massive thing was the Cumbria shootings. The atmosphere was extraordinary.'

Instead, Layla's lawyers concentrated on her injuries. 'The strategy was to show that the scientific evidence proved Layla couldn't have done it,' Mayes explains. Five expert witnesses gave evidence for her. Forensic physician Dr Catherine White examined Layla's injuries – swelling to the back of her head, abrasions on her cheek, injuries to her breasts, scratches on her knee, damage to the perineum and bruising on her hymen. Most of these injuries, White concluded, 'would be very unusual to have been [self-inflicted] . . . particularly in someone without a history of such in the past or a severe mental health problem.'

Mayes says the prosecution managed to paint a brilliantly damning, but she thinks misleading, portrait of Layla. 'Like her explanation of why she had the scissors. It made her look clever. Much cleverer than she is, poor Layla. Looked at in the whole, I think it's impossible she did it. But we lost every bloody point.'

Although fresh counsel pointed out apparent flaws in the evidence, he advised the family there were insufficient grounds for appeal at present because of a lack of new evidence. Other barristers have expressed an interest in pursuing an appeal.

When sentencing Layla, Judge Paul Batty QC said: 'Your behaviour throughout the proceedings has been irresponsible in the extreme and many would say wicked. You tore your own clothing, you cut your body with a pair of scissors, you feigned illness and injury. I'm entirely clear in this case that you craved attention. You wanted your friends to think they had left you in the position where they thought you were the subject of a serious sexual attack. You wanted to teach them a lesson.'

When she heard the verdict, Layla collapsed. She was immediately remanded to the category A prison Low Newton in County Durham. 'It was the worst place I've ever been to in my life,' she writes. 'You were among people like Rose West, and the Baby P killer, and you just think, "What am I doing here?" They were eating dinner with us.

'I'd pretty much broken down by that point. I didn't eat, didn't socialise. They'd unlock my cell and I'd lock myself back up . . . I was getting called names because I'd been on the news, it was just horrible.' After six weeks, Layla was sent to Durham infirmary where her daughter was born and a week later she was transferred to the mother and baby unit at the open prison Askham Grange.

Layla says it's her baby who has kept her going. 'I'm a much stronger person now. After having her I had more to live for – my concentration's on coming out and giving her everything, getting a job.' With good behaviour, she will be released in a few weeks on home detention curfew, required to wear a tag. But after struggling to overcome her dyslexia and obtain her childcare qualification, Layla's only hope of being able to work with children again is appealing against her conviction and clearing her name. 'Childcare is now not an option,' she writes. 'I was also starting my NVQ in elderly care but neither of those are now possible.'

While Layla has regained her strength, the past year has knocked the stuffing out of her mother. Sandra says she stayed strong until Layla was convicted, then she broke down. 'In my mad times, nobody was allowed to drink coffee because Layla couldn't have it, nobody was allowed to eat, Christmas was cancelled, birthdays were cancelled.' Did she want people to suffer like Layla? 'Not suffer. Just share it. I think I was very, very close... to losing it. I never ate or drank for a week, I could hardly move at the end of it. I was constantly stuck in front of the computer trying to find someone who could explain how this happened to her. That's all I still want, someone to explain how my daughter can go through the horror of being attacked to end up in prison with her baby.'

You can see the pain and exhaustion in her face. 'How can you give my daughter three years, when she's never done anything wrong in her life? I still couldn't understand it if, God forbid, she *had* done it, but she hasn't. She's never been in trouble, she's worked hard, she's done everything right. Why was she sentenced to three years in prison? I can't understand it, and nobody will give me the answer.'

Layla Ibrahim was released on home detention curfew last week after serving 13 months in jail.

23 December 2011

Bruised but defiant: Mona Eltahawy on her assault by Egyptian security forces

Mona Eltahawy's tweets about her assault in Cairo made global head-lines. Here she tells her full, extraordinary story for the first time

Mona Eltahawy

The last thing I remember before the riot police surrounded me was punching a man who had groped me. Who the hell thinks of copping a feel as you're taking shelter from bullets? Another man tried to protect him by standing between us, but I was enraged, and kept going back for more. A third man was trying to snatch my smartphone out of my other hand. He was the one who had pulled my friend Maged Butter and me into an abandoned shop – supposedly for safety's sake – and he wouldn't let go of my hand.

It was November. Maged and I had come from Tahrir Square to Mohamed Mahmoud Street, the frontline of clashes between protesters and the military, following a violent invasion of Tahrir by police and soldiers a few days earlier. Almost 40 people had died – including a distant relative – and 3,000 were wounded.

Maged tried to pull me away. 'Enough smacking the groper, let the phone go.' It's clear to us both now that those men we'd met among the protesters on Mohamed Mahmoud Street had entrapped us. They worked with the security services, who were a few metres away, just beyond no man's land, and their job was to hold on to us until the riot police came.

And when they did come, I was the only one left in the deserted shop. I thought Maged had managed to escape, but he later told me he was nearby being beaten, able to see riot police beat me, too. 'You were smart to defend your head,' he said. He needed stitches to his face, and still has contusions to his head and chest.

I suffered a broken left arm and right hand. The Egyptian security forces' brutality is always ugly, often random and occasionally poetic. Initially, I assumed my experience was random, but a veteran human rights activist told me they knew exactly who I was and what they were doing to my writing arms when they sent riot police conscripts to that deserted shop. Bashar al-Assad's henchmen stomped on the hands of famed Syrian cartoonist Ali Farzat. Our dictators tailor wounds to suit their victims' occupations.

As the nightsticks whacked at my arms, legs and the top of my head (in the week that followed, I would discover new bruises every day), two things were at the front of my mind: the pain and my smartphone.

The viciousness of their attack took me aback. Yes, I confess, this feminist thought they wouldn't beat a woman so hard. But I wasn't just a woman. My body had become Tahrir Square, and it was time for revenge against the revolution that had broken and humiliated Hosni Mubarak's police. And it continues. We've all seen that painfully iconic photograph of the woman who was beaten and stripped to her underwear by soldiers in Tahrir Square. Did you notice the soldier who was about to stomp on her exposed midriff? How could you not?

My phone fell as the four or five riot policemen beat me and then started to drag me towards no man's land. 'My phone, I have to get my phone,' I said, and reached down to try to retrieve it. It wasn't the Twitterholic in me that threw herself after the phone, but the survivor. For the first three or four hours of detention, I knew they could do anything and no one would know. In the event, it was near-miraculous that, while I was at the ministry, an activist with a smartphone came to discuss setting up a truce between protesters and security. As soon as he signed me in to Twitter, I sent out, 'beaten arrested at interior ministry'. And then his phone battery died.

Most people detained the same week I was taken in ended up at a police station or jail, but for some reason I was taken to the interior ministry and was then handed over to military intelligence for almost 12 hours. The sexual assault couldn't have lasted more than a few minutes, but the psychic bruise remains the freshest.

The orange midnight air – a cocktail of street lights, an adjacent school on fire, and air that was more tear gas than oxygen – and the black outlines of the helmeted riot policemen invade my thoughts every day, but I feel as though I have dissociated myself from what happened. I read news reports about a journalist whose arms were broken by Egyptian police, but I don't connect them to the splints around my arms that allow only one-finger typing on a touchpad, nor with the titanium plate that will remain in my left arm for a year, to help a displaced fracture align and fuse.

But the hands on my breasts, in between my legs and inside my trousers – *that*, I know, happened to me. Sometimes I think of them as ravens plucking at my body. Calling me a whore. Pulling my hair. All the while beating me. At one point I fell. Eye-level with their boots, all I thought was: 'Get up or you will die.'

They dragged me to the interior ministry, past men in plain clothes who were wearing the same surgical masks that we Tahrir-side civilians had worn against the tear gas. I almost shouted out, 'Are you friend or foe?' Their eyes, dead to my assault, were my answer.

'Shit, I've been caught.' I began to panic. 'Shit, they're probably going to charge me with spying.' I had lived in Israel for a period, where I had worked as a Reuters correspondent.

'You're safe now, I'll protect you.' A senior plainclothes officer reassured me. 'If I wasn't here, there would be no one protecting you from them. See them, over there? Do you know what they'd do to you?' He was pointing to a mob just steps away, itching to get at me. Even as the officer offered hollow protection, the men who had brought me in still went at my breasts. He did nothing.

It was an older man, from the military, who ended it. 'Get her out.'

'Why are you at war with the people?' I asked him. He looked me square in the eyes, fought his tears and swallowed. He couldn't speak. Others asked me again and again: 'Why were you there?'

'I'm a journalist, I'm a writer, I'm an analyst,' I said. But really I wanted to tell them I had longed to touch courage. It lived on Mohamed Mahmoud Street where young men – just boys in many cases, with their mothers' numbers written on their forearms in case they ended up in a morgue – would face off with security forces. Some of those who survived the tear gas and the bullets – rubber-coated and live – lost eyes. Security sharpshooters liked to aim for the head.

For months, Tahrir Square had been my mental touchstone: in New York City, where I live, and wherever I travelled to lecture on the revolution. But it was impossible just to stand by in the square and watch as the Motorbike Angels – volunteers who came on bikes to aid the overworked medics – zipped towards the field hospitals with their unconscious passengers, asphyxiated from the tear gas – and often worse – from the Mohamed Mahmoud frontline.

'If I die, I want to be buried in my Moroccan djellaba. It's laid out on my bed, ready,' tweeted blogger and activist Mohamed 'Gemyhood' Beshir. The hits of tear gas he inhaled pushed him back, so younger men would break his fall and fill in for him on the frontline until he recovered.

Throughout my detention, I demanded medical care for my arms, and showed my captors the increasingly dramatic bruises developing on my hand and arm. Most asked me to make a fist. 'See, it's just a bruise. You wouldn't be able to make a fist if you had a fracture.'

And I told them deliberately graphic details about the sexual assault. Eyes would twitch and look away. No one wanted to hear. 'Why's a good girl like you talking about hands in your trousers? Shut up and silence your shame,' I imagined them saying.

I'll be damned if I carry this alone,I thought. And so I went on and on, until finally they heard, and one of them yelled out: 'Our society has a sickness. Those riot police conscripts who assaulted you, do you know what we've done for them? We've lifted them out of their villages, scrubbed them clean and opened a tiny door in their minds.'

'That's exactly why we're having a revolution,' I responded. 'No one should have to live like that. Who created that misery they live in that you "rescued" them from?'

I also let it be known that I was a US citizen, and asked for a consular representative to be called. I knew that, as an Egyptian-American (I moved to the US in 2000), I would be spared many horrors that countless unnamed Egyptians suffer. But I also anticipated the flip side. 'Aren't you proud of being Egyptian? Do you want to renounce your citizenship,' the military intelligence officer asked me.

Blindfolded, bone-tired and in agony from my fractures, I replied: 'If your fellow Egyptians break your arms and sexually assault you, you'd want someone in the room you can trust.'

The sadistic violence the security forces and army unleashed on Mohamed Mahmoud Street has ripped asunder naive notions that the military were 'guardians of the revolution', or that the 'army and the people are one hand'. No, they broke my hand.

Last week's images from Egypt of the woman stripped down to her underwear and beaten have further unmasked the brutality of the Supreme Council of the Armed Forces (SCAF), the military junta that runs Egypt and which must be tried with crimes against the Egyptian people. I'm unable to look at any of those images of beatings because I feel the nightsticks fracturing my arms all over again. If I hadn't got up when I fell, they would have stomped on me as they stomped on that woman.

I spent the first two weeks back in New York on a painkiller high. It numbed the pain, as well as my ability to write. Once a week I see a psychologist who specialises in trauma; an orthopaedic surgeon has operated on my left arm to realign the ulnar shaft and fix it in place with a titanium plate and screws, and I have regular physiotherapy. But this week's massive women's march in Tahrir has sharpened my focus once again. When a woman who took part wrote to tell me I'd helped to inspire the march because I'd spoken out on Egyptian TV about my beating and assault, I was finally able to cry. They were the tears of a survivor, not a victim.

The Mubarak regime used systematic sexual violence against female activists and journalists, and here's the SCAF upholding that ignoble legacy. But to quote the women in Tahrir this week: 'The women of Egypt are a red line.' My body, and mind, belong to me. That's the gem at the heart of the revolution. And until I return to Egypt in January, healed once again, I will tell that to the SCAF over and over. One finger at a time.

Index

Abbott, Diane 193, 272
abortion 15, 124, 182–8, 244, 251–4
Abortion Act, 1967 124, 185, 186
Abu Ghraib 267, 270
Act of Synod 180
Against Our Will: Men, Women and Rape 34, 37, 164, 170
Ahluwalia, Kiranjit 232, 233
Airlie, Marlene 300
al-Assad, Bashar 382
Alexander, Gerianne 264
Alexander, Sally 220, 224, 225
Alexander, Shaun, 291
Ali, Nusrat 289
Ali, Tariq 224
Allen, Sandra 371, 372, 374–5, 376, 380
Alli 351–2, 357
Allwood, Mandy 187
Ally McBeal 195, 197, 198
Althouse, Ann 309, 310
American feminists 6–8, 10, 29–34, 153–63, 213–15
Amistad 202, 203
Amnesty International 164
Angelou, Maya 96–100, 204
anorexia 353, 368
  see also eating disorders

Anthony, Susan B 13, 195
arranged marriage 64
Association of African Women for Research and Development, The 102
Atkinson, Paul 227–8

Baby Hunger 256
Baby P 379
Backlash 155, 156, 197
Bakewell, Joan 18
Bambara, Toni Cade 122
Bancroft, Audra 281
Banyard, Kat 359
Banyere, Mama Jeanne 259
Barker, Katherine 95
Barnes, Rt Rev. Edwin 179, 180
Bates, Emily 283
Batty, Judge Paul 379
Baudelaire, Charles 198
Beauty Myth, The 243, 243, 244
Beech, Louise 282
'Belle de Jour' 317
Beloved:
  film 200, 201, 202–3, 210, 211, 212
  novel 119–20, 123
  see also slavery

Benderson, Bruce 162
Benn, Melissa 193
Benn, Tony, 84
Beshir, Mohamed 384
Best, George 280
Beyond the Fragments 221, 231
Bird, Derrick 378
birth control 103
Birth Control Trust 188
Bismal, Azmat 283
Black British Feminism 194
Black Dwarf 224, 225
black feminists 12–16, 41, 96–
    100, 231–4
Blair, Cherie 252
Blair, Tony 235, 252
Bluest Eye, The 120, 122
Bluman, Margaret 230
Bly, Robert 161, 167, 169
Bodies 352
Borrowdale, Julie 283
Bosnia 163–70
Boyce, Nicholas 135
bra-burning 10
Braid, Kevin, 291
Breslin, Jimmy 29–30
Brian de Palma, 135
Bridget Jones's Diary 195
British Pregnancy Advisory
    Service 253
    see also pregnancy
Bromley, George 24–5
Brookshaw, Karin 284
Brophy, Brigid 4
Brown, Georgia 20
Brown, Vanessa 301
Brownmiller, Susan 34–8, 164,
    170, 226
bulimia 177

Bush, George W 297
Butter, Maged 381–2

Caldicott, Helen 95
Califia, Pat 160
Campbell, Bea 348
Campbell, Catherine 282
Campbell, Chantelle 284
Carbine, Pat 32
Carey, Mary 126
Carlton Club 27
Carr, Robert 27, 28
Carter, Angela 160
Casey, Michael 333
Castle, Barbara 27, 105–9
catcalls 308, 312–13
Catholic Church 42, 158
Century of Women, A 221, 230
Charles, Prince of Wales 176
Chartres, Richard 180
childbirth 240–51, 253, 274–6, 335
childcare 255
child-rearing 65
Chisholm, Shirley 12–16
Chiti, Jayaprakash 283
Church of England 178
Civil Rights Act, 1964 (USA) 6
Clark, Alan 303
Clarke, Derek 228
clergywomen 136, 178–83
Clinton, Bill 189–92, 201, 244,
    246, 248, 309
Clinton, Hillary 189–92, 330
Cobb, Richard 224
Coleman, Sophie 263
Collins, Joan 129
Color Purple, The 205
Congo 257–61
Congress of Racial Equality 14

Connery, Sean 280
Corpe, Adele 289
cosmetic surgery 356
Courtney, Janet 288
Cox, Natalie 291
Creating Passionate Users 308
Crilly, Mary 293
crimes against women 38–43,
    49–55, 79–82
Crockett, Tina 347, 349
Cross, Stefan 305
Crown Prosecution Service (CPS)
    236, 376–7
Cusk, Rachel 335–41
cyberbullying 307–11

Daley, Rosie 208
Dalton, Paul 278, 287
Dalton, Tae Hui 278, 287
Damera, Anupama 283
Dandridge, Nicola 306
Danish International
    Development Agency
    (Danida) 104
Daughter of Isis, A 363
Davenport, Hayley 286
Davies, Stevie 169
Davis, Angela 122
de Beauvoir, Simone 38, 55, 63–8,
    262
Delf, George 151
Demme, Jonathan 201, 210
Dent, Richard 372, 377–8
Devi, Phoolan 326
Dhillon, Barbara 289
Diana, Princess of Wales 129,
    175–8, 356
Dignity and Daily Bread 229
Diski, Jenny 223

Ditto, Beth 312–13
Dix, Hazel 287
Dobash, Professors Rebecca and
    Russell 279
domestic violence 104, 149–3,
    232, 233, 277–93
Donoghue, James 285
Doshe, Jayshree 21–2
Doshe, Sobhna 21
Doyle, Peter 299, 301–5, 306–7
Drakulic, Slavenka 166–7
Dressed to Kill 80
Dudley, Sarah Jane 286
Duffy, John 235–6, 239
Duncan, Anna 288
Dworkin, Andrea 169

Earhart, Amelia 153
eating disorders 177, 353, 356,
    366–9
  children and 367
  media and 366–9
Ebert, Teresa 156
Edge, Nicola 282
Edwards, Ann 290
Egypt 102, 361–6, 38–6
  security services of 381–6
  Supreme Council of the Armed
      Forces (SCAF) in 386
  Tahrir Square 381, 382, 384, 386
El Saadawi, Nawal 103, 361–6
Eltahawy, Mona 381–6
England, Lynndie 270
equal opportunities 4, 153
Equal Opportunities Bill 28
Equal Opportunities Commission
    106, 254
equal pay 4, 21–6, 58, 196, 254–7,
    298–307

Equal Pay Act 23, 25, 1
Equality and Human Rights
    Commission 330
Ethiopia 102
Evans, Faith 230
Evans, Gareth 287

Faludi, Susan 155, 197, 247,
    358
Farmer, James 14
Farzat, Ali 382
Fat Is a Feminist Issue 352
Faull, Vivienne 180, 182
Fawcett Society 27, 273, 359
Felker, Clay 32–3
Female Chauvinist Pigs 297
female circumcision 101–3, 363
Female Eunuch, The 56, 222, 243
Feminine Mystique 4, 6, 7, 55
feminist literature 358–61
Figes, Eva 55–8
Figes, Kate 193
Filipovic, Jill 308, 310
    Finch, Nicola 286
Finkelstein, Nina 32
Fire With Fire 244
Fish, Constance 282–3
Forward in Faith 180
Foucault, Michel 162
Fountain, Nigel 225, 227–8
Francis, Dr Becky 266
Francis, Icilian 118
Free To Be You and Me 33
French, Marilyn 156
Friedan, Betty 4, 6–8, 55, 195
Friedan, Carl 7
Full Frontal Feminism 359
F-word, The (blog) 359

Gambler's Song Book 135
*Gang That Couldn't Shoot Straight,
    The* 29
Gardiner, Margaret 290
Garner, Margaret 202–3
Garthwaite, Alison 347
Gascoigne, Paul 280
Gaskin, Ina May 241
gay marriage 297
gay men 161–2
Gay News 173
Gebre-Selassie, Alasebu 102
gender identity 262–7
Gilbert, Kay 304
Gillan, Cheryl 184
Giller, Dr Joan 166
Giorgis, Belkis 102
Giroud, Françoise 28–9
Global Solidarity for Secular
    Society 365
God Resigns in the Summit Meeting 362
Godard, Jean-Luc 220
Goldberg, Rabbi David 74
Goodwin, Clive 224
Gordon, Jenni 293
Gore, Al 241, 247, 248
Graham, Katherine 33–4
Graham, Stedman 206
Graner, Charles 270
Gray, John 208
Greenham Common women 89–
    95, 108–9, 127
Greer, Germaine 56, 123–8, 160,
    220, 222, 243
Gulabi Gang 326–8
Gupta, Rahila 233

Helmi, Ahmed 364
Hamilton, Sir Archie 183, 185

Hamilton, Willie 28
handbag, as a female symbol 130
Harbraken, Helena 164, 165
Harewood, Lady 20
Harman, Nigel 269
Harris, Julie 292
Hartley, Nina 268
Hastings, Sue 303
Hearst, Patty 37
Heimel, Cynthia 196
Helmi, Ahmed 364
Helmi, Mona 364, 365
Hemings, Sally 211
Hepburn, Katherine 153, 160
Hetata, Sherif 364
Hewlett, Sylvia Ann 256
Hidden From History 225
Higgins, Lisa 281
hijab 144
Hill, Anita 156
Hite Report 54
Hitler, Adolf 113
Hobbs, May 16–21
Hobsbawm, Eric 225, 226
Hodgkiss, Debbie 284
Hope, David 180
Hopkins, Katie 331
hormones 160–1
Horridge, Melanie 284
Horstead, Gemma 281
housework, wages for 43–9
Hoyland, John 227, 228
Humphreys, Emma 278
Hynde, Chrissie 160–1

I Know Why The Caged Bird Sings 96–
    100, 204
Ibrahim, Layla 370–80
Ibrahim, Sara 370, 372, 374–5

Ibrahim, Taraq 375
Ibuka 344
Independent Police Complaints
    Commission 375
India 325–8
infibulation 101
Integration of Women in
    Development 102
International Planned
    Parenthood Association 103
International Tribunal of Crimes
    Against Women 38–43
Internet 307–11
    pornography 324
Inyumba, Aloisea 343, 344
Iron John 167
Islamic feminists 143–8, 171–5,
    361–6

Jalland, Anne 284
James, Selma 43, 47, 48
Jazz 202
Jefferson, Thomas 211
Jeffreys, Sheila 346, 348, 349
Jenkins, Natalie 288
Jenkins, Roy 28
jezebel.com 324
Jobs for a Change 228
Johal, Anita 232–3
John, Carolyn 375
Johnson, Jacqueline 288
Johnson, Marguerite 97
Johnstone, Nicola 291
Jones, Bronwen 285–6
Jones, Pauline 291
Jorgensen, Kirsten 104
Journey to Beloved 210
Judaism 69–75

Kakutani, Michiko 123
Kalish, Evarist 345
Kanakuze, Judith 342, 344
Kellett-Bowman, Dame Elaine 185
Keningale, Vincent 290
Kennedy, Jane 184
Khalid, Saba 145–6
King, Christine 93
King, Martin Luther 96, 99
King, Oona 272
Kissing the Rod: An Anthology of 17th-Century Women's Verse 126
Kissinger, Henry 31
Kitzinger, Sheila 241
Klein, Naomi 247
Ku Klux Klan 99

Labour Party 271–4
lad mags 294
Lajja (Shame) 171
Leach, Penelope 340
Leonard, Dr Graham 136
lesbianism 39–40, 85–9, 99, 162
    political 346–50
Levenson, Ellie 359–60
Levy, Ariel 358–9
Lewinsky, Monica 189–92
Lewis, Amanda 292
Licorish, Alison 116
Life 187
Life's Work: On Becoming a Mother, A 334–41
Litton Industries 22
Lloyd, Leonora 168–9
Lloyd Webber, Andrew 109
Lohan, Lindsay 314, 315
Longfield, Anne 266
Longstaff, Lisa 376

Longworth, Christine 282
Love Your Enemy? The Debate Between Heterosexual Feminism and Political Lesbianism 346–50
Lusi, Jo 258
Lyle, Sheila 300
Lynch, Chantelle 284
Lyons, Harriet 32

MacCowan, Christine 290
MacDonald, Linda 292
Macdonald, Lorraine 290
McDougall, Linda 184
McKibbin, Stuart 289
Mace, Clare 282
Mackie, Lindsay 53
Madonna 195
Mailer, Norman 29
Maisuria, Ela 292
Major, John 234
Mark, Sir Robert 50
marriage 45, 58, 64–5, 66, 137–9
    arranged 64, 103–4, 143, 145
    gay 297
Marwick, Alice 309, 310–11
maternal profiling 329–30
maternity leave 246, 274–6, 329, 331
Maxim 295
Mayes, Jane 378
Memoirs From the Women's Prison 362
Men's Movement 161
Mezey, Dr Gillian 166, 168, 170
Middleton, Neil 230
miners' wives 109
Ministry of Women 180–1
Miseducation of Women, The 256
Misogynies 134, 151

Misogynist's Source Book, A 136
misogyny 133–6
    online 307–11
Mitchell, Julia 220
Mitter, Swasti 229
Monroe, Marilyn 135
Moms Rising 330, 332
Morgan, Fidelis 136
Morris, Dick 247–8
Morrison, Toni 119–23, 201, 202,
    206, 210
Moss, Kate 368
motherhood 59–63, 124–5, 245–
    6, 329–33, 334–41
Motorbike Angels 384
Ms 30, 31, 33–4
Mubarak, Hosni 382
Mulcahy, David 235–40
Murdoch, Elsie 300
Murray, Jenni 266
Myskow, Dr Lyndsey 264
Mysogynies 151

Namoonty, Bharana Krishna 285
Nasrin, Taslima 171–5
National Abortion Campaign 168
National Organisation of Women
    (NOW) 6, 7
Neglia, Simon 293
Nelson, Maggie 110
Neuberger, Julia 69–75
New Feminism, The 222, 358
New York Magazine 32, 33
Ngozi, Angie 117
Nicholson, Emma 183–4
Nightingale, Florence 3
No Logo 247
Northern Initiative on Women
    and Eating 177

Noughtie Girl's Guide to Feminism
    359
Nyamatanga, Nyarai 287
Nyirabega, Euthalie 345

Object campaign group 360
Obstacle Race, The 160
Odo 136
online abuse 307–11
Operation Black Vote (OBV) 272,
    273
'Oprah's Law', *see* US National
    Child Protection Act
Oram, Kevan 286
Orbach, Susie 351–8
Osliffe, Roger 286–7
O'Sullivan, Sue 86, 87
'Our Bodies, Our Souls' 244, 250
Owens, Paula 292
Oz 227

Paglia, Camille 153–63, 249
Pakistan 173
Pal, Sampat Devi 327–8
Paradise 202
Parker Bowles, Camilla (later
    Duchess of Cornwall) 176
Patel, Pragna 232, 233
Patriarchal Attitudes 55
Paxford, Geraldine 281
Peacock, Mary 32
Pearson, Irena 284
PEN 172
Peppard, Kiki 329–30, 332–3
Peters, Susan 283
Phillips, Trevor 330
Pill 4
Playboy 294, 295
'Poem for Jacqueline Hill' 81–2

Pogrebin, Letty Coton 32
political lesbianism 346–50
politics 26–9, 128–33, 183–5,
    189–92, 271–4, 342–5
  in USA 12–16
  women in 105–9
pornography 50, 80, 267–71,
    294–7, 322–5
Power Plays 266
Prebble, John 36
pregnancy 59–63, 65–6, 124, 187–
    8, 356–7
  'child neglect' and 187
  teen 191, 369
Prescott, John 301
Progressive Judaism 69–75
Promiscuities 243, 244
Promise of a Dream 221, 223, 224,
    225, 227, 229
prostitution 316–22
  forced 166
  jail for 153
  for survival 99

racial discrimination 12–16, 96–
    100, 109–19, 121–2, 309
racial equality 96–100, 192–4,
    231–5, 271–4
Rake, Katherine 273
Rameau, Willie 123
rape 34–8, 49–50, 51, 53, 67, 80,
    98, 103, 147, 205, 235–40,
    267–8, 280, 343–4
  as weapon of war 163–70, 257–
    61
  see also sexual assault
Reagan, Ronald 113, 156
Reay, Vicky 291
Reclaiming the Night 49–55

Redfern, Catherine 359
Redstockings 32
Rees, Christina 180–1, 182
religious extremism 171–5, 362
revolutionary feminists 346
Roberts, Julia 367
Robertson, Gregory 289
Rose, Judith 181
Rose, Sally 285
Roskrow, Felicity 53
Rousseau, Jean-Jacques 159
Rowan, Abigail 288–9
Rowbotham, Sheila 219–31
Rowe-Finkbeiner, Kristin 332
Rowlands, Odell 285
Rowthorn, Bob 227
Roxx, Lara 269
Rules, The 195, 195
Rumbold, Angela 149, 150
Rushdie, Salman 148, 171
Rwandan genocide 342–5

Sartre, Jean-Paul 63, 65, 68
Scargill, Arthur 109
Schwarzer, Alice 66
Second Sex, The 55, 63–8, 243
Secret Diary of a Call Girl, The 316–
    17
Segal, Lynne 222, 226–7
Sellars, Carol 167–8, 169, 170
sex discrimination 16–26, 55–8
Sex Discrimination Act, 1975 57
sexual assault, 370–80, 383, 385
  see also rape
sexual fulfillment (for women) 66
sexual liberation 127, 294–7, 324
*Sexual Personae: Art and Decadence
    from Nefertiti to Emily Dickinson*
    154

Shah, Zoora 233
Shaw, Charles 288
Shephard, Gillian 184
Shepherd, Cybill 253
Shipley, David 244
Siddiqui, Hannana 234
Sierra, Kathy 307–8, 310
Skedd, Mandy 293
Skerritt, Shirley 117–18
slavery 45, 46, 120, 202–3, 210–11, 302
    see also Beloved
Smith, Joan 133–6, 151
Soames, Nicholas 176
Society for the Protection of the Unborn Child (SPUC) 186, 187
Song of Solomon 120, 206
Southall Black Sisters 194, 231–5
Spare Rib 85–9
Spare Rib Reader 86
Spears, Britney 294, 314–15
Spice Girls 194, 195
Springer, Jerry 200, 207, 208
Starlight Express 109–10
Starmer, Kier 373, 376–7
Staunch newspaper 117
Steinem, Gloria 29–34, 127, 157, 195, 248
Stewart, Moira 110
Stiffed 247
Story of O 42
suffragettes 5, 131
Sugar, Alan 331
Sula 120
Sutcliffe, Peter (Yorkshire Ripper) 79–82, 133, 134
Swain, Dr Rosemary 373, 375–6

Tabick, Jacqueline 70
Tahrir Square 381, 382, 384, 386
    see also Egypt
Take Back the Tech 311
Talmudic Law 73
Tar Baby 120, 123
That's My Boy! 266
Thatcher, Margaret 26–9, 88, 106, 107, 108, 128–33, 148, 156, 220, 228, 234
There Are No Children Here 204
third-world women 100–5
Thompson, Dorothy 222–3, 224, 225, 226
Thompson, Edward 224, 225
Thornton, Sara 149–53
Tidy-Harris, Sylvia 276
Tisdall, Caroline 53
Tooley, James 256
toys, gender-specific 262–7
Transport and General Workers' Union (TGWU) 22, 24, 26
Tu, David 258
Tubules, Sue 255
Turlington, Christy 367
Turner, Cheryl 117
Tweedie, Jill 86, 123–8, 226
Tyson, Mike 280

UN Conference on the Decade for Women 101
US National Child Protection Act 201

Valenti, Jessica 359

Wages for Housework campaign 43–8
Walker, Alice 122

Walker, Peter 27
Walking Through Fire 364
Wallace, Kathleen 301
Wallsgrove, Ruth 86, 87–8
Walter, Natasha 193, 222, 295, 358
Watney, Simon 160
Watts, Janet 52–3
Weaver, Reg 24
weight issues 351–8
WeightWatchers 357
Weldon, Fay 148
Well of Loneliness, The 99
West, Rose 379
Wharrier, Christine 299, 304, 306–7
Wheen, Francis 136
White, Dr Catherine 378
White, Nikki 377
Widgery, David 227–8
Widows of the Genocide 344
Wilkinson, Simone 93
Williams, Bevon, 284
Williams, Christeena 116–17
Williams, Professor Patricia 211

Williams, Shirley 18
Wilson, George 284–5
Wilson, Mary 20
Windsor, Barbara 253
Winfrey, Oprah 200–12, 333
Winnicott, Donald 353
Wolf, Naomi 155, 157, 199, 230, 240–51, 295, 323–4
Wollstonecraft, Mary 3
Woman's Consciousness, Man's World 225
Women Against Rape 51, 376
Women and Sex 362
Women Encounter Technology 229
Women in Media 17, 28
Women, Resistance and Revolution 225
Women's Liberation Movement 6–7, 9, 39, 50
Woolley, Simon 273

Yorkshire Ripper (Peter Sutcliffe) 79–82, 133, 134
Young, Hugo 129
Yuval-Davis, Nira 233, 234